Women Entrepreneurs and Socio-Economic Development

——Essays in Honour of Prof. K.S. Chalam——

Women Entrepreneurs and Socio-Economic Development

Essays in Honour of Prof. K.S. Chalam

Prof. D. Pulla Rao
Department of Economics
Andhra University, Visakhapatnam, A.P

SERIALS PUBLICATIONS
NEW DELHI (INDIA)

First Published – 2011

ISBN: 978-81-8387-424-3

Published by

SERIALS PUBLICATIONS
4830/24, 1st Floor, Ansari Road
Darya Ganj, New Delhi-110002 (India)
Phone : 23245225. Fax : 91-11-23272135
E-mail : serials@sify.com
serialspublications.india@gmail.com
Website: www.serialspublications.com

Contents

Foreword

I am very happy to write a few words about the book edited by Prof. D. Pulla Rao in honour of his teacher who was a great teacher, scholar and administrator.

In India, Entrepreneurship was always a male domain, which could not be entered by women. Even today it is rare to find women entrepreneurs, not that Indian woman is not enterprising enough, but because our patriarchal society throws more hurdles in her way than encouragement. But there are a handful of women who have come up after fearlessly crossing all obstructions. They have become achievers in this field.

I am not at all surprised to find the present volume published in honour of my friend and colleague Prof. K.S. Chalam. On many an occasion I have seen him stand up for the cause of women as he has done, for the other weaker sections of society. I consider myself fortunate to have worked with him for 4 years in the UPSC. It was then that I found to be a sensitive human being. I also got an opportunity to attend his both birthday celebrations at Visakhapatnam, where I learnt that he is not only a learned scholar but a bold activist. A 2 day seminar was organized in his honour, which was a great success, I was indeed happy to be informed, that the proceedings of the seminar are being published in 8 volumes.

With the opening of the economy to global players during the last decade of the 20th century, women entrepreneurship has picked up to some extent. I noticed this phenomenon during my assignments in the department of Customs and Central excise, as Commissioner and later as chief Commissioner and Director General. This experience was not exhausted enough from the point of view of women entrepreneurs. The present volume on "women Entrepreneurs and socio Economic Development," has given me a better insight. There are 32 papers, in the volume. Some of the papers are related to the self help groups and their problems and success stories. There is also a paper on Muslim women entrepreneurs, through which we learn that women even from this most neglected and marginalized group have entered the field of entrepreneurship. In this volume, we find papers on women traders, micro finance and dairy cooperatives etc. Through the essays in this book one learns a lot. The basic information which emerges is, that the sectors are demarcated for women entrepreneurs are limited. They find entry into fields limited to ready-made garments, beauty saloons, tailoring etc. One also finds that most women enter the field when they find themselves financially challenged due to some unfortunate incident in the family. It is only then that they are allowed to leave their homes. Women otherwise, are considered only as protectors of the family, as mothers and wives. The so called business women tycoons, who are touted as the most successful women, come from families where business has already been established by fathers, grand fathers or in-laws.

If women get political backing perhaps with the Women Reservation Act, daughters from ordinary families will also forge ahead and we may see a day when 20% of the business in India is controlled by women. Publications, like the present volume can lead the country towards such a direction. The papers in this volume contain valuable information and guidance for the development of women entrepreneurs in particular and for the socio-economic development of women in general. I am sure this Book will generate sufficient discussion and debate for such future studies in the country. I commend this publication. It is indeed a fitting tribute to Prof. K.S. Chalam.

I congratulate Prof. D. Pulla Rao for bringing out a useful and purposeful volume.

Ms. Parveen Talha
IRS (Retd.), Member, UPSC
Ex Director General Customs & Central Excise

Acknowledgements

This book is an outcome of the Seminar on "Human Development and Social Exclusion" conducted in the Department of Economics, Andhra University, Visakhapatnam on the occasion of Shastiabdi Poorti Celebrations of my Guru and Director of my Ph.D work Prof. K.S. Chalam, Member, UPSC, New Delhi. About 350 delegates participated and nearly 250 delegates presented papers and participated in the discussion and deliberations. I am highly thankful to the paper contributors for helping me in bringing out this book which will be of some help to the researchers and also policy makers in India. I am very much beholden to the Prof. K. Rama Krishna Rao, Chairman, Indian Council of Philosophical Research, New Delhi, for his financial assistance. My special thanks are due to our honourable Vice-Chancellor Prof. Beela Satyanarayana and Prof. V. Satyanarayana, Honorary Director, Indian Council of Social Science Research, Southern Regional Centre, Hyderabad for their financial assistance.

My sincere thanks to Prof. L.K. Mohana Rao, Principal, College of Arts & Commerce, Andhra University for inaugurate the seminar session. I express my grateful thanks to Prof. Beela Satyanarayana, Vice-Chancellor, Andhra University, for his inaugural address of the seminar. My sincere thanks are due to Prof. K. Rama Krishna Rao, Chairman, Indian Council of Philosophical Research, New Delhi for sparing his valuable time for preparing and delivering the keynote address. My special thanks to Sri D. Raja, M.P (Rajya Sabha) for attending as a guest of honour and released the Souvenir. My sincere thanks to Prof. Y. Satyanarayana, Vice-Chancellor, Andhra Pradesh University of Law for attending as a guest of honour and delivered valuable message.

I am very grateful to Ms. Parveen Talha, IRS (Retd.), Member, UPSC, Ex Director General Customs & Central Excise for having kindly written the foreword to this book sparing his precious time. I express my thanks to Sri S. Reghupathy, Hon. Minister for Environment and Forests, Govt. of India for attending as the Chief Guest for Shastiabdi Poorti Celebrations of Prof. K.S. Chalam and valedictory function of the seminar session and released the book 'Dravida Udyamam Katha' written by Prof. K.S. Chalam.

I express my gratitude to Ms. Parveen Talha, Member, UPSC for attending the Shastiabdi Poorti Celebrations of Prof. K.S. Chalam and released the book 'Political Economy of Underdevelopment of Kalingandhra' written by Prof. K.S. Chalam.

My heartful thanks to Sri. P. Janardhana Rao, Mayor, Greater Visakhapatnam Municipal Corporation who presided over the function of the Shastiabdi Poorti Celebrations of Prof. K.S. Chalam.

I also thank to Prof. R. Sudarsana Rao, Head, Dept. of Economics and Prof. G. Ramachandrudu, Chairman, P.G. Board of Studies for their continuous support for the successful completion of the seminar.

Finally, my special thanks to the teaching and non-teaching staff, research scholars and students of the Dept. of Economics, Andhra University for their support for the successful completion of the seminar and Shastiabdi Poorti Celebrations of Prof. K.S. Chalam and also in bringing the book to the present shape. I place on record the excellent work done by publishers in bringing the book on time.

Prof. D. Pulla Rao

Introduction

Entrepreneur is considered as the key figure not only in trade and business but even in production in a free economy like India. The importance of entrepreneur has increased several folds during the liberalization period. In fact the skills of an entrepreneur are very important in the expansion of an economy as she takes the innovation and risk to put the technology under operation. As a result of the developments in business and trade, the thin difference between an Investor and entrepreneur is gone now and everyone who is in business and in production is called as entrepreneur. In this context, the importance of women entrepreneur in a traditional society like India is considered as very important. The state is promoting the involvement of women in all activities including entrepreneurial actions by providing assistance to SHG to take up economic activities. But, the progress in this field appears to be not as promising as in other activities like politics and administration. An attempt is made here to learn the current problems of women entrepreneurs and the progress achieved in different parts of the country.

"Women Development Indicators in India: An Overview" by **Dr. T. Chandrasekharaiah and Dr. D. Sai Sujatha** observed that the National Plan of Action for Women adopted in 1976 became a guiding document for the development of women. The data for the study have been taken from Census of India, Sample Registration System and Family Welfare Year Book etc. Women development indicators like literacy rate, work participation rate, workers by sector wise, sex ratio, age at marriage, life expectancy, total fertility rate and couple

protection rate etc for a period of ten decades from 1901 onwards are shown in a table. The findings are showing an improvement in development aspects of women. In order to improve further, active involvement of NGOs and mass public movement are needed apart from government efforts.

Dharmana Rama Rao and Gullipali Rajeswari in their paper on *"Self Help Groups and Women Empowerment"* observed that the concept of women empowerment is complex and different methodologies have been used to measure it. Information on self-help groups was presented in terms of physical achievements, financial results and partnerships as per the data of micro-credit innovation department, NABARD, Mumbai. With respect to the control of resources, changes in behavior and the decision-making reveals that many studies have been made in the right direction and women are in the process of empowering themselves, but a lot needs to change to make women truly empowered.

Dr. M.R. Geeta Bala and Prof. G. Satyanarayana in their paper on *"Empowerment of Women–Self Help Groups"* find that in most of the South Asian Countries, the status of women is comparatively low and their socio-economic conditions are much more disheartening. The Human Development Report's observations and 2001 Census population particulars are presented. The authors have examined the status of women in Andhra Pradesh and History of SHGs in Anantapur District followed by their strengths and weaknesses. Finally, suggestions are made to make SHGs more effective in their functioning.

Dr. A. Lavanya Kumari and Dr. B. Mohana Rao in their paper on *"Women Empowerment through Visakhapatnam Special Economic Zones"* feel that economic empowerment is the initial aspect of women development. Information related to education of women workers in the VSEZ units, decision-making in families of women workers in the VSEZ, average monthly income of women workers in the VSEZ, and saving per month of women workers in the VSEZ units were presented and interpreted. Based on their observations, the authors conclude that the women workers in the VSEZ units are having empowerment and that families are most dependent upon women's economic productivity.

According to **Dr. K. Madhu Babu** in his paper on "*Women Traders in New Economy: Issues and Challenges*" there has been a significant increase in women employed in petty retail trade, hotels and restaurants in the last decade as part of survival strategy of poor urban households. The author has given a brief profile of the East Godavari district where the study was made to examine the viable entrepreneurial trade for women in agriculture and understand the constraints faced and identify the linkages and support system needed. The data is connected with productivity and cost of product for the coir products entrepreneurs, net income from the coir products enterprise, both for trained and untrained and followed by share of income from women's enterprise in total annual household income in terms of different particulars. Main benefits for women were enlisted and it was concluded that despite improvement in their socio-economic status, these women face problems in marketing their product and hence need help in improving their forward and backward linkages.

A. Vamsi Krushna, Dr. P. Jayanand Kumar and P. Raj Kumar in their paper on "*Sustainability of SHGs: A Case Study of Krishna District of Andhra Pradesh*" observed that with the nationalization of commercial banks in 1969 and setting up of regional banks in 1975, the loans extended to the priority sector by institutional agencies increased significantly. The authors examined sustainability and empowerment of women and presented data related to percentage of loans advanced by purpose, occupational distribution of members of SHGs, distribution of members by income group, size of land holding, caste, literacy levels, age and their level of participation in SHG meetings. It was suggested that to make the SHG, financially sustainable it is necessary to advance loans for activities which are not marginalized and which lead to production of goods.

"*Role of Women Entrepreneurs in Social Upliftment*" by **Dr. A.V. Naga Varma, M. Ravi Kumar, M. Anil Kumar and B. Naveen Kumar** state that the government of India has defined women entrepreneurs based on women participation in equity and employment of a business enterprise. The authors have given a description of Palani, well known piligrim centre of South India followed by the socio-economic conditions of people living in Palani. The problems faced by women entrepreneurs are classified under socio-personnel problems, managerial problems, production problems, marketing problems, financial problems and problems of government assistance followed by the observations of some prominent women. Having outlined the hindrances, the authors make some practical suggestions to improve the situation.

According to **Dr. R. Radha** in her paper on "*Globalisation-Impact on the Status of Women*" starts with a question–is globalization weakening or strengthening patriarchy? For the comparative purpose, the status of women during the pre-liberalisation and post-liberalisation periods are taken presenting the basic characteristics showing female capabilities, gender inequality in education and employment scenario in organized and the unorganized sectors, followed by incidence of crime against women in India during 1998-2003 years. Globalization was examined in terms of possibilities and opportunities as well as negative aspects, changing institution of marriage in India, commoditisation of women and impact on the working environment, finally, three steps to democratization for ensuring equal status of women.

Dr. Rais Ahmad and Prof. R. Ramakrishna in their paper on "*Can Microfinance Programmes Empower Women in India?*" observed that men receive the lion's share of income and recognition for their contribution, while most of women's work remains unpaid, undervalued and unrecognized. The authors discuss the concept of empowerment, and strategies for women empowerment, followed by micro finance and women empowerment, SHG Bank Linkage Programme along with information on Self-Help Groups in terms of physical achievements, financial results and partnerships. The responses of the Focus Group Discussions have been classified as efficiency improving activities, community driven development activities and women empowering activities. The authors feel that although women have been empowered, SHGs have not been able to make substantial impact in those key decision areas.

Dr. Y. Rama Krishna and Dr. A.V. Naga Varma in their paper on *"Women Empowerment and Rural Development"* feel that no country can achieve its potential without adequately investing in and developing the capabilities of women. The authors discuss the role of women in rural development and the factors empowering the rural women–social, economic, and technological. Under social factors are included status of women, gender bias and health and nutrition, while economically productive work includes access to resources, micro credit programmes and technological factors include capacity building, exposure to mass media, appropriate training programme and appropriate technology for women. Authors conclude that economic independence, education and competence, willingness, confidence, motivation and encouragement from family, and society contribute to women empowerment.

Prof. R. Rama Krishna, D. Tata Rao and D. Nageswara Rao in their paper on *"Poverty Alleviation and Women Empowerment through Self Help Groups"* observed that the primary aim of the SHG–Bank linkage programme is to integrate informal savings and credit groups with mainstream banking by providing them with credit to enhance their fund base. The authors discussed the two dimensions of the impact of SHGs and the three important external catalysts that facilitated the positive change in the case of Andhra Pradesh, as funding agency, initiative of the government officials and the contribution of organizations from the private and NGO sector, followed by the lessons from Andhra experience in using SHGs as a conduit for poverty alleviation initiatives.

Dr. T.V. Ramana and Dr. P. Subba Rao in their paper on *"Micro Finance–Sustainable Development of Women–A Case Study"* observed that among all the communities women of India are considered as secondary, disadvantaged groups in the family and the society, and hence policy makers, planners and administrators recommend separate income generating activities, for the empowerment of women. The authors discuss micro-credit and development of SHG groups in

Andhra Pradesh. Pattern of occupational shift of the respondents after joining SHGs, women contribution to the total income of the households, reduced income–expenditure gap, and regression results–earnings function for different variable. It was concluded that micro finance brought changes in the life style of the women and supported to increase the earnings, savings and contribution to the family.

Dr. B. Ratna Kumari and M. Anitha in their paper on "*Empowerment and Women Entrepreneurship in Visakhapatnam District*" observed that women's entrepreneurship is gaining increasing importance in public policy circulars. The authors explain the need for the study and research questions to be answered with reference to the EDP–trained and non-trained entrepreneurs and the activities to be undertaken and the emergence of women entrepreneurship, and about District Industries Center. The secondary data was collected from Census reports and DIC office while a structured schedule was prepared and administered to women entrepreneurs in the study area. Different statistical tools were used for the analysis of data. The women entrepreneurs reported to be having a fairly high level of self confidence prior to establish and run their enterprises. Some suggestions were given to help the women entrepreneurs.

Dr. D. Francis, R. Vijaya Krishna and D. Susheela in their paper on "*Developing Women Entrepreneurship in India*" observed that in almost all countries, the governments are providing special provisions for women's development and efforts are being made to extract maximum use of women's talent. The concept of entrepreneurship and characteristics of entrepreneurs were discussed and data on gender-wise work for the participation rate in India, gender wise work participation rates in rural and urban areas for different years and total workers and work participation rates in India for 2001 were presented, followed by suggestions for improving the status of women workers. It was concluded that when women are engaged in gainful employment and contributing to the household and national economy, they should be given due respect and status they deserve in the family and the society.

Dr. B. Ratna Kumari and Mrs. M. Sridevi in their paper on *"Women Empowerment through Dairy Cooperatives"* feel that though women play a significant role in livestock management and production, women's control over livestock and its products in negligible. The authors discuss the role of livestock in the Indian agrarian economy. The socio-economic conditions of sample women dairy farmers regarding the literacy level, occupation, savings, household assets, education level, age, marital status, income from dairying, land holdings and cattle wealth were analysed and conclusions were presented, followed by a comparative study of the cooperative and non-cooperative dairy farmers. Policy implications were discussed to increase women's access and control commensurate to their participation in dairy work.

Dr. K. Somasekhar in his paper on *"Empowerment of Women in the Plan Period: An Overview"* observed that women in general in the country are underprivileged in terms of social status and economic participation, but the plight of rural women is much worse. The authors discussed the concept of empowerment as power, process of empowerment, status of women, need for empowerment. Policies and programmes for empowerment of women during the plan period were discussed followed by the goals and objectives of the National Policy on Women to promote the advancement, development and empowerment of women through various means.

D. Sunder Raj and R. Venkata Ravi in their paper on *"Economic Empowerment of Women: A Group Approach"* observe that economic empowerment helps women to evolve as workers, citizens and human beings. The authors discussed the need for empowerment and efforts towards women development. Economic development of women was examined followed by a discussion of group approach and the impact of group approach. Importance of Self Help Groups was explained and the factors that affect empowerment of women like education, training, conscious raising campaigns and group approach and self-employment training were described. It was concluded that women need to be viewed not as beneficiaries but as active participants in the process of development and change.

Dr. M. Syamala in her paper on *"Empowering Women for Economic Development"* observes that empowerment of women covers aspects such as women's role in the family, society, control over the resources etc. followed by a few important areas which call for empowerment of women in India. Participation of women, education of women, health of women and women's participation in politics were examined. Women in animal husbandry and women in industrial activities were described. The contribution of women in Khadi Village Industries and participation of women in entrepreneurs were presented followed by age group of women entrepreneurs. It was concluded that women empowerment will definitely lead to economic development and well being of not only a family, village, city, state but the whole nation.

Prof. L.K. Mohana Rao in his paper on *"Problems of Women Entrepreneurship in India"* observes that women in many parts of the world make key contributions in the areas of development such as agriculture, health, education, water resources management etc. The concept of entrepreneurship and empowerment of women were examined followed by a description of women entrepreneurship in the Indian scenario. Gender wise Work Force Participation Rate in India for 1901-2001 and employment of women in organised public and private sectors for 1971-2001 were examined followed by a description of major problems of women entrepreneur.

Prof. M. Sundara Rao and Prof. D. Pulla Rao in their paper on *"Micro Finance towards Empowerment of Rural Women: A Study of Tekkali Mandal in Srikakulam District of Andhra Pradesh"* observed that rather than rural men, the rural women perform activities which range from child rearing to household affairs and farm operations. In this study an attempt was made to evaluate the SHG programme in Tekkali Mandal of Srikakulam District. The process of selection involved selection of village, selection of SHGs and selection of household. Data was collected from each SHG member using a structured questionnaire by personal interview method. The data was related to SHG member's participation in developmental activities, SHG members participation in different programmes, amount drawn from Matching Grant Fund by the selected SHGs, amount utilisation on productive and consumption purposes by SHGs and amount repaid by selected SHG members. The authors suggest the need to providing proper guidance and supervision to all the SHGs in the adoption of productive and income generating activities.

Dr. Ch. Appa Rao, Prof. G. Ramachandrudu, S. Prasada Rao and A. Venu in their paper on *"Women Participation in National Rural Employment Guarantee Scheme (NREGS) in Vizianagaram District of Andhra Pradesh"* observed that in recent years no programme for rural areas has received as much attention as the employment guarantee scheme NREGS. Vizianagaram District is one of the most backward and socially disadvantaged sections of the people with lowest female literacy, high poverty levels and highest out migration from the district. Information extracted from the sample respondents relating to socio economic features like age, caste, literacy, type of house, occupational structure, number of workers in the family, impact of NREGS on employment, impact on income, impact on assets, and impact on consumption patterns were studied. It was concluded that programmes like NREGS require proper planning, effective implementation, close monitoring and independent evaluation for delivering maximum benefits to the target groups.

Dr. A.V. Naga Varma, Dr. Y. Rama Krishna and Dr. J. Chandra Prasad in their paper on *"Women Entrepreneurship– The Road Ahead"* observe that the participation of women in economic activities is necessary not only from a human resource point of view but even for the objective of raising the status of woman in society. Major factor influencing women entrepreneurs like economic independence, creativity, own identity, achievement of excellence, risk taking ability, equal status and greater freedom and mobility are examined, followed by a discussion of the socio-cultural barriers and suggestions to overcome them. Finally it was stated that both the government and men should encourage the women to become entrepreneurs in all fields.

Dr. Jagannath B. Kukkudi, Prof. Ramesh Agadi and Dr. Veershetty Rathod in their paper on *"Development of Women Entrepreneurs: An Overview"* observe that women recently began to join the ranks of managers in large numbers. But women at the top management positions are still rare. The authors list out different roles of woman as entrepreneurs, followed by hindrances faced by women entrepreneurs. Recent trends in development of women entrepreneurs and tips for development of women entrepreneurs were mentioned. Information on business opportunities for women entrepreneurs, women in world business and role of women entrepreneurs and five Fredrick Harbiscon functions of a women entrepreneur are presented. It was concluded that unfortunately the government sponsored development activities have benefited only a small section of woman and the large majority of them are still unaffected by change and development activities.

Sanjeeb Kumar Jena and Dr. Jayanta K. Parida in their paper on *"Women Empowerment through Micro Enterprises–A Case Study of Orissa"* observed that micro finance programmes and micro enterprises have been successful in reaching women, particularly given the challenging socio-cultural conditions in which they live. Different rationales for placing a priority on increasing women's access to micro finance services are discussed followed by strengths, weaknesses, opportunities and threats of the Bamboo craft sector in Malkangiri district. Analysis of the different dimensions of women empowerment using ANOVA showing before and after the ME interventions on position of the women with respect to their interaction, interaction patterns of the women entrepreneurs of the MEs at the time of trading, awareness level of the respondents with respect to their rights, independent negotiation in trade, independent mobility followed by paired samples test for change in the earnings of the women artisans of Bamboo crafts were presented and interpreted. Further, change in average monthly expenses, capacity to earning through diversification of trade, physical attainment of education, skill etc, contribution to household, contribution to community decision-making in household and control and ownership over assets and resources were also presented.

Dr. K.A. Rasure in his paper on "*Rural Women Entrepreneurs: A Study*" observed that women entrepreneur is an important change agent in every society. The factors which influenced the entrepreneurship among rural women were classified as technological, personnal, economic, physical and market factors, and major problems encountered by women entrepreneurs were presented in percentages. Guidance from SHG, self-confidence, possession of ancestral property, good transport facilities and response prices and good market potential were the factors influencing entrepreneurship. Among the problems encountered by women entrepreneurs were financial constraints and lack of marketing facilities were found to be the major problems. The author has given suggestions to promote rural women entrepreneurs by reorientation, group entrepreneurship and other strategies.

Dr. M. Savithri in her paper on "*Self Help Groups: A Keystone of Microfinance in India -Women Empowerment and Social Security*" observed that today, Self Help Groups and MFIs are the two dominant form of micro finance in India. Starting from emergence of SHG movement, SHG federation, SHG bank linkage were discussed followed by a table of over all financial snapshot of SHGs in different regions of the country and the grand total of the amount of financing they received was presented and interpreted. Non-financial impact of SHGs was discussed in terms of political and social harmony between different social groups, social justice, community resources, livelihood. A pointed analysis of where government, NGOs, Banks and others including the private sector, can work together to help and answer the needs to SHGs in a measured and effective manner was followed by a discussion of the other side of the coin.

K.R. Rama Mohan and V. Subramanyam in their paper on "*Gender and Displacement: A Study on Project Affected Families under various Irrigation Projects in Andhra Pradesh*" observed that due to construction of irrigation projects in tribal areas, all the inhabitants of the project affected area are displaced from their original habitats to an alien surroundings. The authors discussed the nature of the problem and the role of the state and the media followed by a list of number of affected families of the tribes in each reservoir project- Peddagadda Project, Bhupatipalem, Musurumiki Project etc. Further, state response and the media response was described as faulty and gender insensitive rehabilitation and suggest that gender sensitivity should be there in case of rehabilitation programmes.

Vineeth Sahadevan and A.P. Prajina in their paper on "*Empowering Women through Micro Finance*" observed that Self Help Groups intermediated by micro-credit have been shown to have positive effects on women. This paper aims at examining the socio-economic impact of Kudumbasree among the Kurichiya, one of the scheduled tribes of Kerala. An overview of the Kudumbasree Project was given followed by micro finance operations in Kannavan Colony. The external features and dimensions of the micro finance approach were listed followed by a description of the Kannavam Colony. The basic data about Kannavan Colony was given in terms of number of houses, family, male, female population, SSLC, PDC and DC. It was concluded that Kudumbasree became the life line to Kurichiya women and it has proved without any doubt that women empowerment is the best strategy for the community development.

Dr. R.V.L.N. Ratnakar Rao and Prof. V. Krishna Murthy in their paper on "*Sustainable Development of Women–Issues and Problems*" observed that the Eleventh Plan proposes a five fold agenda for gender equity. A brief description of the National Mission for empowerment of women was given followed by ICDS, NPEGEL, Mid Day Meals in Schools, DPEP and interventions for girls education initiated under the programme. There are other schemes like Kasturiba Gandhi Balika Vidyalaya, TRYSEM and National Rural Employment Guarantee Schemes. Finally the concept of gender budgeting was introduced followed by union budget to ensure gender responsive health care system, maternal health services and obstetrics care etc. It was also added that need based, community run crèches will also be introduced to tackle malnutrition.

P. Jayanand Kumar, M. Sridevi and P. Raj Kumar in their paper on "*Women Entrepreneurship in India– Problems and Prospects*" observed that having realised the importance of the role of women in the nation's development in the Sixth Five Year Plan a special chapter on women's development has been included and explains the plan of action for integration of women in development. The authors define women entrepreneurship, need for women entrepreneurship, functions, characteristics, types and status of women entrepreneurs in India followed by problems of women entrepreneurs and suggestions for improving the status of women entrepreneurs. The authors conclude that as entrepreneurship opportunities will be more in small and medium scale industries, the sector should be given prominence and proper marketing strategy of such products should be planned and implemented which will give scope for women entrepreneurs.

"*Empowerment of Muslim Women Entrepreneurship in Visakhapatnam City*" by **B. Ratna Kumari and G. Zilani Begum** observe that the status of Muslim women in our country is relatively low compared with other women, hence the need to study the Muslim women entrepreneurship. The data and findings are related to the percentage distribution of Muslim women entrepreneurs by age, by marital status, educational qualifications, family size, house type, source of drinking water, toilet facilities, professional/vocational qualifications, business experience, occupation of the respondent's husband, source of credit facilities, initial investment, raw materials, source of materials, marketing problem, financial problem faced, etc. The study recommends that banking policy needs to be implemented in favour of women with greater flexibility.

Prof. V. Krishna Murthy and Dr. R.V.L.N. Ratnakar Rao in their Paper on "*Women Empowerment and Gandhi's Contribution*" observed that the status of women in Gandhi's eyes was that of equal standing as man. His rapport with women including, his written correspondence to the ashram women displays a sincere sense of dignity for women. The authors discuss about Ba and Bapu, Bapu's letters to Ashram Sisters, Gandhi's views on equality, regeneration of women, women leaders followed by four indicators of the status of women. Further, the authors examine the political role of women, women in the Freedom Movement, participation of women in mass movements and Gandhi's efforts, followed by women's status in post-Gandhian era, handicaps and changing perceptions, indicating that on the positive side, more women are doing things that they have not done before and contribute to society's perceptions of what women are and what they can do.

Prof. D. Pulla Rao

Profile of Prof. K.S. Chalam

Prof. K.S. Chalam in whose honour the present book is edited is an Alma Mater of Andhra University. He is a well known Educationist, Political Economist and an innovator of Staff Development Programme in India. He has entered the U P S C in 2005 after a brief stint as Vice Chancellor at Dravidian University, A P.

He served the Department of Economics, Andhra University as a Lecturer, Reader and Professor for more than three decades with dedication and distinction. He was trained as an Economic Planner at Central School of Planning and Statistics, Warsaw, Poland during 1981-1982. He has obtained first rank in the international diploma programme of the school. As a student of Prof. B. Sarveswara Rao, he has strengthened the teaching of Economics of Education and Human Development. He has delivered endowment lectures on Public Sector and on issues relating to educational development at several universities and institutes in the country. He has published so far 20 books in English and 6 in Telugu and about 90 research papers covering areas of Economics of Education, Political Economy, Public Economics, Dravidian Studies etc,. Some of his articles published in Economic and Political Weekly are still cited in several reference works. In his forthcoming book on "Economic Reforms and Social Exclusion" he has made an attempt to bring interdisciplinary approach to study the impact of reforms on the socially excluded groups in India. His book on "Caste-based Reservations and Human Development in

India" published by Sage Publications in 2007 was reviewed in around 20 leading newspapers and journals including the Hindu, the Tribune, etc appreciating the author for the innovative approach used to understand and solve the contentious issue of our times. The reviewers in Pakistan and DFID commended the book as "immense topical relevance, this book will be of interest to students and scholars of development studies....useful to policy makers and practitioners working in this area". The book is being translated into Tamil and Telugu. An honours diploma thesis was submitted by Natasha Azad to California University on this book.

Prof. K.S. Chalam is an internationally recognized scholar, teacher in Staff Development and Economics of Education. He is known in the country as the father of the famous Academic Staff Colleges Scheme as he was the one who initiated the concept in 1985. At a time when the professors of the university system were not given any structured training to improve the quality of higher education, Prof. Chalam initiated a training course with UGC support in 1985. The UGC has recognized his contribution and asked him to conduct the first national workshop to design the proposed Academic Staff Colleges in India. He himself founded the college in 1987 and organized the first orientation course. It became an important part of the system of higher education to improve the Quality of Higher Education. The UNESCO has appreciated the scheme as one of the largest schemes of Staff Development in the world. He was responsible in strengthening the scheme with his 3 important publications on staff development. The latest (2006) book on 'Modern Techniques of Teaching and Staff Development' is a reference volume for all teachers in higher education. He has delivered lectures on Staff Development and participated in deliberations of the Prof. Rastogi Committee. It has helped to consolidate the scheme in the interest of Quality of University Education. Chalam K.S. was the first student trained formally in a university system in Economics of Education in 1972 at Andhra University under Prof. B. Sarveswara Rao. Late J.P. Naik inaugurated the specialization. He has worked for his Ph.D on 'Finances, costs and productivity of higher education'. The study published as a book was reviewed both in India and abroad. Late Dr. Malcolm Adiseshiah acclaimed it as 'an excellent analysis of the economics of education in Andhra Pradesh as such is an important addition to the limited literature in India'. Another reviewer Dijon Jean-Claude Eicher commended it as a "courageous and useful book". He was Professor of Economics in Andhra University and taught the specialization both in the Departments of Economics and Education for a generation of students. He has pioneered interdisciplinary research and published 'Education and Weaker Sections' in 1988. Prof. P.R. Panchamukhi in his review of the book mentioned that 'the interdisciplinary approach to the study of educational problems is a useful framework'. Some of his books are offered as Text books for P.G students. He is one of the very rare research guides who has trained a dozen research students on a variety of issues starting from Human Development in A.P (before HD Report, 1990), Child Labour, Primary Education, Dalit Poverty, Impact of Technology on Agriculture, Liberalization to name a few. He is a prolific writer in Telugu. Apart from 6 Books in Telugu, scores of edit page articles were published in all leading dailies. He has supervised 12 scholars successfully to obtain their Ph. Ds in Economics, conducted research studies funded by UGC, Govt. of A.P, UNICEF, etc.

The contributions of Prof. Chalam are cited by scholars and activists across the globe. He has kept a legacy of teaching at Andhra University. One of the citations of an award rightly remarked that he is a 'scholar with social consciousnesses'. A Volume of papers were contributed in his honour in the name of 'Development of Weaker Sections' in 1998. As the third Vice-Chancellor of Dravidian University for a brief period, he has produced a programme of action for the university. He is also known as the first Director of Swamy Ramanand Teertha Rural Institute, the first institute of NCRI, Govt. of India. His experiments with rural higher education for one year at Pochampally published later in a book are useful as a reference work. He is the founder Editor of 'South India Journal of Social Sciences'.

Prof. K.S. Chalam commands respect among the academicians and activists due to his committed service in public affairs over a period of three decades. He is not an armchair scholar. He has been actively involved in public affairs relating to education and social development. All his studies in economics are interdisciplinary in nature and contain social issues with economic analysis of development. Therefore one of his biographers Avinash Misra called him as Simon Kuznets of India.

He has single handedly projected the underdevelopment of North Andhra with his publications and lectures for the last three decades making the Govt. of Andhra Pradesh to appoint a separate development board for the region in 2007. He is not an idealist but a practical person who got himself married outside his caste and implemented the same principle for the entire family. He has performed more than hundred social marriages in A.P.

Prof. Chalam is not only a serious scholar and teacher, but also a social activist. He served as the National Secretary, Amnesty International during 1984-85, Secretary and Vice-President of Professional bodies like A.P. Economic Association, Indian Political Economy Association etc. He has participated in international debates on caste and race at Durban, Cairo etc. He has presented papers on Education, Poverty, Political Economy at Cambridge, Wisconsin, Manchester, Colombo, Bangkok and at other international fora. He has been on several expert committees at center and State levels and has served on the World Bank teams. He is a builder of institutions. The Academic Staff College that he has nurtured at Andhra University became a model for the entire country. He has started Mahendra Degree College in his native place, Pathapatnam a decade ago to provide higher educational facilities in a remote tribal region. He got his Economics honours from S K C G College, Parlakhemundi, Orissa. He studied in the college as a day scholar walking the distance from his native place in Andhra crossing the border everyday for 4 years. He was the first Telugu person to receive honours degree from Utkal (Berhampur) University in 1968 at an age of 19. He became a Lecturer at a very young age that helped him to develop passion for teaching and research. The passion for teaching made him to continue his advice to the UGC as Hon. Chairman of a 'High Power Committee on Academic Staff Colleges' even after joining the UPSC. He is on several committees including NCRI, ICPR on an advisory capacity. He has an impeccable character and sound knowledge in social sciences that helped him to become Member, UPSC. It is said that his presence in the UPSC made people from lower socio-economic background to get inspired to enter into civil services to serve the country and people. This is reflected in the results of recent Civil Services Examination.

List of Contributors

T. Chandrasekarayya, Assistant Professor, Dept of Population Studies & Social Work, S.V. University, Tirupati, 517 502, AP.

D. Sai Sujatha, Associate Professor, Dept of Population Studies & Social Work, S.V. University, Tirupati, 517 502, AP.

Dharmana Rama Rao, Assistant Professor, Department of Sociology, Andhra University, Visakhapatnam.

Gullipali Rajeswari, Senior Lecturer, Department of English, M.R. College of Education, Vizianagaram.

M. R. Geetha Bala, Lecturer, Dept. of Economics, Sri Satya Sai University, Anantapur Campus, Anantapur, (A.P.)

G. Satyanarayana, Professor, Dept. of Economics., Sri Krishnadevaraya University, Anantapur-5151001. (A.P.)

A. Lavanya Kumari, Department of Economics, Andhra University, Visakhapatnam.

B. Mohan Rao, Department of Sociology, Andhra University, Visakhapatnam.

K. Madhu Babu, Assistant Professor, Department of Economics, Acharya Nagarjuna University, Guntur.

A. Vamsi Krushna, Research Scholar, Dept. of Economics, Andhra University, Visakhapatnam

P. Jayanand Kumar, Lecturer, Govt. Junior College, Chagallu, West Godavari Dt., A.P.

P. Raj Kumar, Research Scholar, Dept. of Economics, Andhra University, Visakhapatnam

A.V. Naga Varma, Faculty Member, PG Courses & Research Centre, DNR College, Bhimavaram-534 202, (A.P.)

M. Ravi Kumar, MA (Economics) Final, PG Courses & Research Centre, DNR College, Bhimavaram-2. (A.P.)

M. Anil Kumar, MA (Economics) Final, PG Courses & Research Centre, DNR College, Bhimavaram-2. (A.P.)

B. Naveen Kumar, MA (Economics) Final, PG Courses & Research Centre, DNR College, Bhimavaram-2. (A.P.)

R. Radha, Assistant Professor, GITAM Institute of International Business, Gandhi Nagar Campus, Rushikonda, Visakhapatnam-530 045.

Rais Ahmad, Chairman, Department of Agricultural Economics & Business Management, Aligarh Muslim University, Aligarh, Uttar Pradesh.

R. Ramakrishna, Professor, Dept of Economics, Andhra University, Visakhapatnam.

Y. Rama Krishna, Reader, P.G. Department of Economics, D.N.R.College, Bhimavaram, West Godavari Dt. (A.P.)

D. Tata Rao, Teaching Associate, Dept. of Rural Development, Dr. B.R. Ambedkar University, Etcherla, Srikakulam. (A.P.)

D. Nageswara Rao, Research Scholar, Dept. of Economics, Andhra University, Visakhapatnam.

T. V. Ramana, Faculty, Department of Economics, Andhra University Campus, Kakinada, Andhra Pradesh.

P. Subba Rao, Reader com Deputy Director, Centre for study of Social Exclusion and Inclusive Policy, Andhra University. Visakhapatnam.

B. Ratna Kumari, Dr. Durgabhai Deshmukh Centre for Womens' Studies, Andhra University, Visakhapatnam.

M. Anitha, Research Scholar, Department of Economics, Andhra University, Visakhapatnam.

D. Francis, Teaching Associate, Dept. of Economics, Dr. B.R. Ambedkar University, Etcherla, Srikakulam, Andhra Pradesh.

R. Vijaya Krishna, Research Scholar, Dept. of Economics, Andhra University, Visakhapatnam.

D. Suseela, Research Scholar, Dept. of Economics, Andhra University, Visakhapatnam.

M. Sridevi, Research Scholar, Department of Economics, Andhra University, Visakhapatnam.

K. Somasekhar, Assistant Professor, Department of Rural Development, Acharya Nagarjuna University, Guntur-522 510. (A.P.)

D. Sunder Raj, RBI Chair of Council for Social Development, Southern Regional Centre, Rajendranagar, Hyderabad–500 030.

R. Venkata Ravi, RBI Chair of Council for Social Development, Southern Regional Centre, Rajendranagar, Hyderabad–500 030.

M. Syamala, Lecturer, Department of Economics, Hindu College, Guntur. (A.P.)

L.K. Mohana Rao, Professor, Department of Economics, Andhra University, Visakhapatnam, A.P.

M. Sundara Rao, Professor, Department of Economics, Andhra University, Visakhapatnam-530 003 (AP).

D. Pulla Rao, Professor, Department of Economics, Andhra University, Visakhapatnam-530 003 (AP).

Ch. Appa Rao, Assistant Professor, Dept. of Economics, Andhra University, Visakhapatnam.

G. Ramachandrudu, Professor, Dept. of Economics, Andhra University, Visakhapatnam.

S. Prasada Rao, Research Scholar, Dept. of Economics, Andhra University, Visakhapatnam.

A. Venu, Research Scholar, Dept. of Economics, Andhra University, Visakhapatnam.

J. Chandra Prasad, Associate Professor in Commerce and former Director, P.G.Courses and Research Centre, D.N.R. College, Bhimavaram – 534 202, A.P.

Jagannath B. Kukkudi, Faculty Member, Department of Studies & Research in Management, Gulbarga University, Gulbarga-585 106, Karnataka.

Ramesh B. Agadi, Dean and Chairman, Department of Studies & Research in Management, Gulbarga University, Gulbarga-585 106, Karnataka.

Veershetty Rathod, Faculty Member, Govt. First Grade College of commerce and Management, Kalgi, Gulbarga District, Karnataka.

Sanjeeb Kumar Jena, Lecturer in Commerce, Aeronautics College, HAL Township, Sunabeda-763002, Orissa.

Jayanta K. Parida, Professor of Commerce, Utkal University, Bhubaneswar-751004, Orissa.

K.A. Rasure, Selection Grade Lecturer in Economics, Nrupatunga Arts and Commerce College, Sedam – 585 222, Gulbarga Dist, Karnataka.

M. Savithri, Assistant Professor, Department of Economics, Nizam College, Osmania University. Hyderabad.

K. R. Rama Mohan, Assistant Director, Centre for Study of Social Exclusion and Inclusive Policy, Andhra University, Visakhapatnam-530003.

V. Subramanyam, Director, Centre for Study of Social Exclusion and Inclusive Policy, Andhra University, Visakhapatnam-530003

Vineeth Sahadevan, Research Scholar, Department of Anthropology, School of Social Sciences, Kannur University, Thalassery Campus, Palayad, Kerala 670 661.

A.P. Prajina, Research Scholar, Department of Anthropology, School of Social Sciences, Kannur University, Thalassery Campus, Palayad, Kerala 670 661.

R.V.L.N. Ratnakar Rao, Dept. of Physical Education, Andhra University, Visakhapatnam.

V. Krishna Murthy, Retd. Professor, Dept. of Education, Andhra University, Visakhapatnam.

Zilani Begum, Research Scholar, Dept. of Economics, Andhra University, Visakhapatnam.

CHAPTER-1

Women Development Indicators in India: An Overview

T. Chandrasekarayya, D. Sai Sujatha

Introduction

The development of a society or a nation depends on the social as well as economically wellbeing of women. The national plan of action for Women adopted in 1976 became a guiding document for development of women. Moreover, a National Perspective Plan for Women drafted in (1988-2000) was advocating a holistic approach for the development of women. Efforts of the Government and Non-Government agencies for development of women over the decades lead to appreciable improvements in the development of women.

In India, half of the population consists of women. They are the hard workers in the country and creating greatest change in living and social conditions for the larger number of people. Hence, the empowerment of women is the key to the socio-economic development of the community and the success lies in development. However, in the modern India women role in many aspects underwent changes, which is essential for sustainable development in which women play a direct and exclusive role in various aspects.

Importance

The study of women development aspects over a period provides in depth knowledge on changing trends of women development indicators, which has a comprehensive effect on women empowerment, and is a great concern for Planners and policy makers. The present paper therefore aims at studying the trends of women development indicators in India.

Data Base and Method

The data for the study have taken from source like: census of India, Sample Registration System and Family Welfare Year Book etc. Major data covers for a period of ten decades (1901-2001). The women development indicators considered are literacy rate, work participation rate, workers by sector wise, Sex Ratio, Mean age at marriage, life expectancy, Total fertility Rate and couple protection Rate. Data on all these female aspects are presented in Table-1.

Female Literacy Rate

One of the important indicators of women development is the level of literacy and educational attainment. It is a component of wellbeing and a factor in development through links with demographic as well as economic and social factors. The increase in the education of women empowerment leads to postponement of age at marriage, reduction in the family size, greater chance of work participation and contributes to greater empowerment. The progress of female literacy in India from 1901 to 2001 is presented in Table-1. Female literacy underwent gradual changes since 1901. It was 0.7 Per cent in 1901, increased to 54.2 per cent in 2001. Thus, the movement of Female literacy in India is encouraging. This increasing rate of female literacy helps to raise the status of women and also contributes to the development of the country. It enable the women to know their rights as well as privileges and helps to empower women. Here it's worth while to note that in Kerala, the early promotion female literacy has contributed to higher status of women. (Mahadevan,1987) which in turn caused to social development.

Table 1
Women Development Indicators in India, 1901-2001

Census Year	Female Literacy Rate[1] (%)	Female Work Participation Rate[1] (%)	Female Workers by Sector Wise[1] (%): Primary	Secondary	Territory	Sex Ratio[1]	Mean Age at Marriage of Female[2]	Life Exception[3] (Years)	Year	T.F.R[3]	Year	C.P.R[4]
1901	0.65	31.7	74.5	13.2	12.3	972	13.1	23.96	1971	5.2	1970	10.6
1911	1.05	33.7	77.1	11.4	11.4	964	13.2	23.31	1974	4.9	1980	22.3
1921	1.81	32.7	78.8	10.2	11.0	955	13.7	20.91	1977	4.5	1988	33.9
1931	2.93	27.6	76.2	9.7	14.0	950	12.7	25.56	1981	4.5	1990	43.3
1941	7.30	—	—	—	—	945	14.7	31.37	1983	4.5	1991	44.1
1951	7.93	23.3	79.6	8.3	12.2	946	15.6	31.66	1986	4.2	1994	45.4
1961	12.95	28.0	82.6	8.6	8.8	941	15.8	40.55	1991	3.6	2001	45.6
1971	18.69	11.8	83.0	7.7	9.4	930	15.8	44.70	1993	3.5	2002	45.7
1981	24.82	19.7	81.6	9.1	9.4	934	17.2	50.00	1996	3.4	2003	47.1
1991	39.30	22.3	81.1	8.1	10.8	927	19.0	59.10	2001	3.1	2004	47.2
2001	54.20	25.7*	—	—	—	933	17.2**	66.10	2005	2.9	2005	46.6

Source:

1. Censes of India, 1991, Series – 1, Final population Totals. & Censes of India, 2001, Series-1, provisional population Totals
2. Shirivastava, O.S. 1996: Demography, and population studies.
3. R.G. of India, 2006: sample Registrations system, New Delhi.
4. Ministry of Health and Family welfare. Family Welfare Year Book.

* Data references to 1999-2000, N.S.So 55th Round

** Data from N.F.H.S. – III,: 2005-06 for 20-49 age group of women, I.I.P.S. Bombay.

Work Participation Rate

Development is assumed to be accompanied by an increase in occupational opportunities for women which in turn perceived to increase the age at marriage and contraceptive adoption there by contributing more towards the development. This is also evident in the state of Manipur; where the economic empowerment has led to the emancipation of women (Durga Prasad, 2005). Table-1 furnishes data on female work participation. It was 31.7 per cent in 1901 drastically decline in several decades and recorded 25.7 percent in 2001. Thus, the female work participation rate has varied greatly over the decades.

Works by Sector-Wise

It is a refined measure than the female work participation rate, because it gives information on women's economic activity by sector wise over a period of time. Table-1 gives data on female workers by sector wise. The dominance of the primary sector in providing employment for females in India is clearly established over time. Further, it has slightly increased in the period of 1961-2001. Moreover, in secondary sector, the participation was slightly better in the beginning accounting 13.2 per cent in 1901. However from 1951, there was a decline till 1991 (8.1per cent) except during 1981 which showed an increase (9.1per cent). On the other hand, in the tertiary sector there was a decline from 12.3 in 1901 to 8.8 per cent in 1961 and after that there was a slight improvement (10.8 per cent) in 1991. The shift from primary to secondary and tertiary sectors leads to an increase the level of economic production. Further, it leads to urban exposure, modernization with greater socio-cultural, political and legal aspects, which in turn enhances the status of women. It is said to note that Indian economy has till now miserably failed in providing employment to females in secondary and tertiary sectors.

Sex Ratio

In most populations of the world, the overall Sex Ratio is favorable to females; while in India, it is adverse to women.

Sex Ratio is defined as number of females per 1000 males. Sex Ratio was 972 in 1901, came down to 941 in 1961 and further declined to 933 in 2001. This is due to female infanticides, induced abortions, differentials in child mortality, the neglect of females not only in the childhood, but also at almost all ages in spite of their pivotal role in national development.

Age at Marriage

Age at Marriages is one of the factors, which shows the empowerment and autonomy of women. The expansion of work opportunities out side of agriculture, especially for women has substantially increased the individuals' economic independence from parents, there by helping the girls to determine there own marriage matters. Table-1 gives the pictures of mean age at marriage for females form 1901-2001. It was 13.1 years in 1901, raised to 15.8 in 1961 and increased to 20.0 year in 2001. Indian mean age at marriage for females has gradually showed an upward movement

This is also due to the prevalence of nuclear families type, weaken of the kinship ties, diversity of economic activities outside the homes. Higher educational levels in urban areas have affected the way of people to look at marriage of the family. Further, the difficulties associated with Job opportunities and living conditions in recent years have also contributed to delay in marriages.

Life Expectancy

Life expectancy is the "average number of years which a person of that age may expect to live". Demographers consider it as one of the best indicator for countries level of development and the overall health status of its population. The developed countries have higher life expectancy (Japan, 86; Hongkong, 85), Where in, females are socio-economically well of (U.N, 2008). Table-1 furnishes data on female life expectancy. It was 24.0 year in 1901, increased to 32.0 by 1951, 50.0 years by 1981, reached to 66.1 years by 2001. Thus, female life expectancy has been increasing fast in recent decades. This is due to general improvement in the health care services.

Total Fertility Rate (TFR)

In demographic sense, it is one of the indices of women's status. U.N (2008) report shows that in developed countries women are socio-economically developed; where in TFR is very low. (Japan 1.3; Hongkong 1.8); while in developing countries it is vice versa. TFR is measured as total number of children born per women in her reproductive period. Table-1 provides data on TFR in India. It was 5.2 in 1971, which were came down to 4.5, 3.5 and 2.9 in 1983, 1993 sand 2005 respectively.

Couple Protection Rate

The couple protection rate has shown an increase where females are better in their socio-economic and cultural aspects. In demography, it is the best indicator of women's status. Though, couple protection rate includes male sterilization, it is marginal compared to female methods. It defined as couples effectively protected from child birth. Table-1 provides data on couple protection rate. It was 11.0 per cent in 1970 which increased to 45.4 per cent in 1994, 47.1 per cent in 2003 and 47.0 per cent by 2005. Therefore, couple protection has been increasing over the decades.

Summary and Implications

The development of society or a nation depends on the social as well as economic wellbeing of women. Though women constitute around half of the population, in spite of the 50 years of planning and development in India, women are not fully drawn in to the main stream of the developmental aspects. Hence, an attempt has been made here to analyse the changing trends of women indicators; which will be useful for planners and policy makers. The main objective of the study is to analyze some developmental indicators of women over a period of ten decades (1901-2001). The data for the present study have been taken from census of India, Family Welfare Year Books, and sample Registration system etc. The women development indicators considered are: Literacy rate, work participation rate, work force by sector, SexRatio, mean age at marriage; Life expectancy; Total fertility rate and couple protection rate.

The findings reveal that the total literacy levels of the women increased drastically over the ten decades (1901-2001) from 0.6 per cent to 54.2 per cent. The work participation rate has decline from 31.7 per cent in 1901 to 25.7 percent in 2001. The data on female workers by sector wise have shown the dominance in the primary sector. In the secondary and tertiary sectors though the participation was better in the beginning; it has declined in the further decades. The sex ratio has shown a declining trend from 972 in 1901 to 933 in 2001, shown an adverse and unfavorable environment for women survival. The mean age at marriage has shown an improvement from 13.1 year in 1901 to 20.0 years in 2001, for a period of hundred years, the age at marriage has shown only a 7 years of upward movement. The life expectancy has increased from 24.0 years in 1901 to 66.1 years by 2001, It was due to general improvement in the health care services and utilization. The total fertility rate and the couple protection rate have shown an improvement over the period of ten decades (1901 to 2001). The findings are showing an improvement in development aspects of women. In order to further improve in these women developmental aspects and other socio-cultural factors in India, active involvement of NGOS and mass public movement is the need apart from the governmental efforts.

References

Shrivastava, O.S.(1996), Demography and Population Studies, Vikas Publishing House, PVT LTD. New Delhi.

Mahadevan, et.al. (1989), "Women in Indian Society"; in Mahadevan eds: Women and Population Dynamics, Perspectives from Asian Countries, Sage Publications, New Delhi; pp. 187-204.

Durgaprasad, G. (2005), "Coherent Family System; Dynamics of Gernder Equity" in Koteswar Raju et.al eds: Organization and management of institutions for family well-being: College community network centre; D.N.R. College Association, Bhimavaram, A.P. INDIA.

U.N. (2008), Population Data Sheet: Economic and Social Commission for Asia and Pacific, Thailand.

Registered General of India (2006), Family Welfare Statistics, Ministry of Health and Family Welfare, New Delhi.

Census India (1991), Series–I, Final Population Totals; R.G. of India, New Delhi.

Censes of India (2001), Series–I; Provisional Population Totals: R.G. of India, New Delhi.

CHAPTER-2

Self Help Groups and Women Empowerment

Dharmana Rama Rao, Gullipali Rajeswari

Introduction

The complexity of the concept of 'women empowerment' is clear from the different interpretations and methodologies that have been used to measure it. It is therefore not surprising that every investigation of the impact of microfinance programmes on women empowerment has its own incomplete interpretation of the concept. Using the World Bank's definition of empowerment along with Kabeer's sensible interpretation of women empowerment within the South Asian context, this paper argues for a more strict interpretation of women empowerment. It is interpreted as the process in which a woman challenges the existing norms and culture to effectively improve her well-being. A distinction is therefore made between the outcomes that lead to greater efficiency within the existing norms, community driven development (CDD) and outcomes that can be directly interpreted as women empowerment.

When a woman is better able to perform such activities, it leads to an increase in her self-confidence and feeling of well being. This might create conditions leading to woman empowerment. Similarly, Community Driven Development activities, undertaken under the initiative of the SHGs-for instance, solving drinking water problems in the village, reduces the demand on a woman's time while leading to better health of all household members, particularly children. However, most of these activities are for the welfare at the household (including women) or community but are not directly empowering.

SHG Bank Linkage Programme

A study conducted by NABARD in the mid-eighties revealed that financial services required by poor households are: safe-keeping of small surpluses in the form of thrift; access to consumption loans to meet emergency needs and financial services and products that did not require collateral (MYRADA, 2002). The Self Help Group Bank Linkage model evolved from the pioneering efforts of NABARD and two NGOs, MYRADA and PRADHAN. Starting with 500 groups in the early 1990s, the cumulative numbers of SHGs that have been financed have increased to 2,238,565, by March 2006. The expansion of the SHG bank linkage programme has been acceleration in the past few years. It has reached an estimated 164.90 million people and disbursed more than Rs.114 billion in cumulative bank loans up to March 2006, using a network of 44,362 bank branches and 4896 NGOs (Table-1).

The government's poverty alleviation programmes such as Swaranajayanti Grama Swarojgar Yojna (SGSY) and the Rashtriya Mahila Kosh implement their programmes through microfinance interventions of NABARD's Self Help Group bank linkage programme.

Using higher rates of savings, borrowings, timely repayment of credit, promptness in attending SHG meetings and decisions by individual members as indicators of enhanced credit access, income generation and socio-economic empowerment of the poor. Puhanzhendi and Badatya (2002), Ramakrishna R (2004, 2005) find that the SHG programme has a positive social impact. Puhanzhendi and Satyasai (2001), Ramakrishna at al. (2008) further argue that the social impact of these programmes on the household is greater than the economic impact.

Table 1
Information on Self Help Groups

A. Physical Achievements	
1. Number of poor families who have accessed bank credit up to March 2006.	32.98 million
2. Estimated number of poor people assisted up to March 2006.	164.90 million
3. Percentage of SHGs comprised of women	90
4. Cumulative number of SHGs financed by banks up to March 2006	2, 238,565
B. Financial Results	
1. Cumulative bank loans disbursed to SHGs up to March 2006.	113,975 million
2. Bank loans disbursed to new SHGs during 2005-2006	23,305 million
3. Increase in credit flow to SHGs over the previous year	50%
4. On-time repayment reported by participating banks	Over 95 per cent
Partnerships	
1. Number of participating banks	547
2. Commercial banks	47
3. Regional Rural Bank	158
4. Cooperatives	342
5. Number of bank branches lending to SHGs	44,362
6. Number of participating NGO and other agencies.	4,896

**Source*: Progress of SHG – Bank Linkage in India, 2005-2006, Micro Credit Innovations Department, NABARD, Mumbai, 2006., ** IUSD = Rs. 43.

Conclusion

Given this detailed investigation of women with respect to the control of resources, changes in behaviour and the decision-making reveals that many strides have been made in the right direction and women are in the process of empowering themselves. But examining the evidence on some key issues both within the quantitative household data and the Focus Group Discussions (FGDs), suggests that a lot needs to change to make women truly empowered.

References

MYRADA (2002), "Impact of Self Help Groups (Group Processes) on the Social Empowerment Status of Women Members in Southern India", paper presented at the Seminar on SHG Bank Linkage Programme, New Delhi.

Puhazhendi, V. and Badatya, K.C. (2002), "SHG Bank Linkage Programme for Rural Poor- An Impact Assessment", paper presented at the seminar on SHG bank linkage programme at New Delhi, Micro Credit Innovations Department, NABARD, Mumbai.

Puhazhendi, V. and Satyasai, K.J.S. (2001), "Economic and Social Empowerment of Rural Poor through SHGs", Indian Journal of Agricultural Economics, Vol. 56. No.3.

Ramakrishna R. (2004), "Empowering Rural Women though Self Help Groups", Indira Devi. M (Ed), Strategies for Sustainability of Self-Help Groups, Visakhapatnam: A.U Press and Publications, p.163-170.

Ramakrishna R. (2005), "Empowerment of Women through Sustainability of Micro Finance", Co-operative Perspective, Journal of Co-operative Management, Vol. 39(4), Jan-March. pp. 1-8.

Ramakrishna R. and Tata Rao D. (2008), "Urban Poverty Alleviation through Self-Help Groups and Micro Credit", Vijayalakshmi B and Swami Das R (Ed) SHGs and Role of Social Work Profession, Seminar Volume, Dept. of Social Work, Andhra University, Visakhapatnam, March, 16th & 17th.

CHAPTER-3

Empowerment of Women-Self Help Groups

M. R. Geetha Bala, G. Satyanarayana

Introduction

The modern world has been witnessing a positive trend in the empowerment of women despite their shortcomings in education and literacy, health and nutrition, training and generation, legislative and judicial reforms. However, the empowering strategies need substantial fine-tuning to ensure that they are effective and result-oriented. The vision for the future should be built on gender perspective; hence, there is a need for a comprehensive and holstic policy for women. This would enable to country to full fill the constitutional mandate of women's equality and the objective of women's total involvement in the development of the nation.

The position of women as central role players in the over all development of a society is proved during the long evolution of societies in different parts of the world. It is also proved that no true development is possible without women's participation. It has been documented in a plethora of studies that in societies where such social and economic empowerment of women was initiated there have been positive implications on economic development, gender equality and social justice.

It is for this reason woman was and is described as better half of a man.

However, in reality, the status of woman throughout the world particularly in developing countries like India does not reflect the above description. In most of the South Asian countries, the status of women is comparatively low and their socioeconomic conditions are much more disheartening than that of men and India is no exception in this context, as women are still suffering in the spheres of social and economic life as second rated citizens.

Among various reasons for the above situation, the level of poverty is definitely identified as major impediments. Further, either limited or marginal employment opportunities in many of the socio-economic activities, low levels of skill, lack of education have all contributed to low economic status to women in India. In addition, malnutrition, poor literacy levels, poor status of health and exposure to various unkind treatments like domestic violence, if not equally significantly restricted women's participation in the development process of the country.

All these factors contributed to the deplorable condition of women in our society. As against this background the study on empowerment of women holds a lot of contemporary relevance in the context of development and poverty alleviation programs. To achieve this empowerment various approaches were adapted and models experimented. One such successful approach is micro credit at the grass root levels. It is this approach that in recent times received wide publicity world over. It is in this context, the study examined the various issues related to empowerment of women in India in general and Anantapur district in Andhra Pradesh in particular.

Importance of the Study

The empowerment of women is one of the crucial elements in social and economic development as it enhances the quality of human resources. Further, the success of development efforts depends on the fruits of development reaching women. The final but one of the most fundamental reasons for promoting the empowerment of women, is the failure of empowering women as well as men to realize their full potential which tantamount to violation of their basic human rights.

The Human Development Report 1995 by UNDP has highlighted the predicament of women with the following observations:

- Women constitute 70 per cent of the world's poor
- 65 per cent of the world's illiterates are women
- globally two-thirds of women's work is unpaid
- The value of women's hidden contribution to the global Economy exceeds S $11 Trillions!
- women hold only 10 per cent of parliamentary posts in the world; and
- Women are allotted less than a tenth of the bank's credit in the world.

The World Bank has observed in its report (1991) that "women are central to the success of poverty alleviation efforts in the short and medium as in the long run."

There are several cogent and pressing reasons for evaluating, promoting and monitoring the level of women's empowerment in India, and it is necessary for ensuring not just their own welfare, but also the well being of the entire household. The role of women in the Indian society is vital. Apart from the matriarchal society, women play a decisive role in most of the patriarchal societies also. The future of children depends, by and large, upon the mother who generally stays at home and takes care of her children's health and education. This is particularly so in countries like India where society and life of people are molded by traditional and religious foundations.

According to the 2001 census, there are 4,948.28 lakh women out of a total population of 10,252.51 lakhs. Of these women, about 3,605.19 lakhs live in the rural areas. The share of women in the country's labour force stands at 31.56 per cent only. The female work participation rate registered an increase from 22.3 per cent in 1991 to 32.3 per cent in 2001. Of the 51.98 million female workers engaged in agriculture and allied activities, 45 per cent are employed as agricultural laborers.

In addition, women's access to land ownership is extremely limited and there is discrimination against women infixing the wage rate due to the seasonal nature of work, women workers get only 90 to 100 days of regular employment in a year.

Gender inequality is felt in many aspects of women's life. Lack of entrepreneurial ability and marketing skills restrict women to the traditional sectors, which do not yield resources, viz., their abilities, interest, skills and other potentials are of paramount importance for mobilization and development of human resources.

Objectives of the Study

As the focus of the present study is to assess the impact of SHGs on the socio economic status on women, the following objectives are considered relevant and essential.

1. To review the socio-economic profile of Micro Credit beneficiaries in the context of different empowerment dimensions in Anantapur District.
2. To examine the socio-economic empowerment of women through micro-credit and to assess its impact on socio-economic variables on income generation activities of women.
3. To take stock of achievements in managerial empowerment through the managerial practices adopted by the groups.
4. To investigate the status of women in pre and post SHG period, particularly in the context of managerial empowerment.
5. To evaluate the existing method of selection of beneficiaries.
6. To assess the influence of SHGs on women empowerment in Anantapur District.

Methodology and Empirical Study

The study was undertaken in 2004-05. This Study confines to the Anantapur District, which comprises 63 blocks with *28,114 SHGs* under the guidance of *83 NGOs*.

A sample of 240 was selected from Garladinne, Pamidi, Kuderu, Kanaganapalli, Heerehal and Nallacharuvu.

- The Multiple regressions are more widely used statistical technique to find the relationships among the considered variables. This can be expressed as a mathematical model.
- $Yi = \beta 1+\beta 2X2i+\beta 3X3i+ \ldots\ldots +\beta k\ Xki+\epsilon i,$

  $i = 1, 2 \ldots.N$
- From the income generation model we can observe that the variables AGB, Own Investment, SHG loan, and supplementary income were found to be statistically significant to some extent. Other variables were not statistically significant. However R square is moderate i.e. 0.376 which is common in cross sectional studies.
- From the investment model, assets and supplementary income were found to be highly significant. Family size and occupation of the respondent are also to be significant to some extent. In this model R square is moderately high i.e. 0.526. So, we can believethat the assets contributing towards their investment, which is a general phenomena in the theory of Investment.
- Basically when a dependent variable is of categorical nature we use either probit or logit models. Binary logit model is used to investigate the various causes for the selection of the activity.
- That the Mcfadden R square is 0.32. The variables age, age of the group, DRDA, supplementary income were found to be statistically significant ($p<0.01$).
- The variable SPLINC shows the negative relation with activity implies that the probability that this activity preferred as secondary since the alternative activities provide them better opportunities.
- We found to know what the factors motivated the members to undergo this training program we employed the logit model.

- That the variables like EDU and AOG are statistically significant. This shows as the level of education is more, people realize the importance of the training program
- It is one of the popular multivariate statistical tools to identify the factors from a given set of variables.
- This is also viewed as a data reduction technique
- To find the factors which are influencing most of their conduct of SHGs, the statistical technique factor analysis was employed.
- Principle component analysis yielded mainly three factors formed out of the Linear combination of the 12 variables with communal extraction .833 and cumulative percentage 71.204.
- F1–Training and guidance, F2–Marketing, F3–financial Independence
- To test the independence of variables, the statistical test known as Chi-Square is used.
- This test shows that they are not able to take decisions of their own regarding the economic matters.
- Members duly depend on their husbands or other family members in taking the decisions on economic related matters.
- Only 18.35% of members expressed that they could take their own
- In this context the NGOs involved in monitoring the SHGs need to conduct periodic awareness camps to enable the SHGs to take decisions independently all by themselves.

Findings of the Study

Having presented the executive summary of the preliminary chapters of the research report, the findings of the study relating to the status of women in Anantapur District, savings level of the SHG groups and members, occupational and production structures of SHG group members, role of SHG women in development activities, and their achievement towards economic and political empowerment in the District.

Status of Women in Andhra Pradesh

1. The female-male ratio (FMR) was very low at 0.927 in India as per 1991 census, but it improved marginally to 0.933 as per 2001 census. The female-male ratio was highly comfortable in Andhra Pradesh at 0.972, which sharply increased to 0.978 between 1991 and 2001.
2. The female literacy ratio in Andhra Pradesh, though increased from 33 per cent to 51 per cent between 1991 and 2001, was still lower than the national averages of 39 per cent and 54 per cent in the respective years.
3. The gender gap in the work participation rate was lower at 21 per cent than that at the all India level, which was estimated at 26 per cent as per the 2001 census.
4. The share of women in the organized sector employment is awfully low at 18 per cent and the males dominated with 82 per cent in the year 2003. The share of women employment in the public sector was still lower at 16 per cent.
5. Women own less than one tenth of total property. Even where women were the formal legal owners, effective management of land, the precious wealth in rural areas, is in the hands of men.
6. Even though after 73rd and 74th Constitutional amendment, the representation of women increased in local bodies such as *Panchayat, Mandal* and *Zilla Prishad* bodies close to one-third, the share of women in Indian Parliament was trivial 8.16 per cent in the year 2004.

History of SHGs in Anantapur District

1. The density of population of the District is 190 per Sq.K.M. The Rural population to the total population of the District works out to be 75 per cent as per 2001 Census as against

76.5 per cent during 1991 Census. As per 2001 censes there are 958 females per 1000 males.

2. As per 2001 census the working force in the total population of District forms 48.83 per cent; out of which 26 per cent were found in the Agricultural Sector.
3. Among different caste groups, backward class women constituted the largest segment of the total members followed by other caste group members, scheduled caste and scheduled tribe women. ST women members accounted for about 7.67 per cent and minorities constituted only 6.18 per cent of the total members in all the self-help groups in the district.
4. There were about 2070 BC women members per mandal in the district. SC members constituted nearly half of the BC members per mandal. In other words, there were about 1159 SC members per mandal in the self-help groups in the district. There were about 890 members belonging to OC, 367 women members belonging to STs and 296 women members belonging to minorities in the district. On the average there were 12 members per group in the district.
5. As on 31st March 2004, there were 24, 432 self-help groups covering about 3, 01,828 women in the district. The total savings of the self-help groups amounted to Rs.4298 lakh. The government sanctioned revolving fund to the tune of Rs.2009 lakh for 14,807 self-help groups in the district.
6. *The Regional Rural Bank* (Sri Anantha Grameena Bank) has focused much attention in extending financial assistance to weaker sections through Micro-Credit. As linking of SHGs with Bank finance has emerged as one of the best alternative credit delivery system to weaker sections, the Bank has focused attention to link more SHGs with Bank finance.
7. The Bank has taken up the role of SHPI (Self Help Promoting Institute) and promoted 191 groups through ten branches during the year and has linked 133 groups involving Rs. 33.20 lakhs with Bank finance.

8. The Banks has extended financial assistance to 3898 Self Help Groups to a tune of Rs. 1222 lakhs during the financial year. As or 31.03.2005, the Bank has 7355 SHG accounts with an outstanding loan of Rs. 1625 lakhs.
9. Besides, revolving fund, the banks in the state provide loans to the self-help groups without much security concerns under SHG-Bank linkage programme which is largely refinanced by the NABARD.
10. Most of the members are in the age group 25 and 49 years. The median age of the members is 39 years.
11. Majority of the SHG members belonged to BC category 53.33%. Over 75% of the sampled SHG members belonged to socially backward communities.
12. Earning additional income for the self and for the family, getting awareness seemed to be predominant objectives in that order for the members to join SHG groups in the District.
13. After becoming the members of SHG groups, the women took up diversified activities, some of them individually and some of them collectively.
14. The SHG groups in the state seemed to have followed healthy democratic practices in their functioning. Majority of groups accounting for about 95 per cent selected the group leaders based on consensus and majority opinion.
15. Groups were homogeneous and cohesive based on caste and neighborhood. The decisions were taken based on consensus after thorough deliberations and discussions.
16. Internal loans out of savings and the corpus were sanctioned to the members mostlybased on needs of the members rather than amount of savings or security of the members.
17. The group leader and peer members exert pressure on the members who failed to pay the loan installment in time. Consequently, there was near 100 per cent recovery of internal loans in regularly functioning SHG groups in the state.

18. Majority of the SHG women felt that it was a very good programme, which enabled them to stand on their own legs, and saved them from the menace of money lenders and to some extent has allowed them to enjoy economic and social independency during the short period of time.
19. In short, the Self-Help Group movement has been pervasive in all the mandals and in all the major villages in Anantapur District.

Strengths

- Groups are homogeneous and cohesive; Group membership is based on Income, Caste and Neighborhood.
- Weaker sections of the society largely benefited from the programme; Member composition is ST=3.3%, SC=19.66%, BC= 53.33%OC= 24.16i%.
- Though a considerable number of SHG women were illiterates, many became literates after attending evening schools.
- The motives behind joining the Self-Help Groups were to earn additional income for self and for the family and to get awareness.
- Women folk proved that they could earn and save even in adverse conditions to project their self-esteem, once they are covered by SHGs in the district.
- Group exercises social pressure to inculcate thrift and regularity in attendance; Non-conformity leads to removal of members from the group.
- There is flexibility in the group management; the Group decides independently on Interest Rate, Prioritizing Loan, and Social Pressure.
- Internal loans were used both for consumption and production purposes.
- The greatest achievement of SHG programme according to the members was the fall in the percentage of women going for loans with the local moneylenders who used to

charge higher rates of interests which were in the range of 24% to 36% p.a.

- The recovery percentage of internal and bank loans were high at 95% due to peer group pressure on the members.
- Self-confidence and assertiveness are found among SHG women members in place of passive and depressed moods in improving the standard of living conditions.

Weaknesses

- There is over dependency on group leaders for collection of savings, loan installments and sanction of bank loans and other benefits from the government. It is reported that some members displayed indifferent attitude on the problems of the group.
- Groups equally or unequally share the revolving fund as soon as it is received from the government and become non-operative or defunt since then.
- Training was provided only to a few members and hence many members were not in a position to undertake gainful economic activities.
- Economic activities were undertaken mostly on individual basis rather than as a group; as a result group spirit, collective action and the sense of 'one for all and all for one' were all at low levels among those members who individually undertook the activities.

Suggestions

- The illiteracy among the group leaders and the members has been doing a great damage to the Self-Help Group movement. The literacy drive needs to be further increased among the members of SHG so that they can depend on their own for the maintenance and accounts of the group.
- Banks should conduct seminar, discussions, etc., periodically and thus create awareness among SHGs members; group members should be influenced to maintain regularity in their savings and formation of among needy groups should be encouraged.

- Rotation of leadership should be encouraged at least for once in two years so that every one would feel responsibility and also it would give them an opportunity to inculcate the leadership qualities.
- An extensive awareness campaign is needed to convince the bankers that the poor are bankable and advancing credit to them is more profitable and secure in terms of recovery.
- It is relevant to suggest that the bankers in the district may adopt Bangladesh Nobel peace prize winner–2006 Md. Yunus' model which to extended financial assistance with out collateral security for helping the millions to escape the poverty trap through a system of small–scale loans. For "lasting peace cannot be achieved unless large population groups find ways in which to break out of poverty. Micro-credit is one such means" (The Hindu–14-10-2006).
- The Bangladesh Grameen Bank, headed by Yunus dubbed as "banker to the poor" has 2,226 branches in 71,371 villages, covering 6.5 million borrowers, most of them women. The micro-credit concept has been copied in more than 40 countries.

References

Hoff Karla, Joseph E. Stigitz (1993), "Imperfect Information and Rural Credit Markets; Puzzles and Policy Perspectives", The economics of rural organization (Eds), Oxford University Press.

Mayoux, L. (1998), "Participatory Learning for Women's Empowerment in Micro Finance Programs! Negotiating Complexity, Conflict and Change", IDS Bulletin, Vol.29, No.4.

Mayoux L. (2001), "Talking the Down Side! Social Capital Women's Empowerment and Micro-Finance" in Cameroon Development and Change, Vol 32.

Hashemi. Syed, M. Sidney Ruth Schuler and Ann P. Riley (1996), "Rural Credit Program's and Women's Empowerment in Bangladesh", World Development, Vol. 24, No. 4

Khandker (1998), "Micro Credit Programme Evaluation! A Critical Review", IDS Bulletin, Vol 29. No.1

NABARD (1998, 1999, 2000, 2001), Annual Reports, Mumbai.

Rajasekhar, D. (1991), Problems and Prospects of Group Lending in NGO Credit Programmes in India. Savings and Development, 20 (1).

Need for New Strategies to Eradicate Poverty, Manak Publishers, New Delhi. Yunus, Muhammad, 1999.

The Human Development Report (1995), (1997).

The World Bank Report (1991).

Census Report (2001).

Andhra Pradesh Annual Report (1998, 1999, 2001).

Annual Report of the Commission of the Rural Development

Adeole. Ayanwale and Taiwo Alini (2004), Micro financing as Poverty Alleviation Measure: A Gender Analysis, JOURNAL OF SOCIOLOGY. 9(2).

Ahmed Syed Masud, Mushtaque Chowdary, Abbas Bhuiya (2001), "Micro Credit and Emotional Well Being Experience of Poor Rural Women from Matlab, Bangladesh," World Development Vol. 29, No.11

Amal Mandal (2005), Swarnajayanti Gram Swarozgar Yojana and Self-Help Group An Assessment, KURUKSHETRA, and January.

Batliwala, S. (1995), The Meaning of Women's Empowerment, Women's World, pp. 23-34.

Bhatia Naveen and Anju Bhatia (2002), "Lending to Groups is it Worth While" *Yojana, February,* pp. 20-22.

Das Gupta, A. (1999), "Self-help Groups and Micro-Credit Rural Banking for Women" *Social Welfare,* March, Vol. No. 45, No. 12, pp. 21-22

Dwarakanath, HD. (2002), "Rural Credit and Women Self-Help Groups" *Kurukshetra,* November, Vol. No. 51, No. 1, pp. 8-15.

Chapter-4

Women Empowerment through Visakhapatnam Special Economic Zones

A. Lavanya Kumari, B. Mohan Rao

Economic empowerment is the initial aspect of women Development. The economic empowerment means greater access to financial resources inside and outside the household, reducing vulnerability of poor women to crisis situation like famine, flood, riots, death and accidents in the family and significant increase in women's own income. Economic empowerment gives women the power to retain income and use it at her discretion. It provides equal access and control over various resources at the household level. Financial self-reliance of women both in the household and in the external environment lead to empowerment of women in other spheres.

Empowerment of women is basically concerned with recognition of women's individuality in the areas of work participation, capability, knowledge, self-respect, self-objectivity, access and control over the resource like capital and technology. Economic empowerment of women implies scrotal diversification of employment possibilities for women, technological up gradation, skill development etc. all these factors are crucial in defining the concept of empowerment of women. The empowerment of women is not only determined by the education and skills but also their socio-economic status.

An 'Export Processing Zone' (EPZ) in simple terms can be defined as an industrial zone with special incentives, set up to attract foreign investors, in which imported material underwent some degree of processing before being exported again[1] The Visakhapatnam Export Processing Zone (VEPZ) is one of the governmental organisations established in the year 1989 in a total area of 366 acres with the aim of promoting export oriented goods and services. Visakhapatnam Export Processing Zone was converted in to Special Economic Zone on First January 2003, by an ordinance issued by the Government of India on 1-4-2000. The total employment provided by VSEZ at present is 2,692 of which 1,090 (40.49 per cent) are women.

The EPZs are achieving their objective of promoting exports and achieving the objective of improving the welfare or working environment of weaker sections especially the women.

The data relating to the educational background of the women workers is collected and is grouped into six categories and the same has been presented in the Table 1. Among the total sample women workers 46.62 per cent are either tenth standard or less than that. About 25 per cent had education up to intermediate followed by 12.22 per cent who are graduates. The remaining three categories technical, diploma and other account for 10.29 per cent, 4.18 per cent and 1.29 per cent respectively.

Table 1
Education of Women Workers in the VSEZ Units

Education	*VSEZ Units*					
	WWD	*MKW*	*BSW*	*LID*	*Total*	*Per cent*
<10th Standard	63(43.45)	18(12.41)	15(10.34)	49(33.79)	145	46.62
Intermediate	19(24.05)	15(18.99)	22(27.85)	23(29.11)	79	25.40
Degree	08(21.05)	07(18.42)	08(21.05)	15(39.47)	38	12.22
Diploma	0	07(53.85)	02(15.38)	04(30.77)	13	4.18
Technical-ITI	11(34.38)	05(15.63)	05(15.63)	11(34.38)	32	10.29
Others	02(50.00)	0	01(25.00)	01(25.00)	04	1.29
Total	103	52	53	103	311	
Per cent	33.12	16.72	17.04	33.12		100.00

Note: Figures in the parenthesis indicate percentages

Decision Making

The decision-making by women regarding various domestic aspects is an indication of economic empowerment of women in the society. The data pertaining to the decision-making at the family level of the women workers had been gathered to understand the pattern of women empowerment. As the sampled women are either a daughter of a father or wife of a husband, the decision makers would be father, husband or both.

The distribution of the collected data (Table 2) indicates that the decisions in the majority of the families are taken by father (54.66 per cent), husband (7.39 per cent) and both father and husband (32.48 per cent). Only 5.47 per cent of women workers are taking independent decisions (by self) at their family level.

The unit wise distribution of data on decision-making at family level indicates clear distinction among the four units of VSEZ. In the case of WWD 47.52 per cent of families are showing that both father and husband take the decisions whereas in LID father (41.18 per cent) taking decisions followed by husbands (39.13 per cent). Independent decision taking families are seen in MKW (35.29per cent) and BSW (29.41per cent).

Table 2
Decision Making in Families of Women Workers in the VSEZ Units

	VSEZ Units					
Decision Makers	*WWD*	*MKW*	*BSW*	*LID*	*Total*	*Per cent*
Father	45(26.47)	25(14.71)	30(17.65)	70(41.18)	170	54.66
Husband	08(34.78)	03(13.04)	03(13.04)	09(39.13)	23	7.39
Both	48(47.52)	18(17.82)	15(14.85)	20(19.80)	101	32.48
Others	02(11.76)	06(35.29)	05(29.41)	04(23.53)	17	5.47
Total	103	52	53	103	311	
Per cent	33.12	16.72	17.04	33.12		100.00

Note: Figures in the parenthesis indicate percentages

Personal Income

The data related to earnings of selected women workers in the sampled units of the VSEZ is grouped into five categories and their respective data are presented in Table. It is inferred from the Table that 32.48 per cent of women workers fall in the category of less than Rs.2, 000/- income per month followed by 28.62 per cent in 2001-3000 group, then 21.86 per cent in 3001-4000 group, and 12.86 per cent in 4001-5000 group. Only 4.18 per cent of women workers are drawing more than rupees Rs.5, 000/- per month. It is further observed from the Table that more than 60 per cent of the women workers are drawing the salary/wages less than Rs.3000/-.

Table 3
Average Monthly Income of Women Workers in the VSEZ Units

	VSEZ Units					
Income(in Rs. p.m)	*WWD*	*MKW*	*BSW*	*LID*	*Total*	*Per cent*
< 2000	10(9.90)	22(21.78)	18(17.82)	51(50.50)	101	32.48
2001-3000	24(26.97)	19(21.35)	16(17.98)	30(33.71)	89	28.62
3001-4000	31(45.59)	08(11.76)	13(19.12)	16(23.53)	68	21.86
4001-5000	29(72.50)	03(7.50)	04(10.00)	04(10.00)	40	12.86
> 5001	09(69.23)	0	02(15.38)	02(15.38)	13	4.18
Total	103	52	53	103	311	
Per cent	33.12	16.72	17.04	33.12		100.00

Note: Figures in the parenthesis indicate percentages

The unit wise data of the earnings of women workers is showing a clear-cut variation between WWD and LID, where higher wages/salary drawing women are more in the former while in the later less salary/wages drawing women are more. The women working in MKW and BSW do not show any specific pattern unlike WWD and LID, but none of the women fall in first three categories which falls below Rs.4, 000/- per month. It is further observed that only about 17 per cent of the women are drawing more than Rs.4, 000/- per month.

Savings

In economic analyses, the income and expenditure go hand in hand not only in assessing the well being but also in estimating the savings, there by showing the economic assets at family level. With this assumption the data related to expenditure (on food and non-food) and savings are sought from the informants. The expenditure on food items inclusive of spending on all edible items is used to know the expenditure per month, and the same has been categorised into seven groups which ranges from less than Rs.2,000/- to Rs.5,000/-. This data is presented against the selected units and the same has been presented in Table.

Table 4
Savings (per month) of Women Workers in the VSEZ Units

	VSEZ Units					
Savings(in Rs. p.m)	*WWD*	*MKW*	*BSW*	*LID*	*Total*	*Per cent*
< 500	07(30.43)	06(26.09)	04(17.39)	06(26.09)	23	9.06
501 - 1000	19(26.39)	12(16.67)	17(23.61)	24(33.33)	72	28.34
1001-1500	09(25.00)	02(5.56)	07(19.44)	18(50.00)	36	14.17
1501-2000	15(28.30)	11(20.75)	04(7.55)	23(43.40)	53	20.87
> 2001	39(55.71)	08(11.43)	12(17.14)	11(15.71)	70	27.56
Total	89	39	44	82	254	
Per cent	35.05	15.35	17.32	32.28		100.00

Note: Figures in the parenthesis indicate percentages

Table 4 shows that the savings of women respondents per month in the VSEZ units. It is observed that 78 per cent of the responds are saving from Rs.500-1000, followed by 27.56 per cent are saving above Rs.2, 000 per month. Nearly 35 per cent of the respondents are saving between RS.1000-2000 per month. Among units of the VSEZ the proportion of savings of WWD unit is highest to the per cent of 35.05, followed by LID (32.28 per cent), BSW (17.32 per cent) and MKW (15.35 per cent).

Conclusion

To conclude, traditionally Indian women were involved in household work and reproduction of children. However, in recent times due to financial constraints and due to changing attitudes, women have to work outside their home to earn a living. The attitude in the society has not changed completely as men seldom do the household work. Women work outside and when they come home, they have to do the domestic work too. After independence, the Government of India provided for specific constitutional guarantees to enhance the status of women. Such guarantees are to be given without any discrimination on the basis of religion, race, caste, sex or place of birth. Despite these safeguards and guarantees, women's status still appears to be mostly confined to traditional household activities such as cooking, cleaning, washing, child rearing, etc. However in recent years involvement of women seems to be increasing outside the arena of traditional household activities. It was seen in the women of all the four units in the VSEZ.

The VSEZ mainly employs young unmarried women. All are literate and it signifies the changing trend of urban industrial working women. The family background of the respondents shows that the workers belong to nuclear families. The occupations of the head of the household shows that neither they are engaged in prestigious occupations nor minimal jobs. Half of the samples workers play a major role in decision-making regarding family expenditure. The labour force participation of women and their proportion contribution to total family income are the highest in households with the lowest economic status. In other words, the families are most dependent upon women's economic productivity. Finally, it can be concluded that the women workers working in these units are having empowerment through the Special Economic Zone.

References

ILO (1998), Labour and Social Issues Relating to Export Processing Zones, p. 3.

Government of India (2001), *Planning Commission Report*, Ministry of Finance.

UNIDO (1995), *Export Processing Zones: Principles and Practices*, Vienna, UNIDO, p.7.

CHAPTER-5

Women Traders in New Economy: Issues and Challenges

K. Madhu Babu

Women's role in economic development, in most countries of the world, cannot be undermined. In the Third World Countries, especially, where agriculture still constitutes the main source of livelihood and the main area of work for most people, women's contribution is quite high. Boserup[1] found that in such economies there is a high rate of participation of women in the agricultural production. The strategies undertaken for the development of agriculture in these economies were more concerned with the increase in productivity through mechanization of the agricultural production process and neglected the sex specific composition of the rural labour force. Overtime, men gained from the technical changes that came about in agriculture while women were marginalized. One study puts female unemployment at six to seven times that of man[2]. They remained mostly as low paid casual labourers.

India's female population, as per 2001 census, is 496 million and constitutes 48.26 per cent of the total population. In the rural areas, 30 lakh women have lost jobs in agriculture and livestock. Women have last 1,47,000 jobs in the textiles sector during 1995-2001. Female under-employment is also increasing at a faster rate than for men. India has 397 million workers, out of which 123.9 million are women. 106 million of these workers are in the rural areas and the remaining 18 million workers in urban areas[3]. The organized sector, women workers in India are even more dismal-almost 96 per cent of the women workers are in the unorganized sector. The female work participation rate has increased overall from 19.7 per cent in 1981 to 25.7 per cent in 2001[4]. In the rural areas it has increased from 23.1 per cent to 31 per cent and in the urban areas it has risen from 8.3 to 11.6%. There has been a significant increase in women employed in petty retail trade, hotels and restaurants in the last decade as part of survival strategy of poor urban households. These are typically low paying jobs where women work for long hours without any special benefits and face harassment[5]. This is one factor why in India women's participation in the labour force has been relatively low and stagnant while in most countries it has been increasing, during the last few decades.

Yet another disadvantage to female agricultural workers is the male-female wage differential. Despite the legislations like the Minimum Wages Act and Equal Pay for Equal Work, wage discrimination against women is wide spread in India, especially in the agricultural sector. Agricultural work is seasonal in nature. During the off season women in agriculture have to struggle hard to find alternate source of income. In drought prone area their plight is worse and they migrate to urban areas in search of work. Sometimes only male members of the family migrate leaving behind women and children to find for themselves in extreme conditions.

Most of the problems of rural women emanate from poverty compelling them to live a life of hardship and drudgery. The government of India, since independence, is making concerted efforts to bring women into the mainstream of development through its various programmes and scheme. But the improvement in rural women's condition is painfully slow. The First Five Plans emphasized on the welfare of women. It was only in the Sixth Five Year Plan that there was a shift from welfare to development. The International Women's Decade

1975-85 had its impact on the planning process in India. The Ninth Plan took a major step by incorporating "Empowerment of Women" as one of the main objectives of development during the plan period. The year 2001 was declared as the Women's Empowerment Year, and India has already adopted National Policy for Empowerment of Women. During the Ninth Plan a special Women Component Element was introduced under which more than 31 per cent of the funds in women related sectors were specifically earmarked for women's programmes. Several other initiatives have been launched to provide comprehensive package of up-gradation of skill through training, extension of input and market linkage in the traditional rural sectors.

Several institutions have been involved in imparting training and in helping women to take up viable entrepreneurial trades. These include social welfare departments, special departments for development and welfare of women, Indian Council for Agriculture Research (ICAR), state agriculture and extension departments and Non-Governmental Organizations (NGO's). In this background the present paper has been made to examine the viable entrepreneurial trade for women in agriculture and understand the constraints faced and identify the linkages and support system needed for enhancing the viability and feasibility of the trade.

The ICAR launched the All India Coordinated Research Project (AICRP) in Home Science in the year 1983 in State Agricultural Universities Human Capital of Rural Women. The agro based technologies undertaken by the Home Science department under AICRP include preparation of processed food items like jams, jellys, energy drinks, poultry management, preparation of handicrafts using natural fibres, etc. The impact of the project was very encouraging in some districts and average in some. Therefore, purposively selected East Godavari District for the present study in preparation of coir products. There 182 members of women workers engaged in coir industry in the sample villages. Among these total women one third consisting of 60 members are selected purposively for the study. We selected two villages viz., Gokhavaram and

Kalvacherlu from this district and from the two villages selected 60 women entrepreneurs in coir products, 40 trained and 20 untrained. Thus on the whole we selected 60 women entrepreneurs by simple random sampling method from the lists obtained from the respective KVK's and Coir Board Organizations. The study year was 2005-06.

Brief Profile of the Selected District

East Godavari district is one of the developed districts in the state of Andhra Pradesh located on the east coast. The district has good potential for development of industrial activities due to abundance of raw material such as agricultural produce, forest produce, minerals, livestock and fisheries production. The district contributes about 10 per cent of the total food grain production of the state. The district is blessed with an average annual rainfall of 1218 mm, which is higher than state average. The cropping intensity is 135 per cent. Main crops grown in the district are paddy, sugarcane, pulses, cotton, tobacco, topioca, etc. The coconut is also major plantation product in the district.

The district has organization of around 46,000 women groups under DWCRA and has scope for taking up micro enterprise for them. As a part of this, two special Swarnajayanthi Gram Swarojgar Yojana (SGSY) projects are under implementation in the district-one for the development of coir and the other for 'Fashion Designing' with a project outlay of Rs.25.00 crore and Rs.23.97 crore respectively. The coir project is under implementation in 22 mandals covering all the mandals in Konaseema area and Fashion Designing Project in 57 mandals of the district. The Coir Development Project is expected to benefit 28,000 women while Fashion Designing Project will benefit 13,680 women.

Socio-Economic Characteristics of the Sample Women

The distribution of sample women by social class indicate that 55.84 per cent belong to OBC's (Other Backward Castes), 31.66 per cent belong to the 'general category', Scheduled Castes (SC's) from only 12.5 per cent and none belong to Scheduled

Tribes (ST's). Majority of the women (40 per cent) are in the age group of 25-35 years, 34.17 per cent are between 35 to 55 years of age, 22.5 per cent are in the age group of 15-25 years and 3.33 per cent are above 55 years. About 68 per cent women are married, 15 per cent are widowed, 5 per cent are divorced and 12 per cent are unmarried. Literacy levels are very low among the sample women. About 73 per cent are either illiterate or have primary level of education, 25 per cent have secondary level of education and less than one per cent have graduation level of education.

About 50 per cent reported having subsidiary occupation but for cent per cent of the sample women the enterprise is their main occupation. In the total sample 12.50 per cent households have neither homestead land nor farm land.

Entrepreneurial Activity of the Sample Women

The women entrepreneurs in coir products were trained by the KVK in East Godavari District. The women were trained in the preparation of coir rope and coir mats. Coir is the locally available raw material. The women use simple equipment viz., coir motorized ratt, which was designed and developed by the KVK. None of the sample women own the machine. They work in groups in the KVK premises, voluntary agency premises or rented sheds using common machines. Majority acquire the raw material from the Coir Board or local private coir industry on buy back policy. Very few purchase the material from the local traders and sell in the local market.

Productivity and Cost of Production of Coir Products

Now it is of interest to examine the productivity and cost of production of coir products of sample women. To start a micro enterprise in coir products, one needs some simple machinery and some space to work. This forms the fixed capital. The machinery used is simple and needs little space. But since the machine costs around Rs.1.25 lakhs, none of the sample women could afford to buy it. They work in groups on common machinery.

The productivity and the cost of production for trained and untrained sample women entrepreneurs is given in Table-1. The trained women are using on an average 127 kgs of raw coir per month and they are producing an output of 110 kgs i.e., per 100 raw coir, the output is 86.55 kgs. The scale of activity of the untrained women is comparatively low. They are using on an average 65 kgs of raw coir per month and producing 55 kgs of output i.e., per 100 kgs of raw coir, the output is 83.89 kgs. The productivity of the trained women is slightly better than the untrained women. The average quantity of raw material i.e., coir used by the trained women is 127 kgs per month. The price of raw coir is about six to seven rupees per kg. The sample women of Kalvacherla village who acquire the raw material from the KVK or Coir Board are paying Rs.6.00 per kg, while the women in Gokhavaram village who acquire the raw material from coir industry are paying Rs.7.00 per kg per month. Cost of production for the trained women is as follows. The cost of coir is Rs. 811 for the 127 kgs average that trained women used, average cost of colours is Rs. 15.00 and the expenditure towards power is Rs. 81.44, Rs. 30.80 for transport and Rs. 21.60 for rent. The total cost of production for each trained women entrepreneur using 127 kgs of raw coir amounts to Rs. 959.84. At this rate the total cost per 100 kgs of raw coir is Rs 755.77. The untrained sample women entrepreneurs are paying higher price for raw coir as most of them acquire the raw material from the coir industry and the expenditure towards rent is also high. As a result the total cost per 100 kgs of raw coir is Rs. 806.54, which is higher by Rs.50.77 compared to the trained women.

Income from the Coir Products Enterprise

It is also interest to analyze the income from the coir products. The quantity of output produced by the trained women entrepreneurs in a month is 110 kgs. The sale price per kg of output is about Rs.16-17. The total income is Rs.1811 and the net income per women in a month is about Rs.852 (Table-2). The net income per 100 kgs of raw material is around Rs.675. For the untrained women the net income per 100 kg of raw

Table 1

Productivity and Cost of Product for the Coir Products Entrepreneurs

	Quantity of		*Cost Production Rs.*					
	Raw Coir used Kgs	*Output Produced Kgs*	*Coir*	*Colours*	*Power*	*Transport*	*Rent*	*Total Cost*
Trained								
Avg. per women entrepreneur per month	127.00	110.00	811.00	15.00	81.44	30.80	21.60	959.84
Avg. per 100 kgs of raw Coir	100.00	86.55	638.58	11.81	64.12	24.25	17.00	755.77
Untrained								
Avg. per women entrepreneur per month	65.00	55.00	436.00	6.66	41.60	14.00	26.00	524.26
Avg. per 100 kgs of raw Coir	100.00	83.69	670.76	10.25	64.00	21.53	40.00	806.54

Table 2
Net Income from the Coir Products Enterprise

	Quantity of Output (kgs.)	*Sale Price per Kg*	*Total Income (Rs.)*	*Total Cost of Production (Rs.)*	*Net Income (Rs.)*
Trained					
Avg. per women entrepreneur per month	110.00	16.48	1811.48	959.84	851.64
Avg. per 100 kgs of raw coir use	86.85	16.48	1431.29	755.77	675.52
Untrained					
Avg. per women entrepreneur per month	55.00	16.20	906.40	524.26	382.14
Avg. per 100 kgs of raw coir used	83.89	16.20	1382.51	806.54	575.97

material is Rs.576 lower by 100 of the trained women. This is because the untrained women's productivity is lower, the cost of production is higher and the sale price is also little lower.

Impact of the Enterprise on Household Income

The impact of the women's enterprise on the household income of the sample households is presented in Table-3. The impact of the women's enterprise on the household income of the sample households is quite impressive. The contribution of the income from coir products enterprise is 28.03 per cent in the total household income. The comparison of the per capita incomes of the sample households with the poverty line income indicate that the per capita incomes in the selected enterprise groups are well above the poverty line income even without the income from the enterprise. Majority of the sample women from all the enterprises reported that there was an improvement in the assets and comforts in their households and they were able to provide better educational facilities to their children due to the enterprise.

Table 3
Share of Income from Women's Enterprise in Total Annual Household Income–Total Sample

	Coir Products	
Particulars	*Rs.*	*Percent*
Farm Income	108280	9.34
Income from Annual Husbandry	51000	4.40
Wage Income	414400	35.74
Income from regular employment	102000	8.80
Petty Trade / Small Business	136600	11.78
Other Sources	22090	1.90
Total Household Income Excluding Income from Women's Enterprise	834370	71.96
Income from Women's Enterprise Annual	325000	28.03
Total Household Income Including Income from Women's Enterprise	1159370	100.00
Per capita Income without including Income from Women's Enterprise	469.83	-
Per Capita Income including Income from Women's Enterprise	652.80	-
Poverty line for Rural A.P.	294.25	-

Main Benefits for Women

1. Almost all the sample women expressed that their self esteem increased after taking up the entrepreneurial activity and majority reported that their role in the family decision making increased.
2. Social respect. As the women's income increases and they become well trained and well educated, they gain social respect villages are coming to centres, taking their advice and using their services.
3. They were able to take decisions regarding children's education, children's marriages, purchasing of assets in the households, etc.
4. Employment in their village.
5. Self respect. Working with technology makes them feel proud, and
6. As they are all SHG/DWCRA members majority of them developed leadership qualities and they were able to interact with several persons related to their entrepreneurial activity.

Main Challenges

The following are the main problems, faced by women entrepreneurs:

1. The expected encouragement is not materializing at village level.
2. There should be demand for the products they make. In the absence of local demand at least there should be some agency to buy their product or facilitate the marketing.
3. About 52.0 per cent of the sample women reported that there is local demand for their product but 48.0 per cent answered in the negative. Though there is local demand, the women selling in the market on retail forms only 12 percent in the total. Forty four percent expressed that they have difficulty in marketing the product.

4. About 32 percent reported difficulty in procuring the raw material.
5. When asked whether women face problems in entrepreneurial activities 48 per cent reported in the positive and 52 per cent in the negative. Those who felt that there are problems complained of marketing problems, procuring raw material.

Conclusion

The contribution of Rural women to the economy is quite significant. Over 80 percent of the working women in rural areas are engaged in agriculture and allied activities. They usually perform drudgery prone activities and do not get equal wages with male workers. Given a chance women agricultural workers prefer to take up alternate economic activities. The Government is also laying stress on empowering rural women by identifying alternate economic activities. The present study reveals, the enterprises taken up by the women are found to contribute significantly to the household income. Despite the fact that there is improvement in their socio-economic position, these women do face problems especially in marketing their products. As the sample women are all DWCRA members they do not face problem for their working capital. If they can get bank loans, some women prefer to start the enterprise on their own on a larger scale. Hence, it may be concluded that women entrepreneurs need help in improving their forward and backward linkages.

References

1. Boserup, Ester, Women's Role in Economic Development' George Allen and Unwin 1970, London.
2. Ajit Ghose, "Current issues of Employment in India". EPW, Vol.34. No.36, 4th September, 1999.
3. Padma, Women Workers in India in the 21st Century–Unemployment and Underemployment: www.cpiml.ICI.org, 2004.
4. S. Rothbock,et.al, "Labour in the New Economy-2001.
5. Padma, "Women Workers in India in the 21st Century-Unemployment and Underemployment: www.cpiml.ICI.org, 2004.

Chapter-6

Sustainability of SHGs: A Case Study of Krishna District of Andhra Pradesh

A. Vamsi Krushna, P. Jayanand Kumar, P. Raj Kumar

Introduction

With the launching of the programme of nationalization of commercial banks in 1969 and the setting up of regional rural banks subsequently in 1975, the loans extended to the priority sector by institutional agencies increased significantly. To an extent these steps made up for the inadequate role played by cooperative institutions in rural credit. But all is not well with priority sector/rural credit supply. The progress achieved by the institutional agencies is hampered by the ever increasing size of the overdues. Overdues are the loans which are not recovered before the stipulated period. These can choke the credit flow and hence the credit institutions will find it more and more difficult in future to survive. The sustainability of credit supply from formal agencies has therefore become an issue of concern (Rajaram Dasgupta, 2001).

The mounting size of overdues has the effect of making the institutional agencies ration credit. The poor people as a class are more likely to suffer in the process than the rich. The poor as also the rich may be equally guilty of not repaying the loans in time. Yet the poor are bypassed while advancing loans for (1) they have little bargaining power and (2) the transaction costs involved in advancing and recovering small amounts far exceed those associated with large advances (Puha Zhendhi, 1995).

Developments along the above lines leave the poor in about the same position as they were in 1969. The importance of SHGs arises from the fact that the poor are ill served by the formal agencies. SHGs also assume importance in view of the fact that money lenders subject the poor to severe exploitation by charging exorbitant interest charges. When the poor borrow from banks after their initiation into SHGs, they can ensure that the transaction costs of the formal agencies is reduced. Cost of lending decreases for the agencies since loans are advanced to a group. Further and more importantly, since the members of SHGs are of homogeneous economic class and since peer monitoring is the rule in the groups, loans advanced will be recovered promptly (Stiglitz, 1990; Samar Datta and Raman, 2001). The presumptions that SHGs can bring down cost of lending, reduce overdues and can come to the aid of those who need credit the most–the poor–made NABARD to extend all out support to their expansion. (Rajaram Dasgupta, 2001) Also, the fact that most SHGs are formed by women, who by nature are thrifty and honest, made every one see SHGs as having a great future. The progress achieved by SHGs in Andhra Pradesh is particularly heartening. SHGs have grown from strength to strength in the State and the policies of the Government with their emphasis on empowerment of women have much to do with this. By 2000-2001, the number of SHGs exceed 1 lakh.

The progress of SHGs exceeded all expectations so as to leave every one complacent about their future. At the national as also at the international level these micro-finance institutions are being considered particularly suitable to finance the poor and the needy. (Basley and Coate, 1995; Ghatak and Guinnane, 1999). But is it possible that this complacency is a little misplaced? After all SHGs finance petty non-agricultural ventures, which are not skill intensive and therefore their success cannot be guaranteed. Much of the credit supplied through SHGs gets used up for consumption purposes and therefore is not productive. If members of SHGs ever happen to feel that the credit coming forth from the SHGs is not yielding adequate or no returns and repayment of loans borrowed from them is inescapable, they may stop patronizing them (Katar Singh and Raji Gain, 1995; Dadhich, 2001, 2003). The continuing existence of SHGs–their sustainability–therefore depends upon how well the low skill intensive products turned out by the members of SHGs are received in rural areas. There is no guarantee either that agricultural prosperity will contribute to the success of SHGs. While the existence of SHGs can help mobilize savings during periods of agricultural prosperity, the very prosperity can dampen the demand for the inferior goods produced by the micro-entrepreneurs. Indications are that the rural non-farm employment, after recording a significant growth in the 1980s, has decelerated in the 1990s in Andhra Pradesh, according to the estimates of National Sample Survey Organisation (Chadha and Sahu, 2002). This does not portend well for the SHGs in the State.

In the light of the above discussion we have tried to focus on the scope for sustainability of SHGs taking as sample the SHGs of Puttagunta Village of Nandivada Mandal in the Krishna district. The village has all the characteristics of being classified as a prosperous one. The irrigated area of the village constitutes 40.34 per cent of the total cultivable area. Is this environment ideal for setting up and continuation of SHGs? As argued above there are competing postulates.

Sustainability

If one is to go by the number of groups ever set up in the village, the record is remarkable. As many as 45 SHGs were constituted. The earliest groups to have been formed was in December 1990. But it was only during the period 1995-1999 that most groups were formed. The Telugu Desam party which had been at the helm of affairs at the state level during the period, with its women-centred policies, seemed to have aided the formation of a large number of groups during the period. It is however not known whether the elections to the posts of president of SHGs, though invariably contested, were fought, either explicitly or implicitly, along party lines.

Though the SHGs grew in number to reach a total of 45 at one time, at the time of the survey in the year 2007-2008 the number of active SHGs in the village was merely 12. Besides, there were 3 passive groups. That leaves 30 as the dissolved SHGs. That is 2/3rd of the SHGs ever set up were dissolved. By any standard this is a large proportion and beckons at the sustainability issue. Agricultural prosperity does not seem to contribute to the sustainability of SHGs of the village.

Table 1
Percentage of Loans Advanced by Purpose

Purpose	*Active Groups*	*Passive Groups*	*Total*
Consumption	1912	1404	3316
%	55.15	65.00	58.93
Production	1555	756	2311
%	44.85	35.00	41.07
Total	3467	2160	5627
%	100.00	100	100

We do not have data on the activities for which loans are disbursed to members of dissolved groups. We conjuncture, however, that most of them are marginal activities with little scope to emerge as money–spinners. Even the activities funded by the presently active groups do not seem capable of generating much surplus to the members of SHGs. Loans are taken by members for family maintenance, petty trading-including vegetable sale, tea powder sale, tea-stall. Loans are also taken for investment in basket making, activities facing stiff competition from urban manufactures. There are those who borrowed for setting up an STD booth, a flour mill and a dairy enterprise. Some artisans–especially carpenters–have also borrowed from active SHGs. It is noticed that of the total advances made more than 50% have gone for consumption purposes (Table-1).

Table 2
Occupational Distribution of Members of SHGs

Particulars	*Active Groups*	*Passive Groups*	*Total*
Agricultural Labour	74	14	88
%	46.25	31.11	42.93
Marginal Farmers	39	20	V
%	24.38	44.44	28.78
Non-form activities and Rural artisans	47	11	58
%	29.38	24.44	28.29
Total	160	45	205
%	100.00	100	100

The occupational pattern of the members of the active SHGs is of interest. 47 out of 160 (29.38%) members reported that they depend upon non-farm activities for a living. In respect of the 3 passive groups the corresponding figure is 11 out of 45 (24.44%). Thus a large majority of members of the SHGs are dependent upon agriculture for a living and their incomes if anything would fluctuate much more widely than the incomes of those in non-farm activities. This may have a telling effect on the sustainability of SHGs (Table-2).

Empowerment of Women

The yardstick used to assess the performance of an SHG should not always be its financial standing. Even if an SHG does not seem capable of sustaining itself financially, every effort should be made to put it on the rails particularly when it empowers the economically and socially disadvantaged by giving them a new identity in the society and when it gives them a sense of belonging. The saving habit that is inculcated by SHGs among women should also be taken cognigence of, for, the money saved can make them feel independent. The interaction among the members of SHGs facilitated by group meetings can make women think progressively about their children's education, family health, etc.

There is no denying the fact that the SHGs of the village comprise mostly the economically poor. Rough calculations show that about 50% of them fall below the poverty line (Table-3). If one is to go by the distribution of landholdings, the condition of the members would be even more precarious– about 90% of them have either no land or are only marginal farmers (Table-4). Though some persons of forward castes could be found among the members of SHGs, their proportion is not very high (Table-5). These details go to show that the SHGs (active and passive) of the village are largely in the service of the economically and socially weaker sections of the village. Illiteracy has not deterred them from joining SHGs (Table-6). To put it differently, even the illiterates and the under privileged see advantages in joining SHGs. The members of the SHGs are mostly young and therefore they can be expected to be dynamic as well (Table-7). It should be possible to tap

Table 3
Distribution of Members of SHGs by Income Group

Particulars	*Active Groups*	*Passive Groups*	*Total*
Below Rs.12000	59	V	68
%	36.88	20.00	33.17
Rs.12001-24000	73	12	85
%	45.63	26.67	41.46
Rs.24001-48000	16	17	33
%	10.00	37.78	16.10
Rs.48001 and above	12	7	19
%	7.50	15.56	9.27
Total	160	45	205
%	100	100	100

Table 4
Distribution of Members of SHGs by Size of Land Holding

Particulars	*Active Groups*	*Passive Groups*	*Total*
Marginal farmers	62	9	71
%	38.75	20.00	34.63
Small farmers	19	7	26
%	11.88	15.56	12.68
Medium farmers	8	4	12
%	5.00	8.89	5.85
Big farmers	0	1	1
%	0.00	2.22	0.49
No Land	71	24	95
%	44.38	53.33	46.34
Total	160	45	205
%	100.00	100	100

Table 5
Distribution of Members of SHGs by Caste

Particulars	*Active Groups*	*Passive Groups*	*Total*
OC	36	11	47
%	22.50	24.44	22.93
BC	76	23	99
%	47.50	51.11	48.29
SC	48	11	59
%	30.00	24.44	28.78
ST	0	0	0
%	0.00	0.00	0.00
Total	160	45	205
%	100	100	100

Table 6
Distribution of Members of SHGs by Literacy Levels

Particulars	*Active Groups*	*Passive Groups*	*Total*
Illiterates	56	20	76
%	35.00	44.44	37.07
Primary	73	16	89
%	45.63	35.56	43.41
Secondary	19	71	26
%	11.87	5.56	12.68
Higher	10	2	12
%	6.25	4.44	5.86
Above	2	0	2
%	1.25	0.00	0.98
Total	160	45	205
%	100	100	100

Table 7
Distribution of Members of SHGs by Age

Particulars	*Active Groups*	*Passive Groups*	*Total*
No. of Groups	12	3	15
Members	160	45	205
Age group			
Below 25 years	24	8	32
%	15.0	17.78	15.61
25 to 35 years	88	17	105
%	55.0	37.78	51.22
Above 35 years	48	20	68
%	30.0	44.44	33.17
Total	160	45	205

the hitherto untapped entrepreneurial skills of these women. The interaction among members which is so essential for spread of knowledge about health, education and more particularly for governing the activities of the SHGs seems good with over 2/3rd of the members reporting it to be so (Table-8). The cumulative savings on an average amount to Rs.15,150/- per SHG in respect of active ones, and Rs.10,800/-

Table 8
Responses of Members Classified by their Level of Participation in Meetings of SHGs

Participation in Group Activities	*Active Group Members*	*Passive Group Members*	*Total*
Good	100	8	108
%	62.50	17.78	52.68
Average	44	16	60
%	27.50	35.56	29.27
Poor	16	21	37
%	10.00	46.67	18.05
Total	160	45	205

per SHG in respect of passive ones. These are not large amounts considering that most SHGs were set up during 1995-99.

Conclusion

The importance of SHGs arises from the fact that the poor are ill served by the formal institutional agencies (viz., banks, RRBs, and even cooperatives). These institutions refrain from lending to the poor because of the high transaction costs involved in lending to them. SHGs also assume importance in view of the fact that money lenders subject the poor to severe exploitation by charging exorbitant interest charges. By forming into SHGs the poor can get over these two problems. Inasmuch as the poor borrow and repay money to banks as a group, the cost of lending decreases. Since the members of SHGs are of homogeneous economic class and since peer monitoring is the rule in the groups, loans advanced will be recovered promptly. This makes SHGs sustainable and the ever increasing number of SHGs has much to do with this fact.

NABARD's role in the expanding number of SHGs is not to be belittled either. SHGs have grown from strength to strength particularly in Andhra Pradesh. The performance of the groups is not, however, uniform across all districts. Our study covering 45 randomly selected SHGs of Krishna district of the state shows that 30 of them have been dissolved soon after they were set up. This raises the issue of sustainability of the groups. However, wherever the SHGs are functioning well, they benefited the most disadvantaged–the poor, the lowly placed in social hierarchy. SHGs are giving them a new identity in the society. Saving on a monthly basis, which was unknown to women is now a reality. The hither to untapped entrepreneurial skills of women are to the fore. To make the SHGs financially sustainable it is necessary to advance loans for activities which are not marginalized and which lead to production of goods that have few substitutes in urban manufactures.

References

Besley, T., and Coate, S. (1994), "Group Lending, Repayment Incentives and Social Collateral", *Journal of Development Economics*, Vol.46, No.1, January.

Chadha, G.K. and Sahu, P.P. (2002), "Post-reform Setbacks in Rural Employment Issues that Need Further Scrutiny", *Economic Political Weekly*, No.21, Vol.XXXVII, May 25-31.

Dadhich, C.L. (2001), "Micro Finance–A Panacea for Poverty Alleviation", *Indian Journal of Agricultural Economics*, Vol.56, No.3, July-September.

Dadhich, C.L., Book Review of Krishan Jindal and Sharma, K.C. (2003), "Micro Finance Institutions: Issues in Sustainability", *Indian Journal of Agricultural Economics*, Vol.58, No.2, April–June.

Ghatak, M. and Guinnane, T. (1999), "The Economics of Lending with Joint Liability: Theory and Practice", *Journal of Development Economics*, Vol.60, No.1, October.

Katar Singh and Raji Gain, T.S., "Evolution and Survival of SHGs: Some Theoretical Propositions and Empirical Evidence", *Working paper No.4*, BIRD, Lucknow.

Puha Zhendhi, V. (1995), "Transaction Costs of Lending to the Rural Poor", The Foundation for Development Cooperation, Brisbane, Australia.

Rajaram Dasgupta (2001), "An Informal Journey through Self-Help Groups", *Indian Journal of Agricultural Economics,* Vol.56, No.3, July-September.

Samar, K., Datta and Raman, M. (2001), "Can Heterogeneity and Social Cohesion Coexist in Self-Help Groups?", *Indian Journal of Agricultural Economics,* Vol.56, No.3, July–September.

Stiglitz, J.E. (1990), "Peer Monitoring and Credit Markets", *The World Bank Economic Review,* Vol.4, No.3, September.

Chapter-7

Role of Women Entrepreneurs in Social Upliftment

A.V. Naga Varma, M. Ravi Kumar,
M. Anil Kumar, B. Naveen Kumar

The growth of industrialization, education and domestic system has brought about significant changes in the tradition bound Indian Society. Now increasing proportion of women are seeking gainful employment in industrial field. It is a fact that man alone cannot break the evils of poverty, unemployment and inequality. Active and equal participation of women is indispensable in fighting against this social evils.

The global evidences prove that women have been performing exceedingly well in different spheres of activities. It is traced out as a extension of their kitchen activities to 3 Ps., pickles, powder (masala) and pappad manufacturing with growing awareness and spread of education over the years women have started engrossing to modern activities like engineering, electronics and energy popularly known as 3Es.

The Government of India has defined women entrepreneurs based on women participation in equity and employment of a business enterprise. Accordingly a women entrepreneur is defined as "an enterprise owned and controlled by a women having a minimum financial interest of 51% of the capital and giving atleast 51% of the employment generated in the enterprise to women".

Palani, as a well known piligrim centre, it is one of the oldest towns in South India. For the last 200 years it has been one of the centers of South Indian Culture and civilization. In India the history and culture of a region often centers around a temple. This is particularly true of South India where the temple has made a unique contribution not only to the religious life of the people but has also served as the nucleus around which the social and cultural life of the people. This town is known through out the world, as the abode of Lord Muruga.

Palani, the head quarters of the taluk, is one among the six taluks of Anna District, the others being Dindigul, Kodaikanal, Nilakottal, Vedasanthur and Natham. It was formerly called the Aiyampalle Taluk. Its area is 625 Square miles. The Palani town is situated at about 350 meters height from the sea level.

The life of the Hindus is more or less simple. Most of them engaged in some professions connected with the temple like guides, sellers of Puja articles, vibuthi making, panchamirtham etc., and other activities of the people are silk leaning and twisting, Handloom fabrics, power looms puppet making, manufacture of chemicals and pesticides, production of garments soaps and detergents, fair price shops, day to day requirement shops i.e, grocery shops, milk depot, flower shop, vegetable shops etc.

However, most of them are agriculturists and roadways transport operators. There are more than thirty private Siddha clinics in Palani. Siddha medicines have been prepared in the traditional method and exported to various countries.

Percentage analysis were used for socio economic background and problems faced by the women entrepreneurs (See Table-1).

The Problems faced by women entrepreneurs in the country emanate from a multitude of sources and are manifold. Entrepreneurship is not a "bed of roses" to the women. Their task has become more tedious and full of challenges since thy have to encounter public prejudices and criticism. Women face certain problems not as a entrepreneur but as a women.

Therefore, when compared to men the problems of women entrepreneurs are more in number.

They are classiefied under: 1. Socio-Personal Problems 2. Managerial Problems 3. Production Problems 4. Marketing Problems 5. Financial Problems 6. Problems of Government Assistance. This is the observation of Ms. Poonam Barua, Convenor, Forum for Women in Leadership."

The above situation has prompted Ms. Swati Piramal, Director (Strategic Alliances) Nicholas Piramal India Ltd. To observe that "Under representation of women in leadership positions threatens the goals of progress of a country."

Ms. Preethi Malhotra, President of the Institute of Company Secretaries of India (ICSI) has also observed: "Corporate Boards (in India) need to be compelld to be manned by women as well. However there is a ray of hope. Women gradually start realizing their strength. In this context, Ms. Renuka Ramnath, Managing Director and CEO, ICICI, Venture Funds Management observed:

"If you are n a position of power, there you have to ask yourself what you are doing with that power and is it being harnessed well and who is benefiting from it. This assertive statement is likely to increase the number of women executives in India, in the near future.

The Corporate Sector in India has finally woken up to the idea of giving a fair colour to its gender profile at the top. Even though the country's report card on women at the top management has not been impressive so far, companies are now moving with a sense or urgency in this regard. Recently, a Forum of Women leaders namely WILL (Women in Leadership) has been formed at the Infosy's camp, for the purpose of initiating a dialogue on getting capable women leaders at the top. This forum broached a host of initiatives like setting up of research committees, scholarship for women etc., The deliberations at the Forum (in a recent meeting) reveal some pertinent and interesting data.

At Present, women constitute 40% of the top management team in HSBC. Zensa has worked hard to improve its figures to 10-15% up from nil five years back. Three years back, in

Motorola women engineers constituted 20% of the total engineers. Now they constitute 30% of the total strength. In 2006, women constituted 50% of the total number of management trainees".

A few accomplishments by women in Corporate Sector are note worthy. For instance, Akila Srinivasan's case can be cited. At present, she is the Managing Director (MD) of Shriram Life Insurance. She is the only woman CEO in the conservative Rs.17,220 Crore Shriram Group. She has been instrumental in striking global alliances for her group companies. These include Melewar Group of Malaysia for an education venture, Singapore's Sem bawang for a logistics joint venture and the Sanlam Group of South Africa for life Insurance. It is due to her meticulous work that the company has recently managed to mop up a premium of Rs. 114 crore. 85000 Life Insurance Policies were sold. The Company incurred expenses of Rs. 25 Crore in this regard the lowest expense ratio in the industry

Mallika Srinivasan, Director, TAFE has turned her Chennai based tractor company into Rs. 4000 crore giant with more than 22% of the market share. The achievement of Shikha Sarma, Managing Director and Chief Executive Officer (MD & CEO) of ICICI Prudential into Number 1 Private Life Insurer. Her constant and continuous work has given ICICI Prudential a notional market value of Rs. 28,315 crore, the highest of all private life insurers. In a similar way, Swati Piramal, Director, Nicholas Piramal, one of the biggest Pharmaceutical Companies has turned the company into a $350 million company.

Having outlined the hindrances in "Women Executive Empowermnt" the authors make a few suggestions to get this concept translated into reality. Firstly there should be a change in the traditional mindset of the men executives to go beyond comfort-zone of appointing only men as executives. Secondly, the concept of "flexi work" should be given due emphasis. Working women with children and family commitments can be allowed to choose their own convenient working hours within the regular frame work of working hours. Thirdly, the "work from home" concept should be encouraged. With the extensive use of computers, this can be made easy. Fourthly, women should be aware of their rights. The Government and NGOS (Non-government Organizations) can play an effective roles in this context. Fifthly, the organizations should become gender neutral. Gender–neutrality implies that women should not be suppressed merely because of the female gender. Organizations can follow the steps practiced by concerns like ICICI, Tata Consultancy Services (TCS) and Infosys Technologies. Finally, meritocracy should never be sacrificed. Ultimately, the appointment of women to top positions as executives on merit basis matters much.

With increased educational back ground, women no longer belong to weaker sex. The observation by William Shakespeare that "Frailty, thy name is woman", no longer holds good. Women should make the above citation obsolete and irrelevant in the modern context.

Refrences

Business Today – October 7, 2007.

Business Today – June 17, 2007.

Business Economics – January 1-15, 2007.

The Hindu Business Line, October 29, 2007.

The Economic Times, October 19, 2007.

Business Today, October 7, 2007.

The Economic Times, Dec.3,2007.

Outlook Business, 17 Nov, 2007.

Chapter-8

Globalization–Impact on the Status of Women

R. Radha

When we are talking about globalization and women, a major question which needs to be answered is-Is globalization weakening or strengthening patriarchy? In other words, are women, as a result of globalization, gaining more rights; or because they are now more visible in their claim for gender and social equality, have the forces of conservatism reacted, making their struggle an uphill one?

The process of globalization sweeping the world is exerting its unnoticed forces to redefine 'marriage' and 'family'. Institution of marriage and the existence of a 'family' as a unit have found a new meaning. This new meaning is very often dictated by the market forces. The notion of family is shrinking, from large joint families, to nuclear families to individual or 'autonomous family' constituted by single person.

This move that has been precipitated by the process of globalization has both positive and negative fallouts. On the one hand, this new found freedom promoted acceptance for such a process and allows the nuclear family to democratize and negotiate.

Many traditional values and norms take new forms which may be detrimental to old social arrangements, such as providing family support systems to women. According to studies, one of the definite fallouts of globalization and marketization has been growing incidence of domestic violence on women. This paper tries to assess the impact of globalization on women in the Indian society and their living status by analyzing some of the basic indicators viz., life expectancy of women, health, education, standard of living, maternal mortality rate, professional live of women and tries to present the positive and negative effects of it.

For the comparative purpose of the status of women during the pre-liberalization and post liberalization periods, the years 1990 and 2005 are taken for comparative purposes. As economic reforms started in India during the year 1991 thereby the selection of years would be appropriate so as to depict the conditions of women in the pre-liberalization and the post liberalization periods. Three tables Table-1, presenting the Basic Characteristics showing the Female Capabilities, Table-2 presenting the Gender In-Equality in Education and Table-3 presenting the Employment scenario in organized and the un-organized sectors were given.

Table 1
Gender Inequality in Education

Variable	*1990*	*2005*
Adult Literacy Rate, Female (% aged 15 and older)	32	47.8
Adult Literacy Rate (Ratio of female rate to male rate)	0.711	0.65
Gross Primary Enrolment Ratio (%)	81	116
Gross Primary Enrolment Ratio, female (Ratio of female to male)	0.71	0.94
Gross Secondary Enrolment Ratio (%)	27	50
Gross Secondary Enrolment Ratio (Ratio of female to male)	0.54	0.80
Gross Tertiary Enrolment Ratio female (%)	5	9
Gross Tertiary Enrolment Ratio (Ratio of female ratio to male ratio)	0.42	0.70
Public Expenditure on Education (% of GDP)	0.7	0.9

United Nations Human Development Report: 2008, 1990

Table-1 presents the Gender In–equality in education, Adult Literacy rate which was 32% in 1990 rose to 47.8% in 2005, education is the backbone of a nation, and growing literacy levels is the symbols of development. The Gross Primary Enrolment ratio was 81 in 1990 rose to 116 in 2005, as in the case of secondary enrolment ratio which was increased from 27% to 50%. The Gross Tertiary enrolment ratio was registered at 5% rose to 9%. And the percentage of Public expenditure on Education too rose from 0.7% to 0.9%. So as the result of globalization the female literacy rate rose from 1990 to 2005 which is a positive indicator and one of the positive effects of globalization.

Table 2
Basic Characteristics Showing Female Capabilities

Variable	1990	2008
Life Expectancy; Females as a % of males	100.3	105
Adult Literacy Rate; Female as a % of males	43	92
Births attended by skilled attendants	33	98
Institutional deli varies	-	83
Maternal Mortality Ratio reported	340	48
Infant Mortality Rate (Per 1000 live births)	98	23
Under- five Mortality rate (Per 1,000 live births)	149	27

United Nations Human Development Report: 2008, 1990

The basic indicators present two years data i.e. 1990 and 2006 which are taken for comparative purpose. The 7 basic indicators are compared which show a considerable rise in the indicators, with respect to life expectancy which shows a gradual increase in the life of female and literacy rates also have shown a rise which is depicted in the increased births attended by skilled attendants. There was also a considerable decline in the maternal mortality rate and infant mortality rate, as in the case of under five mortality rate which was registered at 27 for 1000 live births.

Globalization can be a major force for prosperity only if it is backed by adequate national policies and conducive social and economic environment. A large group of working women of India is in the rural and unorganized sectors. Socially the majority of Indian women are still tradition bound and are in a disadvantageous position. Since globalization is opening up the Indian economy suddenly at a very high speed, without the required economic and social policies to provide the much required safety net, women who have been involved with

Table 3
Employment in Public and Private Sectors

(Lakh persons as on 31st March)

	1991	1994	1995	1996	1997	1998	1999	2000	2001	2002	2003	2004	2005
Public Sector													
Male	167.1	168.8	168.66	167.94	168.31	166.55	166.04	164.57	162.79	158.86	156.75	153.07	150.86
Female	23.47	25.65	26	26.35	27.28	27.63	28.11	28.57	28.59	28.87	29.05	28.9	29.21
Total	190.57	194.45	194.66	194.29	195.59	194.18	194.15	193.14	191.38	187.73	185.8	181.97	180.07
Private Sector													
Male	64.42	63.41	64.31	67.2	67.77	67.37	66.8	65.8	65.62	63.83	63.57	62.02	63.57
Female	14.34	15.89	16.28	17.92	19.09	20.11	20.18	20.66	20.9	20.49	20.64	20.44	20.95
Total	76.76	79.3	80.59	85.12	86.86	87.48	86.98	86.46	86.52	84.32	84.21	82.46	84.52
Public & Private Sector													
Male	229.52	232.21	232.97	235.14	236.08	233.92	233.84	230.37	228.4	222.71	220.32	215.09	214.42
Female	37.81	41.54	42.28	44.26	46.37	47.74	48.29	49.23	49.29	49.49	49.35	49.34	50.16
Total	267.33	273.75	275.25	279.41	282.45	281.66	281.13	279.6	277.89	272.06	270	264.43	264.58

United Nations Human Development Report

production in the traditional ways, have to cope with numerous problems and yet try to avail of the opportunities which an open economy promises.

Table -3 presents employment in public and private sectors of male and female from 1991 to 2005. In both the sectors (Public Sector & Private Sector) the predominance of male is clearly seen. The employment of female is 14.043 percent of males in 1991 during the initial stages of reforms this gradually raised to 17.36 percent during 2000 and in the year 2005 it reached up to 19.36 percent in the Public Sector.

When the employment of women in the Private Sector is analyzed 64.42 lakhs of male were employed during 1991 whereas female constitute only 0.04 % of them, this has gradually rose to 0.031% in the year 2000, which remained same at 0.03% in the 2005. The analysis of Public and Private Sectors combined together presents 0.04% of female participation in 1991, which gradually rose to 0.06 % in the year 2000 and to 0.04 % in 2005. So the growth of employment both in the organized and unorganized sectors with respect to female work force is consistently lower. This situation clearly depicts that globalization had an impact on the growth of employment opportunities especially in the unorganized sector but the rise is minimal, when the female employment scenario is analyzed.

In India today, globalization has had positive and negative implications within the male-dominant society. Even though India's constitution grants women legal citizenship, women get very little respect and standing in this country. With the help of the media, women's organizations have helped to advance women in the workforce, creating an increase in the standing of women. Even though globalization is broadening the workforce for women, it can have a negative impact by exploiting women in dangerous jobs, in which they are overworked. Globalization can have a positive or negative effect on women in India, but with globalization there is the power to uproot the traditional views towards women so they can take an equal stance in society.

Possibilities and Opportunities: On the positive side globalization has contributed to bring about welcome changes in the lives of women who have been able to avail of the opportunities, which have opened up in the various sectors of development. These are

- Prospects of higher and quality education have become feasible for those women who can afford them, economically and socially.
- Employment in technological and other advanced sectors, which have global bearing, has opened up for suitable qualified women.
- With changing attitude towards women, especially in the urban areas, women enjoy more egalitarian set of gender relationship.
- Augmentation of women's movements through exposures at the international level will help bring to about major changes in the economic, social and political lives of women.
- Reduction in gender inequalities will have positive effect on women's empowerment in the socio-economic context.
- Attitudinal changes towards women's role in the family due to good education, benefits of family planning and health care, child care, good job opportunities etc. will surely help in the development of more confident and healthy women.
- Positive approach to economic and cultural migration will facilitate women to be exposed to better prospects at the international level.

On the Negative Side...

- The traditional role of women in agriculture, livestock and animal husbandry, Khadi and village industries including handicrafts, handlooms fisheries, et, is being undermined because mechanization and automation is becoming prevalent in the market based economy which will adversely affect the village based traditional economy.

- Privatisation and reduction of public services will reduce regular employment opportunities for women.
- Globalisation has increased the number of low paid, part-time and exploitative jobs.
- Occupational sex segregation will be a stark reality in the open economy. This will tend to result in worse working condition, lower pay and inferior career opportunities.
- Curtailment of state provisions in child care, community care and social security, will increase the dual burden of employment and family responsibilities for women in general.
- With male migration on the increase from the rural to urban sectors, the women have to bear the triple burden of caring, farming and paid employment in the rural sector.
- In the neo liberal work practices, contract work, unsocial hours of work, cooperative practices, and payment by result make it very difficult for women to cope with their multiple responsibilities.
- With the disappearing social and financial safety nets and government subsidy, the poverty alleviation programmes, universal education, and women oriented health programmes will be adversely affected.
- Trade liberalization will allow MNCS to enter into food processing and other feminised industries which will lead to reduction in low skilled women labour.
- Privatisation of education and training will increase the cost of getting educated. When family budgets are readjusted, the female children will be the main casualty because most of the resources will be spent to educate the male children.
- Migration of women especially for economic reasons often gives rise to exploitation and trafficking of women at the local, regional and global levels.
- Open market economy leads to price rise in food and other basic necessities. Women who have to directly deal with family subsistence have to cope with such changes.

The plights of Indian women are similar to those of women in other developing regions such as Africa and Asia. Globalization has made many international corporations richer by the billions. However, what most people are not aware of is that women in these developing countries are suffering enormously due to this expansion of corporate empires. According to estimates from World Development Indicators, "Women work two-thirds of the world's working hours, produce half of the world's food, but earn only ten percent of the world's income, and own less than one percent of the world's property (Tomlinson)". Let us now analyze the impact of globalization on different variables of the Indian society.

Globalization and Changing Institution of Marriage in India:

Indian marriage systems are going through a major transition due to the impact of globalization on basic social values and institutions. The institution of marriage can be assessed by comparing and contrasting traditional and contemporary marriage patterns. The traditional pattern was marked by prominence of arranged marriages which were primarily oriented towards creating alliances between two families through "classical matchmakers" such as family priests and relatives. In such a marriage there was only a minor role for the bride and bridegroom in the context of decision-making regarding the marriage. Contemporary marriage, however, is based more on an understanding between the about-to-be-married man and woman along with attention to the views of family elders. New "mediators" such as the media (matrimonial columns) and marriage bureaus have also emerged, contributing to the rise of a nationwide, and sometimes transnational, system of information and choice-making in the context of marriage. Marriage Bureaus are popping up like mushrooms. Depending on how much you are willing to pay, they do anything from giving the "right advertisement" in the media, scrutinizing the resumes, sending the selected resumes for your approval, arranging the meeting of the two families, and also undertaking private investigation to check for the character and the details mentioned in the resume of the prospective. But the element of responsibility or concern is missing in this new matrimonial dotcoms which many times are proving in fake and false details of which the responsibility is not taken by them ultimately here the loosers are women and their lives.

Marriage, Market and Dowry Related Violence

The major influence that has been cast by globalization is an over-exposure to, and increased presence of worldly pleasures and luxury items, which are now essential items of dowry. The markets are flooded with household goods such as refrigerators, televisions, audio systems, DVD players etc. The bride's family is expected to give the latest model of these branded items as dowry or gifts at the time of marriage. It is an issue of prestige and the status of the family depends upon it. Dowry (and bride price in certain communities) has always had a universal presence in Indian marriage. The story does not end here. The bride's family is also expected to throw a lavish and extensive marriage part. The bride's family is also expected to pay for all the rituals that precede the marriage and that happen at the time of marriage. Polishing schools a new concept, are also flourishing, and it has become the fashion to attend these schools before marriage. Since most households are large families, where the boy shall be staying with his parents even after marriage, the innovators in the marriage market have started "Training Schools for Prospective Daughters-in-law", where the girls are being trained on how to get along with their mothers-in-law and how to fit exceptionally well into the traditional role of an ideal daughter-in-law. These schools are gaining tremendous popularity amongst the middle-class. The India daily soap opera industry is highly influenced by the marriage institution, and barring a few T.V. serials, which have few takers, the entire visual media is dominated by the "Mother-in-law & Daughter-in-law" episodes. These T.V. daily soaps on one hand show the "New Woman", who is independent, intellectual, and a decision-maker and on the other hand show women as traditional, homemaker, and the ideal daughter-in-law. This new image of women, for which the serial directors are largely responsible, (though they would say that they make films only about what the people want to see), puts them in a double-edged bind. A woman is supposed to work and earn for the family as well as do the household chores with the same vigour and enthusiasm as their non-working mothers-in-law display or used to display. This double jeopardy is a result of the new marriage norms that have been slowly evolving. The boy looks for a girl who is beautiful, smart, intellectual, and sporty because she has to accompany him at all company dinners and parties and yet she should be traditional because she has to get with his mother and father and fit into the traditional role. The roles of men are changing, but for women they are causing an excess burden. A look at the marriage advertisements shows that the boys' families look for a fair, slim, convent-educated, professional girl from a respectable family. Some even hint at the expected dowry.

The latest National Crimes Record Bureau data shows that dowry deaths and torture by husband has been increasing. If we include all the marriage related violence, the table 2 shows that there is a consistent increase in cases related to dowry deaths and violence by husband and his family on the bride. Moreover, among all categories of CAW, Cruelty by Husband and Relatives has shown an increase of 10% between the years 1998-2003.

Table 4
Incidence of Crime Against Women in India

	Incidence					
	1998	*1999*	*2000*	*2001*	*2002*	*2003*
Dowry Death	6975	6699	6995	6851	6822	6208
Torture(Cruelty by Husband & his Relatives)	41376	43823	45778	49170	49237	50703
Dowry Prohibition Act	3578	3064	2876	3222	2816	2684

Source: NCRB 2003

Thus, the globalization and economic power infact are precipitating domestic violence because there is a greater demand of resources. There is an increasing need of commodities and luxuries.

Globalization and the Commoditization of Women

The market has also affected culture, which is increasingly being commercialized and commoditized. The rise of individualism and consumerism actually accompany globalization and the need for TNCs to sell their products to accumulate a greater surplus by them. Firms and individuals follow this trend in their pursuit of materialism and the creation of status symbols. In the same vein women are being commoditized as never before. Economic globalization in the form of 'market democracy' has also created the image of the New Asian Women. She is professional woman, entrepreneur, manageress executive who is articulate, glamorous and assertive. This image is in every women's magazine that is avidly read by the middle class and aspiring working-class women who do not have the means to buy designer clothes and skin-whitening products.

Privatization and the Rolling Back of the State

Under the guise of free market restructuring, the privatization of public services as well as basic necessities. Because women are still expected to be responsible for child care and family maintenance, they will bear the disproportionate weight of these constraints. Women as homemakers have to balance the extra costs due to increasing charges for public utilities, education and health care as a result of cuts in public subsidies. Not only will their double burden be intensified, there will also be mounting pressure to assume multiple roles both as paid and unpaid labour, eg., taking care of the elderly, the retrenched, taking on extra work in the informal sector. Those adversely affected will be poor women who will have decreased or no access to such amenities or will have to struggle more to gain access to these services for their family.

Globalization and Increase in the Cyber Crime Against Women

The absence of judicial activism and deficient cyber laws against the fast-spreading scourge of cyber violence against women could not be ignored. Digital revolution was proving to be a double-edged weapon against women. "On one side, it is providing tremendous benefits to women. On the other, its misuse is violating their human rights. It is aggravating conventional forms of violence like trafficking and female foeticide. The charges of blackmailing girls and women regarding their old contact and photographs and threatening them to put their photographs one net have been increasing seen.

Globalization–Impact on the Working Environment

53% of the working women in India fear for their safety. In New Delhi itself about 53% working women feel insecure, especially during night shifts in all major hubs of economic activity across the country. Most of them are employed in the BPO/ITeS, hospitality, civil aviation, medical and textile space. Their concern is that safety norms set up by their respective establishments are not adequate and given the increase in crime, their insecurities and fears are only going up.

According to the Assocham Social Development Foundation (ASDF), an assessment was carried out revealing that 48% of women who are engaged in the small-scale sector are extremely worried about their safety and nearly 26% in the medium sector and 23% in the large-scale establishments are scared to step out after the sun sets.

- 34% women in the low skilled category are worried about their well being; 29% in the moderately skilled section and 8% among high skilled workforce.
- The fast growing BPO/ ITeS, hospitality, civil aviation industry has generated parallel employment for cab drivers who have often been responsible for rash driving, accidents, eve teasing, rape and even murder.
- 86% women on night shifts face commuting problems because of lack of adequate transport arrangements by employers. Those working in Kolkata, Mumbai and Pune face maximum commuting hurdles while those in Delhi, Hyderabad and Ludhiana the least.

- In Bangalore, 75,000-95,000 women work in night shifts. There are around 2,200 IT firms in Bangalore, of which 1,600 are registered with the Department. In Bangalore, around 56% women respondents in a survey carried out amongst women working in night shifts in the IT, aviation, hospitals and BPO sector feel unsafe. Delhi topped the list with 65% of women followed by 35% in Hyderabad, 28% in Chennai and 26 % in Mumbai.
- BPO/ITeS is not the only sector with post-sunset shifts. Women nurses have been doing night rounds as also those working in media, airlines, hotels and other service industries.

Conclusion

There have been increased economic opportunities for women in this globalized era but mounting threats. The fallouts of the process of and market forces on growing domestic violence against women can be combated effectively if the family and society give equal power to women and the state mediates and facilitates the democratization of the family by enacting gender just laws and formulating and implementing gender just polices and programs. Women participation and access to resources is actually a manifestation of the democratic processes that exist within the Family, the Society and the State. The more democratic the structure, the more is the power given to women.

There are three steps to democratization for ensuring equal status of women... they are

- Democratize of family to allow women to be equal partner in decision making.
- No discrimination between sexes in society.
- Equal representation of women in state.

It has been seen that when the society imposes sanctions against the perpetrators of violence, the women is empowered to exert for their rights. Only when the family and the society are democratized, the status of the women is strengthened. At this time, it becomes the duty of the state to facilitate and strengthen the process. The solution lies in the fact that women empowerment approach to combat violence against women should be well integrated and interwoven into in all policies and programs of the governments. Women should be equal partners not only at the public places but should have adequate control of their own resources which can only give due status for them in this gloabalized era.

References

Dr. Ranjana Kumari, "Globalization and Socio-Cultural Dimension of Domestic Vuiolence", Centre for *Social Research* 2, Nelson Mandela Road, Vasant Kunj, New Delhi-110070.

Asmita Basu, "Violence against Women: a statistical overview, and Challenges and gaps in data collection and methodology and approaches for overcoming them Needs of users of data collection" *Expert Group Meeting,* UN Division for the Advancement of Women, Geneva, Switzerland.

Eliminate Violence against Women: Some facts, *www.indiawomenstat.com*

Working for Workers, The Hindu, Sunday, Dec 31st , 2006

Raja Mitra, "Emerging State-Level ICT Development Stategies", The World Bank, NW, Washington.

Domestic Violence Act, The Portal of Hope.

Indira Jaising, Domestic Violence Act, Nov, 02, New Delhi.

Human Development Reports–Various Issues.

Chapter-9

Can Microfinance Programmes Empower Women in India?

Rais Ahmad, R. Ramakrishna

Introduction

According to 2001 Census, 48 percent of the total population in India are women and among the working population women constitute only about 32 per cent in India. These figures explain not only the prominence of women in the population structure but also indicate the deprivation of women in empowerment. Human Development Report 1995 of UNDP was recognized very much the contribution made by women– Of the total burden of work, women carry more than half; ¾ th of men's work is in paid market activities compared with only 1/3 rd of women's work; Men receive the lions share of income and recognition for their contribution, while most of women's work remains unpaid, undervalued and unrecognized. Women empowerment, therefore, is a topic, which attracted attention by social scientists, politics, administrators, financial institutions and even NGOs in the present day scenario.

The true women empowerment takes place when women challenge the existing norms and culture, to effectively improve their well being (Bali Swain, 2006). While doing so, it carefully interprets the World Bank's definition of empowerment within the South Asian contexts and makes comprehensible distinctions between community driven development, efficiency improving activities that are culturally considered to be women's domain and activities which truly empower women (Bali Swain, 2007).

Concept of Empowerment

What do we mean by empowerment? When does the well-being of a person improve? Nobel Laureate Amartaya Sen (1993) explains that the freedom to lead different types of life is reflected in the person's capability set. The capability of a person depends on a variety of factors, including personal characteristics and social arrangements. However, the full accounting of individual freedom goes beyond the capabilities of personal living. For example, if we do not have the courage to choose to live in a particular way, even though we could live that way if we so chose, can it be said that we do have the freedom to live that way, i.e. the corresponding capability?

In the feminist paradigm, empowerment goes beyond economic betterment and well-being, to strategic gender interests. As Mayoux (1997,2001) suggests, empowerment is a process of internal change, or power within, augmentation of capabilities, or power to, and collective mobilization of women, and when possible men, or power with, to the purpose of questioning and changing the subordination connected with gender, or power over. Empowerment can range from personal empowerment that can exist within the existing social order. Thus this kind of empowerment would correspond to the right to make one's own choice, to increased autonomy and to control over economic resources. But self-confidence and self-esteem also play an essential role in change. Empowerment signifies increased participation in decision-making and it is this process through which people feel themselves to be capable of making decisions and the right to do so. Personal empowerment can lead to changes in existing institutions and norms, however, without the collective empowerment the personal empowerment and choices are limited, as Sen explains.

The World Bank defines empowerment as "the process of increasing the capacity of individuals or groups to make choices and to transform those choices into desired actions and outcomes. Central to this process are actions which both build individual and collective assets, and improve the efficiency and fairness of the organizational and institutional context which govern the use of these assets" (*http://info.Worldbank.org*). Thus, as the World Bank (2001) report confirms, societies that discriminate on the basis of gender pays the cost of greater poverty, slower economic growth, weaker governance and a lower living standard of their people. The World Bank also identifies four key elements of empowerment to draft institutional reforms: access to information; inclusion and participation; accountability; and local organistional capacity (*http://Inweb18.worldbank.org*).

In reality, empowerment is a process of awareness and capacity building leading to greater participation, better decision-making power, etc., Mere provision of LOANS to women does not guarantee their empowerment. But what is needed is ..... Improvents in attitude to women's role at household level and at community level; Increasing women's participation in household decisions; Increasing women income levels and control over income leading to greater levels of economic independence; Access to support networks and markets which will enable them to protect their interests. However, there are some limitations to women empowerment. Firstly, within schemes, impacts are often vary significantly between women i.e., in most cases the poorest women are bypassed in lending programmes. Secondly many aspects of gender inequality cannot be dealt with through micro credit viz., violence, unequal division of domestic responsibilities, etc. Lastly, impact on empowerment cannot be inferred from financial services or repayment levels. For instance, women may repay by taking loans elsewhere and getting into serious debt trap. So, the said limitations point to the need for more strategies to achieve women empowerment.

Strategies for Women Empowerment

Nature and Type of Enterprise Supported

- Encourage enterprises to examine the role of women within the enterprise.

Financial Systems are to be Transformed to Work for the Majority

- Accurate management information systems.
- Institutional structures that can support sustained service delivery to low income clients.
- Operations that manage small transactions efficiently.
- Transparent financial reporting that conforms to international standards.
- A wide range of retail intermediaries to provide financial services. All these are essential for effective management.

Quality of Credit and Non-Credit Services Offered

- Focus on service to low income clients.
- Emphasis on character based lending for smaller loans and project appraisal for L.T. loans.
- Develop complementary services that will support women's participation viz., child care etc.

Quality of Planning and Management Issues Offered

- Use ongoing evaluation to provide an opportunity for women to voice concerns and other suggestions for change

Quality of Financial Services Offered

- Extend smaller loans with flexible repayment schedules.
- Ensure that the provision of credit is supported with additional business skills viz., marketing, risk identification etc.
- Minimise gender specific constraints.

Quality of Training Offered

- Broaden the range of skills for women entrepreneurs.
- Increase helps confidence.
- Incorporate gender equality issues into training.

Of all the strategies to empower women on these complex fronts, there is a need for the growth of gross root organizations in which women have been active agents in the process of their empowerment.

Micro Finance and Women Empowerment

The micro credit schemes using SHGs were designed against the background of the failure of earlier studies to empower poor particularly women. With the help of some Bangladesh Banks, Yunus conducted an innovative experiment in 1976, emphasizing group delivery of credit and exploring what constituted a manageable group size for effective financial intermediation. The Central Bank of Bangladesh later facilitated Yunus' work by arranging funding from International Fund for Agricultural Development (IFAD).

In Yunus' experiment, group collateral substituted for physical collateral. The group guarantee to repay individual loans, becomes the hallmark of micro lending. Using the mechanism, poor people with no physical collateral, were able to form group to gain access to institutional credit. The mechanism also allowed credit, to reach the poor, especially poor women. The central premise, of this targeted credit approach, is that, lack of access to credit, is the greatest constraint on the economic advancement of the poor. Yunus believed that, with appropriate support, the poor could be productively employed, in income generating activities, including processing and manufacturing, transport, storage and marketing of agricultural products, and poultry and live stock raising. After almost seven years of experimentation, with a variety of group-based mechanisms, his idea took formal shape, as a bank with its own charter. With the government holding about 90 percent of the shares in paid-up-capital, Grameen Bank was established in 1983, to work exclusively for the poor, defined as individuals, owning less than half an acre of land.

Micro-Credit institutions, evolved their own design features, such as class, eligibility for membership in the group, ranging from landless to minimum land holding; prior entrepreneurial experience to no experience; monthly repayments to weekly repayments: individual lending to group-based lending; requirement of collateral to no collateral and group lending contracts to no group lending contracts. The programme of linking SHGs to Banks which was started on pilot basis in India in 1991-92, made rapid progress over the years. The cumulative number of SHGs credit linked with banks increased from 32,995 during 1992-1999 to 22,38,565 during 2005-2006 covering more than 164.90 million poor households (Table-1). More than 90% of SHGs linked to banks were exclusive women SHGs.

Table 1
SHG-Bank Linkage–Cumulative Progress

Up to End March	*SHGs Financed*	*Bank Loan (Rs.m)*
1992-1999	32,995	571
1999-2000	1,14,775	1,930
2000-2001	2,63,825	4,809
2001-2002	4,61,478	10,263
2002-2003	7,17,360	20,487
2003-2004	10,79,091	39,042
2004-2005	16,18,456	68,985
2005-2006	22,38,565	1,13,975

SHG Bank Linkage Programme

Over the past decades, despite its large network of rural bank branches has failed to reach the poorer sections of the society. The All India Debt and Investment Survey showed that the share of non-institutional agencies in outstanding cash dues of the rural households was 38 per cent (GOI, 1981). The main limiting factor in reaching formal finance to this group was the high transaction costs and lack of appropriate credit and saving products. A study conducted by NABARD in the mid-eighties revealed that financial services required by poor households are: safe-keeping of small surpluses in the form of thrift; access to consumption loans to meet emergency needs and financial services and products that did not require collateral (MYRADA, 2002). The Self Help Group Bank Linkage model evolved from the pioneering efforts of NABARD and two NGOs, MYRADA and PRADHAN (MYRADA & PRADHAN, 1992). Starting with 500 groups in the early 1990s, the cumulative numbers of SHGs that have been financed have increased to 2,238,565, by March 2006. The expansion of the SHG bank linkage programme has been an acceleration in the past few years. It has reached an estimated 164.90 million people and disbursed more than Rs.114 billion in cumulative bank loans up to March 2006, using a network of 44,362 bank branches and 4896 NGOs (Table-2).

The Government of India, National Policy for the Empowerment of Women (2001), declared various measures aimed towards achieving greater equality between men and women. In 1993, the Indian government ratified the International Convention on the Elimination of all Forms of Discrimination Against Women (CEDAW). The government's poverty alleviation programmes such as Swaranajayanti Grama Swarojgar Yojna (SGSY) and the Rashtriya Mahila Kosh implement their programmes through microfinance interventions of NABARD's Self Help Group bank linkage programme. Apart from the large number of households that this programme services, the following features make the NABARD SHG model unique:

1. The distinctive process of formation of the SHGs and the freedom that they have in deciding the terms of their lending and borrowings within the group, once they receive the loan.
2. The use of the existing and extensive infrastructure of rural bank branches for disbursing microfinance services.
3. Three distinctive ways of linking the SHGs to the banks through NGOs with the NGOs playing a major role in promotion of the SHGs and their training.
4. The Government's poverty alleviation programmes such as SGSY and the Rashtriya Mahila Kosh

Table 2
Information on Self Help Groups

A. Physical Achievements	
1. Number oi poor families who have accessed bank credit up to March 2006.	32.98 million
2. Estimated number of poor people assisted up to March 2006.	164.90 million
3. Percentage of SHGs comprised of women	90
4. Cumulative number of SHGs financed by banks up to March 2006	2, 238,565
B. Financial Results	
1. Cumulative bank loans disbursed to SHGs up to March 2006.	113,975 million
2. Bank loans disbursed to new SHGs during 2005-2006	23,305 million
3. Increase in credit flow to SHGs over the previous year	50%
4. On-time repayment reported by participating banks	Over 95 per cent
Partnerships	
1. Number of participating banks	547
2. Commercial banks	47
3. Regional Rural Bank	158
4. Cooperatives	342
5. Number of bank branches lending to SHGs	44,362
6. Number of participating NGO and other agencies.	4,896

**Source:* Progress of SHG–Bank Linkage in India, 2005-2006, Micro Credit Innovations Department, NABARD, Mumbai, 2006.
** IUSD = Rs. 43.

implement their programmes through microfinance interventions.

Using higher rates of savings, borrowings, timely repayment of credit, promptness in attending SHG meetings and decisions by individual members as indicators of enhanced credit access, income generation and socio-economic empowerment of the poor. Puhanzhendi and Badatya (2002) find that the SHG programme has a positive social impact. Puhanzhendi and Satyasai (2001) further argue that the social impact of these programmes on the household is greater than the economic impact.

SHGs and Women Empowerment

The truly empowering activities are those that reflect the changes that women have effectively made to better their lives by resisting the existing norms of the society. Based on the conceptual framework above the responses of the Focus Group Discussions (FGDs) have been classified as follows

Efficiency Improving Activities

- Sending children to school regularly;
- Improved nutrition in the household;
- Taking better care of health and hygiene of their children;
- Taking care of other group members in time of health and psychological crisis.
- Helping in social functions.

Community Driven Development Activities

- Cleaning the village road, village pond and village school;
- To solve the drinking water problem;
- Helping to start a school for their own children and children of the village:
- Building a bridge over a small rivulet, thereby connecting the village road to the outside world.
- Build a small patch of the village road;

- Starting a store with groceries, vegetables and other basic requirement within the village at reasonable prices;
- Starting an adult literacy programme in the village;
- Participating in the sanitation programme of their village;
- Help Government in immunization programmes;
- Monitoring the school and primary health care centre in their village;
- Street light for the village and its maintenance;

Women Empowering Activities

- Overcoming the resistance from husband and other members of the family to join the SHG;
- Increased participation in decision-making within the household to issues that were usually considered outside the domain of women;
- Improved status and increase in respect within the household;
- Feeling fearless, open and confident;
- All group members learn to sign their names and some have joined adult literacy programmes;
- Adopting family planning measures;
- More mobile, can move out of the house and the village more frequently;
- Talking to the male persons in their village, which they were not confident to do before because of cultural reasons;
- They have more information about the government programmes due to their exposure and can apply for them for their own betterment and the benefit of the community.
- Actively participating in the decision to send their children to school;
- Eradication of prostitution;
- Some women can actively engage in the decision of their marriage with the elders in her household;

- Awareness about politics and engaged in political participation by way of voting or directly, by standing as a candidate in the local elections.

Political participation, especially at the local level has been seen as a key factor in empowerment of women. In India, the government has passed legislation to ensure reservation of seats for women in the local institutions viz.,Panchayats. SHG respondents showed greater awareness of reservations for women in Panchayats and jobs, and an increased level of participation in village politics. However, this empowerment did not show any significant impact on some of the key decision-making areas of family planning, children's marriage and the buying and selling of land. These decisions, which have traditionally been within the male domain, reflect that although the women have been empowered, SHGs have not been able to make substantial impact in these key decision areas.

Conclusion

Based on the evidence along with a more strict interpretation of women empowerment, it is difficult to believe that a minimalist microfinance programme would have sustainable impact on the empowerment of women. SHGs, where a majority of groups are linked with the help of NGOs that provide support in financial services and specialized training, have a greater ability to make a positive impact on women empowerment. If women empowerment is to be pursued as a serious objective by SHG programmes in particular and the larger microfinance community in general, greater emphasis needs to be placed on training, education and creating awareness in order to achieve a larger and more lasting empowerment.

References

Amartya Sen & Nussbaum M.C. (ed.) (1993), *Capability and Well-Being, in the Quality of Life.*

Bali Swain (2006, 2007), Department of Economics, Uppsala University, Sweden.

Census of India (2001), The Registrar General & Census Commissioner, 2A, Mansingh Road, Delhi, India.

Mayoux L. (1997), "The Magic Ingredient? Microfinance and Women's Empowerment", A Briefing Paper prepared for the Micro Credit Summit, Washington.

Mayoux, L. (2001), "Tackling the Down Side: Social Capital, Women's Empowerment and Micro-Finance in Cameroon", Development and Change, Vol.32.

MYRADA (2002), "Impact of Self Help Groups (Group Processes) on the Social Empowerment status of Women Members in Southern India", paper presented at the Seminar on SHG Bank Linkage Programme, New Delhi.

Puhazhendi, V. and Badatya, K.C. (2002), "SHG Bank Linkage Programme for Rural Poor-An Impact Assessment", paper presented at the seminar on SHG bank linkageprogramme at New Delhi, Micro Credit Innovations Department, NABARD, Mumbai.

Puhazhendi, V. and Satyasai, K.J.S. (2001), "Economic and Social Empowerment of Rural Poor through SHGs", Indian Journal of Agricultural Economics, Vol. 56. No.3.

Refer to Social Capital, Empowerment and Community Driven Development at http://info.worldbank.org/etools/bspan/PresentationView.asp?PID=936&EID=482

Refertohttp://Inweb18.worldbank.org/ESSD/sdvext.nsf/68ByDocName/WhatIsEmpowermentFourAreasofPractice.

UNDP Human Development Report (1995), New York.

Chapter-10

Women Empowerment and Rural Development

Y. Rama Krishna, A.V. Naga Varma

Women empowerment is a global issue, which has gained momentum in recent decades. In India, besides ratification of international conventions, there are provisions in the Constitution and several legislative Acts have been passed to ensure women empowerment. It, however, appears that on this front the situation on ground is far from satisfactory.

Women as an independent target group, account for 495.74 million and represent 48.3% of the country's population, as per the 2001 census. No country can achieve its potential without adequately investing in and developing the capabilities of women. In the interest of long-term development it is necessary to facilitate their empowerment. In many developing countries, including India, women have much less access to education, jobs, income and power than men. Even after five and half decades of planned development Indian women, except a privileged minority, have not achieved expected success in the mainstream of life. If we don't improve the status and role of women, our country will be unable to have a competitive edge over others.

The position of women and their status in any society is an index of its civilization. Women are to be considered as equal partners in the process of development. But, because of centuries of exploitation and subjugation, Indian women have remained at the receiving end. In this context, in order to provide a big push, institutional support is necessary to empower Indian women in general and rural women in particular. Women empowerment demands a "Life-cycle" approach where empowerment is viewed as a process and not as an event.

Good Governance is not possible without participation and empowerment of rural downtrodden women. UNDP Report indicates that while 67% of global income is earning by women and a mere 1% of global property is owned by women.

Women are engaged in a wide variety of occupations especially in the unorganized sector. In the rural unorganized sector, women care for cattle, sowing, transplanting, harvesting, weaving, working in the hand-looms and producing handicrafts mostly as low paid wage earners or unpaid family workers. They are also engaged in producing and selling a variety of goods such as vegetables, fruits, flowers, cooked food, groceries etc.

Empowerment of women involves many things, economic opportunity, property rights, political representation, social equality, personal rights and so on. Historically the world over, either by law or by custom, the status of women is undermined by asymmetrical power relationship in decision-making, personal and social rights, access to resources and entitlement. Women in many countries still lack rights to inherit property, own land, get education, obtain credit, earn income of work outside home, and control their fertility: they are still widely under-represented in involvement in decision-making at the household or social level. Empowerment by means of modest income-generation projects is clearly insufficient to ameliorate the prospects for a high quality of life for women.

In reality rural farmwomen are invisible in statistics, they remain unreached and unattended in planned developed efforts and are with no access and control on the resources. Rural Indian women are extensively involved in agricultural activities. However, the nature and extent of their involvement differs with the variations in agro-production systems. The mode of female participation in agricultural production varies with the land-owning status of farm households. Their roles range from Managers to Landless laborers.

Women in many countries still lack right to inherit property, own land, get education, obtain credit, earn income or work outside home, control their fertility. They are still widely under-represented in decision-making at the household or social level. Empowerment by means of modest income generation projects is clearly insufficient to ameliorate the prospects for a high quality of life for women.

Role of Women in Rural Development

- In India, food security as a national objective was placed on the policy agenda much earlier than in other developed and countries. Women's key role in the production of major grains and minor millets illustrates their invaluable contribution to food security. Women are often the major and frequently the sole providers of the household food supply. As major buyers of family food security, as primary providers of nutrition to the young children, women are the major decision-makers in ensuring nutrition to the next generation.
- Women are the key figures in small holdings which provide livelihoods to the majority of the rural people. With rapidly declining environmental conditions and the consequent male migration, women in female headed households are emerging as the managers to the much degraded farm lands.
- Women are heavily engaged as agricultural workers. About 80 percent of all economically active women in India are engaged in agriculture. They work longer and harder than men. They also work on more tasks than men. Usually, the low income, low skilled and low productivity jobs are female specific. Almost always, labor intensive, back breaking and time consuming activities are the domain of the weaker sex.

- Women are typically involved in post-harvest processing of food and non-food products. Their contribution is substantial even where they are mostly confined to the homestead. They are also active in barter, exchange and trade of agricultural produce and processed products.
- In animal husbandry women have a multiple role. An estimated 75 million women are engaged in the India dairy sector. Their activities vary widely ranging from care of animals, grazing, fodder collection, cleaning of animal shed to processing milk and livestock products. Through women play a significant role in livestock management and production, women's control over livestock and its products is negligible.
- In India, nature and extent of women's participation in fishery varies across the states. About one million women as compared to 1.80 million men are involved in the fisheries.

Factors Empowering the Rural Women

Educational

Education is the key which opens the door to life, develops humanity and promotes national development. Education can be an effective tool for women's empowerment. It enables rural women to acquire new knowledge and technology required for improving and developing their tasks in all fields. Therefore, at least one Functional Literacy Centre should be opened in each Gram Panchayat as functionally literate and adult education necessary.

Social

Empowering women contribute to social development. Economic progress in any country whether developed or underdeveloped could be achieved through social development. Hence, women's empowerment cannot be ignored, while devising various policies for rural and social-economic development.

Status of Women: Even country has made progress in developing women's capabilities, but inequalities continue to exist between women and men. The low status of women is the outcome of a variety of causes in which patriarchal values reinforced by tradition, media and other socio-political institution play a major role. Thus, tee institutional bases of women's oppression have to be sensitized to accept the gender equality and moreover, women's perception of themselves would also need to be changed.

Gender Bias: Cultural traditions and economic necessity have always mean a significant role for women in agriculture. In India it is not uncommon that women do not have control over the land. Even, where women constitute a larger share of a agricultural producers there are cultural constraints to easy communication between men and women, because almost all extension workers are men.

Health and Nutrition: Health and nutrition are two very important basic needs for empowerment of rural women. To achieve real and quicker development in health sector, an extensive as well as intensive "Health Education and Awareness Campaign" (HEAC) need to be given topmost priority and it should mainly stress on nutritional education, benefits of immunization, family planning etc.

Economic

Empowering women with economically productive work will enhance their contribution to agricultural development.

Access to Resources: The farm women need to have control over limited resources like land and livestock, so that they could take away decisions and implement them in any way that is required. Ownership and control over productive assets will create a sense of belonging and owning. It will thus help to take responsibility in family and local group activities. Other impact of control is to enhance their decision-making ability to meet some physiological needs like self-esteem and confidence.

Micro-Credit Programmers: Micro-credit programmes extend small loans to poor people for self-employment projects that generate income allowing them to care for themselves and their families. In most cases, micro-credit programmes offer a combination of services and resources to their clients in addition to credit for self-employment. Access to productive resources is critical for enhancing women's economic choices. Since, formal credit institutions rarely lend the poor, special institutional arrangements may become necessary to extend credit to those who have no collateral to officer their enterprises. In order to have access to credit, setting up self-help group, local banking system by women, Non-Governmental need to be established. The policy challenge is to support effective grass-roots credit schemes and intermediaries and ensure that low-income have assured credit from the formal financial system.

Technological

Though women are involved in almost all agricultural operations, in rural areas yet, they have inadequate technical competency due to their limited exposure to outside world. This has compelled them to follow the age old practices which in turn result in poor work efficiency and drudgery and need computer, internet latest information's.

Capacity Building: Capacity building and empowerment are important for which there should be decentralized capacity building among the rural women particularly farm women. Empowerment projects should go beyond the provision of basic social services for all. They should include components vital for enabling the poor to participate in economic activities. It is important to develop the skills among farm women in order to increase their productivity and to keep them abreast of modernization and technological changes for being competitive in the market.

Exposure to Mass Media: The transfer of technology approach, which mainly includes mass media are also not paying due attention towards dissemination, of adequate and timely agricultural and marketing information to the farm rural women. Therefore, there is outmost need to provide adequate coverage to the programmes related to women and they must get exposure to mass media for improving their communication and meditation skills to strengthen their capacity to contact and mediate with external world.

Appropriate Training Programmed: Training is an important component of HRD which enhances knowledge, skill and attitude. For building technical competency among farm women, need based skill-oriented training programmes to reinforce their role in farm activities need special attention. The training programmes should initially be organized on their felt-needs and then be switched over to unfelt but essential needs. To achieve this sacred task, infrastructural facilities in terms of more numbers of KVKs, FTCs and BRLP should be established in the district on priority basis.

Appropriate Technology for Women: In order to cater the technological needs of farm rural women, women specific technologies should be developed. While evolving agricultural technologies, indigenous practices used by women should be paid due attention for blending with the frontier ones for greater adoption. Also there is need to strengthen linkage between various research and extension organizations engaged in transfer of technology.

Conclusion

Women are very important segment in development at local to global levels. Economic independence and education and competence, willingness, confidence, self-motivation, encouragement from family and society contribute to empowerment of rural women.

References

B.V. Chalapathi & B.V. Raghavulu (2005), "Decline of Good Govertance- Decentralization" in *Third Concept.* Vol. No 19, Augest, New Delhi, p.39

Premalatha Pujari, Vijaya Kaushik (1994), *Women Power in India,* Vol.3. Kanishka Publishers, New Delhi, p. 24

Dr. Sr. Rosa K.D., Women Empowerment and Family set-up–page 18.

Sayed Afzal Peerzade, Empowerment of Women A Study –page 291.

Chapter-11

Poverty Alleviation and Women Empowerment through Self Help Groups

R. Ramakrishna, D. Tata Rao, D. Nageswara Rao

Introduction

Andhra Pradesh has used Self Help Groups (SHGs) extensively as a primary tool of poverty alleviation and empowerment. A SHG is small group of persons who come together with the intention of finding a solution to a common problem such as medical issues, livelihood generation with a degree of self-sufficiency. Early programs sought to provide self-employment, empowerment, and incorporate rural poor women into the development process. Following on successes in earlier programs, which were modified to make them more meaningful, the state has promoted significant increases in SHGs using a social mobilization approach. The state-sponsored Velugu program working in over 860 mandals in 22 districts, aims to reach 2.9 million of the poorest of rural poor. Both the number and structure of SHGs in Andhra Pradesh has been scaled up. Capacity building is an important component in the scaling up of Andhra Pradesh's poverty alleviation initiatives. Training includes participatory training methods, SHG formation and strengthening, book keeping and financial management and also helps members and leaders develop linkages with banks and other institutions.

The primary aim of the SHG-Bank linkage program is to integrate informal savings and credit groups with mainstream banking by providing them with credit to enhance their fund base. Once an SHG has demonstrated its capacity to sustain and to absorb outside credit, loans are extended to it from the formal banking structure. Using existing financial infrastructure to meet the needs of micro credit initiatives has saved on duplication and transaction costs and has also been instrumental in changing perceptions about the credit worthiness of the poor. Andhra Pradesh has chosen social mobilization and inclusiveness as methods of addressing poverty alleviation. The process uses social mobilization as an institutional mechanism to help the poor interact with government machinery so that public resources and services are better accessed. Besides group mobilization, the programs focus on expanding the assets of the poor and creating economic opportunities connected with people's livelihoods.

Impact Analysis

The impact of SHGs can be seen in two dimensions. The first is in poverty alleviation. This impact cannot be captured at one point of time in a conclusive manner. There has to be a sustained upward trend in moving away from poverty for the families of SHG members and the process of poverty alleviation should be studied. The second dimension of the impact of SHGs, is the empowerment of the poor and of women in particular. An increase in incomes, livelihoods or assets does not necessarily lead to 'empowerment' in the true sense. Any intervention, such as participation in a SHG and access to micro credit, will shift five spaces in a person's life- economic, physical, socio-cultural, political and mental. Impact will lead to empowerment if the non-mental spaces are instrumental in increasing mental spaces in such a way that action and voice are generated to improve the quality of life. There is absolutely no doubt that SHGs have lead to an expansion in the economic spaces of members (Mayoux, L 1997, 2001; Ramakrishna, R 2004, 2005; Ramakrishna, R. and Tata Rao, D 2008; Puhazhendi,

V. and Satyasai, K.J.S., 2000, 2001). Empowerment can be reached through social inclusion (Ramakrishna et.al, 2008) and therefore, Social inclusion, information and people's participation are significant catalysts that empower people through positive shifts in spaces.

Learning, Experimentation and External Catalysts

In Andhra Pradesh, one noteworthy observation relates to the linkages between different approaches towards development, poverty alleviation and empowerment. While incomes have to be augmented through livelihood generation interventions, for which credit is an important component, attention also has to be paid to the determinants of human poverty in terms of health and education requirements. When one talks of interventions involving the government, NGOs and the poor, the first significant external catalyst that facilitated positive change in the case of Andhra Pradesh, is the funding agency. It is evident that the SHG route to development and empowerment is seen as worthwhile to invest large amounts of money and efforts into. The timely assistance offered to programs has given the impetus to extend and deepen intervention. The second catalyst can be identified in the context of the initiative the government officials have taken which are outside their job requirements of implementing projects. The capacity to have a vision, to place it before the government and find ways to translate thought into action are 'external' to the given understanding of the role of the administrative services. These have proved critical in the progression of Andhra Pradesh towards pro-poor strategies. The third one can be seen in the contribution of organizations from the private and NGO sector. These have proved significant to the up scaling of SHGs. The opening of markets of SHGs by the private sector, training and capacity building inputs by organizations make for significant external catalysts.

Lessons from Andhra Experience

The primary lesson learned from the Andhra experience is that there is value in using SHGs as a conduit for poverty alleviation initiatives. However one has to understand the limitations of this use and gauge the ways in which these can be surpassed to get more out of such an approach. The need for small homogenous groups to be formed is simultaneously the strength and the weakness of SHGs. It is critical to choose wisely the common denominator that brings people together in a group. When this common feature is poverty, the identification of the poor as also the understanding of poverty is the most important exercise. Second, when micro credit is the pivot around which organization takes place, its ability to alleviate poverty/empower is limited. In Andhra Pradesh however, these limitations have been overcome by integrating micro credit with a powerful 'plus' component of social and economic infrastructure. The danger here lies in that while it seems almost Utopian on paper, during implementation, community institutions like SHGs may not be equipped to take on such complex tasks.

Third, SHGs should not be seen only in their capacity to route micro credit. Their political potential is powerful. SHGs and federations form the training ground to make leaders and potential political aspirants. This critical mass has tremendous potential to work for the betterment of the regions they represent. Andhra Pradesh has unleashed an extensive wave of mobilization and sharp attention has to be paid to the danger of other vested interests co-opting such a critical mass. Fourth, the potential of women SHGs for women's empowerment depends upon several other supportive measures like education, health, housing and infrastructure. While all five spaces may expand positively, there is a limit to the capacity for credit based SHGs to empower women. Further since gender related discrimination requires interventions that will not alienate men and forming only women groups may well do just that unless other methods of awareness building are used.

Fifth, partnerships are fundamental for development. This kind of inclusiveness where institutions and actors both public and private, work in synergy, has considerable potential for poverty alleviation. It can bear positive results if care is taken to protect the interests of all the participants. Sixth, the Andhra experience has shown how the linkage between the national, regional and local environment can be made with political will. The political economy within which the up scaling has taken place is a democracy there is a trade-off between the state acting in the interest of the people so as to maintain their own position and protecting their vested interest at the cost of the people. Monitoring and evaluation should be conducted with indicators that are able to capture the complex matrix of socio-cultural, economic and political variables that influence empowerment.

Seventh, the Andhra experience has brought to the fore the close nexus between accountability and people's participation. Involving people at every level of decision making within the program transforms 'beneficiaries' into participants and ultimately everyone benefits. Such channels of communication can be opened by the political state as has been done in Andhra Pradesh. Finally, Andhra Pradesh has shown that, to approach a complicated problem such as poverty, a complex mix of methods is required. At one level, use has to be made of existing structures and at the same time new edifices have to be created. What is important however is that these two should somewhere be able to synchronize?

Summary and Conclusions

There is absolutely no doubt that SHGs have lead to an expansion in the economic spaces of members. However the composition of the members reveals that the coverage of the poorest-of-the-poor is low, while the coverage of non-poor is considerable. The financial status of households and savings capacities has improved due to improvement in access to formal credit institutions, since SHGs are linked with banks. However, one has to understand the limitations of this use and gauge the ways in which these can be surpassed to get more out of such an approach.

- SHGs political potential is powerful. Federations form the training ground to make leaders and potential political aspirants;

- The potential of women-SHGs for women's empowerment depends upon several other supportive measures like education, health, housing and infrastructure;
- Partnerships are fundamental for development. This kind of inclusiveness where institutions work in synergy, has considerable potential for poverty alleviation.
- The linkage between the national, regional and local environment can be made with political will.
- Involving people at every level of decision making within the program transforms 'beneficiaries' into participants and ultimately everyone benefits.
- A complex mix of methods is needed to solve complicated problems such as poverty.

References

Mayoux, L. (1997), *"The Magic Ingredient? Microfinance and Women's Empowerment"*, A Briefing Paper prepared for the Micro Credit Summit, Washington.

Mayoux, L. (2001), *"Tackling the Down Side: Social Capital, Women's Empowerment and Micro-Finance in Cameroon", Development and Change,* Vol.32.

Puhazhendi V. and Satyasai K.J.S. (2000), *"Micro Credit for the Rural People: An Impact Evaluation", Study Report,* National Bank for Agriculture and Rural Development, Mumbai.

Puhazhendi, V. and Satyasai, K.J.S. (2001), *"Economic and Social Empowerment of Rural Poor through SHGs", Indian Journal of Agricultural Economics,* Vol.56. No.3.

Ramakrishna R. (2004), *"Empowering Rural Women though Self Help Groups"*, Indira Devi. M (Ed), *Strategies for Sustainability of Self Help Groups,* Visakhapatnam: A.U Press and Publications, P. 163-170.

Ramakrishna R. (2005), *"Empowerment of Women through Sustainability of Micro Finance"*, Co-operative Perspective, *Journal of Co-operative Management,* Vol. 39(4), Jan-March. Pp.1-8.

Ramakrishna R. and Tata Rao D. (2008), *"Urban Poverty Alleviation through Self-Help Groups and Micro Credit"*, Vijayalakshmi B and

Swami Das R (Ed) *SHGs and Role of Social Work Profession*, Seminar Volume, Dept. of Social Work, Andhra University, Visakhapatnam, March, 16th & 17th.

Ramakrishna R., Tata Rao D and Jayasheela Prakesh (2008), *"Empowerment of Weaker Sections and Role of SHGs", Strategies for the upliftment through Inclusive Policies, National Seminar on Social Exclusion and Inclusive Policy with special Reference to Weaker Sections of India*, Centre for Study of Social Exclusion and Inclusive Policy, Andhra University, Visakhapatnam during 28th-29th March.

Chapter-12

Micro Finance-Sustainable Development of Women : A Case Study

T. V. Ramana, P. Subba Rao

Introduction

Development of any nation depends upon the utilization of human resources including women. Demographically speaking women constitute nearly 50 percent in the total population in the country. They are able contributors to growing national income with their multilevel works. However, due to non-recognition of women, and whatever efforts have been made by the governments are meant for development of the community through men-folk only even though they are equal partners with men in the process of food production etc. in rural areas. It may be one of the reasons to slow development, poverty and unemployment in the country. Among all the communities, women of India have different characteristics compared to the rest of the world and considered as secondary, disadvantaged group in the family and the society until recent

Efforts to Uplift the Disadvantaged Women

After independence, the government of India has introduced a number of legislations and employment generation programmes to enlarge lifestyle of the women. *Micro finance* is one of the schemes providing small amount of credit to the Self Help Groups has drawn the attention in the country and recognized as anti- poverty programme.

Significance of the Present Study

In rural areas, poverty until now has continued. Consequently, earnings of the husband (head of the family) are inadequate to sustain the needs of the family like hygienic food and better education to their children. If the housewife becomes an earner, she can mould her family in a progressive manner. As such, there is an imperative need on the part of women in the family to supplement the earning of the male members by undertaking income generating self-employment activities.

It is found from studies that earnings of male, allocated only 30 percent to their family and the remaining amount, utilized for intoxicants and other harmful activities. While, the earnings of women have utilizing cent percent to the family needs. These results could motivate the policy makers, planners and administrators to recommend a separate Income Generating Activities (IGA) for the empowerment of women. Micro finance supports to exploit the local resources effectively for income generation, efficient use of labour, support to stabilize family size, improve education of children. It can be holding up perception and attitude change, social and cultural change thorough group formation by women in the rural areas.

Objectives and Technique Used in the Study

The empirical literature on the outreach of micro finance, a positive improvement was found in the life style of the respondents. Keeping this in mind the present study examines the impact of Micro Credit through SHGs on socio economic conditions like-*out side contact, role in decision making in the family, economic contribution to the family, occupational change, mobilize financial resources through savings etc of women in the study area.* Main determinants of income of women have also attempted. Lastly, suggests ways and means to progress as a part of the strategy for sustainable development of women.

The study has been conducted in Kakinada Rural Mandal, East Godavari district of Andhra Pradesh. Primary data was randomly collected from 100 members of Self Help Groups from the 10 villages who have assisted micro finance for the last 4 years. Secondary data was collected from concerned departments, various journals and newspapers. OLS *multiple regression models* were used to test the hypothesis of determining factors of monthly earnings of women. Simple *averages* and *percentages* are also used at appropriated places in the study. *Cross section analysis* method is followed in table analysis. In order to elicit the views of Self-Help Groups scheme, the researcher focused group discussion and they came out with some important suggestions for improving the programme.

A Brief Note on Evolution of Micro Finance Market in India

Micro credit is an old phenomenon and began formally with the nationalization of commercial banks in 1969 and gained strength after the introduction of Regional Rural Banks in 1975. Later IRDP taken momentum through micro finance under poverty alleviation programmes in 1980s. These programmes provided finance to individuals but not groups. This system was expended until the early 1990s but failed to reach the poorest due to many reasons like improper utilization of credit, gender inequality, improper identification of borrowers, lack of manual trust etc. Mean while group approach (SHGs) of micro finance was identified as a noble mechanism for empower the disadvantaged women.

Micro Credit- SHGs in AP

In Andhra Pradesh, all SHG women were covered under micro credit with saving of one rupee per day and the financial institutions extending loans up to 4 times to the amount of group savings (Table-1). Besides the matching grant (stopped recently), Interest Subsidiary (Pavala Vadddi- 0.25 % of interest) Scheme was started during the year 2004-05 with an objective of providing loans to SHGs under Bank Linkage Programme. Nearly Rs. 5000crores at Rs 0.25 interest rate, released under this scheme and 100230 groups were benefited in end of the 2007in the financial year.

Table 1
Development of Self Help Groups in AP

Particulars	*Unit*	*Amount*
Cumulative Savings	Rs.in crores	244.49
Cumulative Govt Assistance	Rs.in crores	648.06
Cumulative Interest Occurred	Rs.in crores	154.50
Cumulative Corpus	Rs crores	1747.05
Per Capital Group Savings	Rs	19865
Average Individual Savings	Rs	1444
Per Capital Group Credit	Rs	42500
Average Individual Credit	Rs	3036

Source: Commissioner ate for women Empowerment Hyderabad.

Micro Finance-Self Help Groups in AP

Self-Help Group is a small voluntary association of 15 to 20 members of poor people preferably from the same socio-economic background. The functions of SHGs are:- to create a common fund by the members through their regular savings, flexible working system and pool the resources in a democratic way, the Loan amount i.e., micro finance is small and reasonable so that easy to repay in time, the rate of interest is affordable. A number of social issues including gender and family, child labour, disability and health related to poverty alleviation were addressed in SHGs.

This programme has spread over the entire villages in the state. There are 4.76lakhs women SHGs in Andhra Pradesh covering nearly 65.40 lakhs poor women. A tremendous growth has been registered in the state.

Expansion of SHGs in the Study Area

Rural women in East Godavari District BPL has occupied the first with 59,000 groups in the state and benefiting the rural poor women from the scheme. Almost all (except very few) groups have taken Micro finance and successfully running the Income generating activities. As far as Kakinada Rural mandal (Study area) is concerned, there are 1428 SH groups (2.42 percent in total SHGs of the district) and approximately 2.20 lakh members are benefited. The main activities of the groups in Kakinada mandal is small business, Fish & Dry Fish business, Vegetable Business, Petty Trade Cloth Business, Milch Cattle, Milk Business and Tailoring.

Major Findings of the Study

Micro Credit-Socio Economic Conditions of Women

No doubt that micro financing through SHGs has became a powerful instrument to improving socio and economic conditions of women. The details regarding reasons for joining in SHG shows these particulars. Many of the members joined the SHGs for getting financial assistance (23.42 percent), promote personal savings (23.42 percent) social status (21.58 percent) and (14.74 percent of respondents) for job from various productive and income generating activities. They also targeted the social, cultural and political improvement (16.84 percent as others) through SHGs in the study area.

Change in Social Conditions

An age group of 25-30 and 45- 50 are active participants in the scheme. The scheme has benefited very much to the widowed and separated women. Nearly 46.16 percent of respondents who belong to Scheduled Castes are illiterates. It may adversely effects on income generation through IGAs.

As the opined of the SHG members, due to the social activities of the SHG, they are aware of family planning and need/benefit of small family. Further, institutional deliveries also increased among the group members. Meanwhile, among the social groups, SCs have highest average size of family recorded with 5.4 members followed by 4.3 and 4.1 in case of BCs and OCs respectively. The average size of family of all respondents is 4.6 in the study area

Participation in social activities of Mahila Mandal , out side contact for business, decision making in the family are also some major factors to determine the social empowerment of the women. SHG activities have pushing them to participate voluntarily or by force in social activities. Interestingly, 62.50 percent of respondents were taken membership while they joined in the scheme.

Out Side Contact

As far as out side contact is concerned, about 53 percent of the respondents visit villages monthly and half-yearly to town. Across the Castes, 55.56 percent of SCs visit town weekly but it is 22.22 percent each in BC and OCs respectively to the purpose of business activities and social interaction. Low level of out side contacts is found in upper castes (OCs) as they said-traditions, lack of interest to their family heads and insecurity feelings.

Decision-Making

As far as decision making in the family is concerned, only 10.25 percent of them reported that they used to take partake in major decisions. Moreover, 23.08 percent of the respondents pointed out that their In-laws used to take major decisions. Meanwhile, after joining SHG, 62.82 percent of the women reported that they also engross in decision-making process along with their husbands and now thrash out and sound out before taking any decisions. The *chi square test* value shows a positive association between SHG efforts and decision-making of the respondents.

Modification in House Equipment

About 34 percent of the respondents posses Pucca houses built under government scheme registered for the women, 25 percent tiled, 17 percent semi-pucca, 16 percent were Tached/ temporary houses. Nevertheless, nearly 50 percent of the tached houses are possessed by SCs alone. They possessed various items of house equipment like Watch, Stove, Rice Cooker, Electric Iron, knitting machine, TV set, Light- furniture and other house related equipments (house decoration etc) prepared after joining SHGs.

Awareness from out side contact, visit of offices for meetings etc, demonstration effect, and earnings from Group activities caused improvement in the equipment after joining SHGs. 'Deepam' a special programme for SHG members introduced by government of Andhra Pradesh and sanctioned Gas connections to some of the members. However, 30 percent of respondents (majority of them are relating to SCs) not utilized properly and some were handover to neighbors due to hike in price of LP Gas.

Occupational Change of the Respondents

There is a significant occupational mobility among the respondents mainly from agriculture to business activities like Petty Trade (PT) kirana shop etc., Milk Business (MB), Milch Cattle (MC), Small Business (SB) like vegetable vending, and Dry Fish (DF) (Table-2). The participation of respondents in agriculture reduced from 71.79 percent to 30.77 percent after they joined SHGs. Incase of Petty Trade (PT) positively increased from 3.85 percent to 17.95 percent, milk business/ Milch cattle increased from 5.13 percent to 15.33 percent. The respondents who are in Small Business, their percent increased from 7.65 percent to 17.55 percent, also raised from 8.97 percent to 17.97 percent respectively in Dry Fish business. This trend changed earnings of the respondents.

Growth in Working Days

Number of Working days increased after participation with help of financial support to the SHGs. The percentage growth in employment increased by 50 percent each in case of SCs and BCs and 58.33 percent in case of OCs respectively. Overall percentage growth in employment is recorded at 52.78 percent.

Income Earnings and Contribution to the Family

The contribution of women to the family is another impact of micro finance through SHGS (table-3). Before joining SHG, the incomes of majority of respondent's (32 percent) were under the income group of RS.600-1000. However, this was reduced to 18 percent after joining SHG due to increased their incomes. The percentage of respondents under Rs 1000-2500 increased to 42 percent from 15 percent. The income of 12 percent of respondents is increased and recorded in the income group of Rs. 3000-3500. By and large, nearly 59 percent of the respondents have increased their incomes after joining SHGs. The newly joined (32 percent) respondents have also getting earning at

Table 2
Pattern of Occupational Shift of the Respondents After Joining SHGs

Before / After	AL		PT		MB/MC		SB		DF		Total	
	No.	%	No.	%	No.	%	No.	%	No.	%	No.	%
AL	24	30.77	11	14.10	8	10.25	6	7.69	7	8.97	56	71.79
PT			3	3.85			2	2.56			5	6.41
MB/MC					4	5.13					4	5.13
SB							6	7.69			6	7.69
DF									7	8.97	7	8.97
Total	24	30.77	14	17.95	12	15.38	14	17.95	14	17.95	78	100.0

Source: compiled from field data

reasonable manner through IGA of the SHG. As results, *nearly 1/3 of amount has been contributed to the total incomes of the families. Now,* women are more honors/ respected, and engaged in house hold chores.

Regularity in Re-payment of Loans

The SHGs obtain loan from credit institutions at 1-2 percent of interest rate. The attained loans ranged from Rs1000 to Rs 15000. Demands for money/loan extremely take place in purchase materials and inputs, increase in consumption of the family. Micro finance has also given grant a stay of execution from moneylenders.

Table 3
Women Contribution to the Total Income of the Households

Category	*Average Income of Family Members*	*Earnings & Contribution*		*Total Income of Family*
		Amount	*Percentage to Total*	
Scheduled Caste	3600(24.11)	2100(29.77)	36.84	5700(25.93)
Back Ward Caste	5130(34.36)	2300(32.60)	30.96	7430(33.80)
Other Castes	6200(41.53)	2655(37.63)	29.98	8855(40.27)
Total	14930(100.0)	7055(100.0)	32.09	21985(100.0)

Source: compiled from field data

About 56 percent of the respondents repaid installments in time and 10 repaid in advance. Meanwhile, about 34 percent of non-participants in IGA are unable to repay the loan in time due to their economic problems, ill health of breadwinners, and lack of work facilities in some seasons.

Regular Practice of Saving

Micro finance facilitates small savings from rural women who were hither to considered incapable of having any capacity to save. Interestingly, About 50 percent of the respondents were not in saving practice before joining. Cent percentage of respondents entered into the saving practice after they joined in SHGs.

Reduced Income- Expenditure Gap

Expenditure on food items of the households significantly increased after joining SHGs. The percentage change in expenditure after joining of SC, BC and OCs is recorded as 58.96 percent, 36.57 percent and 27.03 percent respectively. The percentage increase in non-food items expenditure of SCs and BCs is higher than the OCs recorded as 48.18 percent, 40.66 percent and 56.94 percent respectively. Expenditure on intoxicants increased very much as registered by 50 percent, 50 percent and 44.44 percent in 3 categories. Meanwhile, incomes of the families have increased significantly due to the contribution of the respondents and the gap between income and expenditure has been gradually declined (Table-4).

Table 4

Micro Finance-Reduced in Income- Expenditure Gap

(in Rs)

Category	*Before joiningSHG*			*After joiningSHG*		
	Income (I)	*Expenditure (E)*	*I-E*	*Income (I)*	*Expenditure (E)*	*I-E*
Scheduled Caste	3600	3970	-370	5700	5950	-250
Back Ward Caste	5060	5130	-70	7430	7180	+250
Other Castes	5060	5580	-520	8855	8700	+155
Total	13720	14680	-960	21985	21830	+155

Source: compiled from table3.

Determinants of Monthly Income of the Respondents

In Indian traditional society, women are under control of male in all stages of her life. Therefore, monthly earnings of women can be determined not only the credit facilities but also many factors. A careful study was conducted with the following parameters tested with the OLS multiple regression model.i.e.

$$MEOR = b_0 + b_1\ NOPR + b_2\ AGER + b\text{-}_3\ EDRY + b_4\ EXPR + b\text{--}_5 + SKIL + b_6\ TIRF + b_7\ YNGA + b_8\ CRDT + b_9\ MRKT + U$$

Where- MEOR (monthly income of respondents) is considered as dependent variable. Remaining are independent variables viz, NOPR (Nature of occupation of the respondent), AGER (Age of the respondent) EDRY (Education of the respondents in years) EXPR (Experience of the respondents) SKIL (skill dummy, taking value 1 for skilled and 0 otherwise). TIRF indicates average total income of the family, YNGA shows age of the youngest of child, CRDT- credit amount sanctioned, and MRKY as marketing dummy, taking values 1 for direct sales to consumers and 0 otherwise, U= Error term.

Measured Independent Variables

The mean age of the respondents was around 33 years and education by secondary level. The average family income owned by them was Rs.4545 and the mean monthly income of the respondents amounted Rs. 2340. The mean work experience of the sample respondents was reported to be less than four years under the scheme. For simplify the study, it is proposed that 51 percent of the respondents shifted their previous work. About 49 percent of the respondents sold their products directly to the customers. The average age of the youngest child is seven, which represents in family constraints for women. Lastly, the average SHG credit sanctioned was Rs.12000 according to the study.

Hypothetical Explanation on Selected Factors

Monthly income of the respondents is expected a negative correlation with the husband's/family income. Larger the family income, less participation of women resulted less income. It is expected that the incomes from other than SHG activity sources is lower than SHG activities. At the same time, Age (work force) of the respondents have positive correlation with earnings of them. Similarly, age of the youngest child may act negatively on monthly income of the respondents. They should take care of them at that stage. Education and experience helps to take decisions technically than illiterates. So, positive correlation is assumed between monthly earnings and the factors. Further, better marketing to the products and credit facilities may have positive correlation on income earnings of the respondents.

Regression Results

The results of regression analysis are shown in Table 5. A shift in occupation by the respondents reveals at 1 percent level of significance. Age of the respondents and skill are observed to positive signs and experiences of them have a negative coefficient. Interestingly, increase in family income is adversely affecting the incomes of women as expected coefficient. Similarly, local marketing of products emerged statistically insignificant. Hence, there should a need of advertisement to their production.

Table 5
Summary of Regression Results- Earnings Function

Variables	*Coefficient*	*t value*
NOPR	-264.12	-2.69*
AGER	1.01	0.14
EDRY	21.29	1.67
EXPR	-21.03	-1.36
TIRF	0.24	5..64*
YNGA	2.19	-0.49
CRDT	-0.007	2.94*
MRKY	-52.37	-0.47
Constant	284.12	0.63
R^2	0.38	
R-2	0.31	
F- Value	4.73*	

Note: * indicate significance at 1 percent level

Problems

However, problems also followed the respondents as two sides of the one coin. Taking more time to get loans from the bank, low profits to their sale of products, low profits due to high price inputs are major problems identified in the study. Competition from nearest wholesale shops has adversely affecting the sales of the respondents.

Non-cooperation of group members in willing to sanction of huge amount of loan to purchase milch animals and dry fish are effecting adversely on loan seekers. Long distance of market caused high transport cost and reduces profits from their sales of milk, vegetable, dry fish etc.

The collecting savings and loan is very meager amount. This may not up scale their activities. Difference in loan purpose also collapsed the goal of income generation of some groups. Hence, the micro credit on the income, employment and levels of living of their member is marginal. Many of them are not able to cross the poverty line. It requires an additional; injection of investment.

Conclusions

The study concentrated on the impact of microfinance on SHGs in the study area. It is identified from the study that a radical improvement was identified in all fields of women. They got strong decision-making power along with their husbands in the family. Cent percent of the respondents were making saving regularly. They have had a power of credit winner than rural male. Increased working days, earnings, and it lead to reduce in income-expenditure gap from minus level to surplus. Institutional deliveries have also increased and educational facilities extended to their children. They obtained self-confidence and made face-to-face discussion with officials, which was recognized as a landmark in history of women. Voluntary participation in community activities like construct roads, planting trees conserving environment, campaign against eradication of social evils like dowry, child marriages , support to widows and destitute are few to mention empowering issues. The micro finance is taken changes in the life stile of the women and supported to increase the earnings, savings, and contribution to the family. At the same time many factors influence the earnings of the women. The multiple regression results shows clearly in the study.

Policy Suggestions

1. The study identified that the activities undertaken themselves by respondents with their knowledge. No modern methods in their activities, ultimately they face losses. They should conduct awareness camps to choose remunerative activity. It can reduce waste of monetary resources. Major portion of micro finance should be given

only according to profit motive other wise the funds are likely to be lost.

2. Many of SHG members are using the credit for consumption purpose only. This may not be provided additional returns from credit. Hence, possible efforts must be prepared by the concerned authorities to take up income generating activities at least with half of sanctioned credit.
3. Formation of SHGs by SCs and minorities are limited in the study area. Therefore, the concerned authorities should take care to achieve goal that equal distribution of credit facilities.
4. At present, the group members have to save for a minimum period of six months to get loan. This provision may discourage the IGAs; hence, it should reduce the period at least for three months.
5. Strict supervision is needed by the concerned bank officials for proper utilization of finance on productive purpose; it can avoid diversion of funds for other useless purposes.
6. Unless training of technical skills imparted to the women by SHGs they will not get meaningful self-employment in their villages. Technical skills are required in addition to finance e.g. training to make milk products and store facilities etc.
7. The banks should provide sufficient time to repayment of loan and they must be supervising the economic activities. Because better monitoring of SHGs will yield better results.
8. Micro credit cannot push the rural into debt traps. It should come in the form of a participatory model and not as a profit model. It should be bottom up and not top down. The effectiveness of SHGs would be considerably enhanced if a symbiosis could be worked out between them and panchayat Raj Institutions. The given policy implications may help to further improvement through micro credit of the women

Chapter-13

Empowerment and Women Entrepreneurship in Visakhapatnam District

B. Ratna Kumari, M. Anitha

Introduction

In India, entrepreneurship has been dominated by male governed economy, where the role of women as entrepreneurs has been negligible. However in the recent past women entrepreneurs has been playing an increasingly important role in promoting growth and economic development of country's economy (Syal P., Dhameja S.K. 2003).

Women's entrepreneurship is also gaining increasing importance in public policy circulars. National governments and international organizations are coming to realize that promoting women economic development through women entrepreneurs plays a critical role in economic growth, particularly at the grass roots level. First and foremost, it enhances the tempo of the economic growth, provides greater prosperity to the small scale entrepreneurs and their workers. Moreover, it directly provides employment and economic independence to women and improves their social educational and health status. Vast majority of the population of India still lives in rural areas and depend for their economic sustenance on agricultural and allied economic activities. Although much has been written about aspects of women's empowerment and entrepreneurship in India, not very much has been done when it comes to quantifying the extent of women's business ownership and their contribution to economic growth. Relationship of economic activity among women to a country's economic growth shows that there is a distinct and strong correlation between women's entrepreneurship (Ray D.,) 2003.

Due to the growth of industrialization, urbanization, education and democratic system in the country, the traditional bound Indian society is now undergoing a change and women are now seeking gainful employment in several fields in increasing numbers. Still it can't be said that the women entrepreneurship movement has taken off the ground and it is felt that the movement is still in transition period.

Women entrepreneurs may be defined as the women or a group of women who initiate, organize and operate a business enterprise. However such innovator are rarely sound in the underdeveloped countries, the enterprises for these people may be small and unimpressive when judged by standards of the developed countries. But the high propensity to imitate can set in motion the chain reaction which leads to cumulative progress. Thus in the Indian context, entrepreneur is an adopter and imitator than a true.

Innovator

Word 'entrepreneurship' broadly stands for self-employment. It mainly involves identification of opportunities with in the economic system. It involves assumptions of risks and responsibility in designing and executing a business strategy of starting a new business venture. Entrepreneurs are skilled organizers of various activities such as identifying the needs for various products (or) services, originating or generating ideas on how to provide the desire products or services, evolution of planned out ideas and present a business enterprise opportunity, and finally, a plan of action to translate idea into a commercially viable proposition. Entrepreneurship has been attracting more and more attention of policy makers, academicians and business practitioners since early nineties. The main reason behind this is that the creation of new enterprises has a great potential to contribute to a balanced and accelerated economic growth and creation of employment opportunities.

Need for the Study

Under informal sector in which unorganized activities, particularly in the urban areas of the developing economy, has gained importance in research policy on women entrepreneurs and urbanization. The limited scope for growth of entrepreneur's potential opportunities of the informal sector has been recognized in many developing countries.(Istanbul, Turkey, 3-5 June, 2004). There are numerous women who are found in entrepreneurial field but in micro enterprises which are not visible. Since they are not visible, their contributions also not accounted. Without their contributions, many household would have remained in poverty and hunger. Instead of taking wage employment, many women confined to self-employment, investing on a minimum amount possible, expecting of realizing short term returns.

With this back drop, it is realized that a study of such women who run micro enterprises felt necessary and the present study has been conducted. Since such micro enterprises are run by women in urban areas, it was decided to undertake the natural outcome of the industrial growth, emerge as a response to large scale industrial enterprises, industrialization and urbanization. However, a considerable population in urban areas may engage in activities to the demands of the urban and rural population. Necessary, in the event of declining agricultural operations, failure of agriculture etc, people tend to choose to other occupation. As a response of the above factors, urban micro entrepreneurial activities emerge run both by men and women. Hence cities like Visakhapatnam, suits to the above questions to be answered have been, chosen as the study area for the present study.

Women have been in focus of the policy makers and development planners, since the seventh five year plan, entrepreneurship development programmers [EDP] have also been organized for women. In fact in the rural areas, the Industries Centre [DIC] has been the nodal agency in conducting EDP to promote first generation entrepreneurs on the one hand and to generate self employment opportunities among the unemployed youth. Women have also been included as partners and special women EDPs had also been conducted in 1990s.

Research Questions

It was realized that there is a need to conduct a study on women entrepreneurs, how the EDP trained differ from the non-EDP trained entrepreneurs, what are the nature of activities undertaken, how they differ from owned enterprises, is there a common pattern chosen among the women owned enterprises, whether all EDP trained women were able to start the enterprises, if they failed to start, what factors prevented them to start the enterprises, how does the trained entrepreneurs perform in comparison with non-EDP trained entrepreneurs, whether EDP training with extension of financial support contributed positively for the emergence of women entrepreneurship, whether they perform better than the women who have not had such training, the obstacles faced by the two groups etc were raised as research questions. In order to analyses these questions, the present study has chosen to conduct a research among the women entrepreneurs in Visakhapatnam District of Andhra Pradesh.

Empowerment

Empowerment is the process— —and the result of the process— where by the powerless or less powerful numbers of the society gain greater access and control over material and knowledge resources, challenge the ideologies of discrimination and subordination, and transform the institutions and structures through which unequal access and control over resources is sustained and perpetuated (Annonuvo, 1997).

Women's empowerment has been viewed by several people at several points of time in several ways, which have been described and categorized as traditional, conservative and radical views. But the alternate view for all these puts emphasis on women collectively coming together to recognize and address the gender issues which stand in the way of their advancement. Empowerment in this context involves the transformation through a process of enlightenment, concretization and collective organization and therefore necessitates collective action by women to discard the patriarchal beliefs and attitudes they have learned in their system (Longwe, 1997).

Entrepreneurship

Rural India offers plenty for self-employed as the data reveals the fact that only 6.2 per cent in rural areas are regular salaried, 56 percent self-employed as compared to 40.1 and 42.1 percent respectively in urban areas.

It is very well known that women constitute the biggest source of potential workers in rural areas. About 86 percent of the rural women are working in agriculture; 36 percent have their own land and another 36 percent work as agricultural laborers; about 14 percent are engaged in other jobs (Renu, 2001). They are paid less wages, involved in drudgery work both in farms as well as at home.

While reviewing and analyzing the rural entrepreneurship, Hansra et al. (2002) chose the definition of an entrepreneur as a person who either creates new combinations of production factors such as new methods of production, new products, new markets, find new source of supply and new organizational forms; or as a person who is willing to take risks; or a person who by exploiting market opportunities eliminates disequilibria between aggregate supply and aggregate demand; or as one who own and operates business. Entrepreneurship is defined as a force that mobilizes other resources to meet unmet market demand, the ability to create and build something from practically nothing, the process of creating value by pulling together and package of resources or exploit an opportunity.

The essence of entrepreneurship rests in creating something new. Entrepreneurship need not involve anything new from a global or even national perspective, but rather than the adoption of new technologies and new enterprises producing goods not previously available at a location. Entrepreneurship is not about setting rich quick, nor is it science that any 'born entrepreneurs' can achieve. And it is not confined to "for profit" ventures (Handle and Rushworth, 2002).

Women Enterprises

Government of India defines women enterprise as an enterprise owned and controlled by women having a minimum financial investmen of 51 per cent of the capital giving at least 51 per cent of the employment to women. This definition has been criticized for underlining to give 50 per cent of employment to women. As a result a new definition has been evolved later in 1992. Women enterprise is defined as those enterprises owned and controlled by women but men also supporting with in the business. Enterprises set up by women should be provided with incentives and support on the basis of their ownership and management characteristic and not linked with employment of women.

Micro Enterprise

Micro enterprise is defined in this study as an enterprise with an investment ranging from below Rs. 10000 to above 1 lakh. The 'micro entrepreneurs' are those who run and control the enterprise by women.

Statement of the Problem

Many enterprises (industries) are managed and run by women entrepreneurs since several year. District Industries Centre (DIC) has given assistance and guidance for women entrepreneurs to run their enterprise unit. As a part of women empowerment process, many women entrepreneurs started their entrepreneurial activity, but so for evolution has been made on this particular activity of women. With this intention, present evolution study on women entrepreneurs of Visakhapatnam district was taken up by Dr. Durgabai Deshmukh Centre for Women's Studies.

District Industries Center (DIC)

A District industries centre is an institution at the district level, which provides all the services and facilities to entrepreneurs at one place so that they may set up small and village industries. These services and facilities include the identification of a suitable scheme, the preparation of a feasibility report, arrangements for the supply of machinery and equipments, provision for raw materials, credit facilities and input for marketing and extension services, quality control, research and entrepreneurial training. The DIC would also ensure that small industries continue to be viable units. For this purpose, it provides all the facilities to the entrepreneur under one roof at district level.

Research Design

The study is primarily descriptive in nature. The research was tried to present a scientific description of a variety of facts pertaining to women entrepreneurs, their socio-economic background, the nature of entrepreneurship, the nature of their enterprise, and their entrepreneurial activity including the influence of their work on their families.

Objectives of the Study

To evaluate the emerging trend of women entrepreneurs in Visakhapatnam district, the present study has the following objectives.

- To study the socio-economic and demographic background of women entrepreneur in Visakhapatnam district.
- To study several aspects of the nature of the entrepreneurial activity taken up by the women.
- To explore into phenomenon of entrepreneurship among women (its nature, origin and stages of entrepreneur's entry into entrepreneurial activity, Motivating factors, pre-or post-marital phase of entry and its correlates, Extent of self confidence among the entrepreneurs and its correlates, and facilitating factors)

- To examine the positive and negative consequences of the entrepreneurial activityon the women entrepreneurs and their families.
- To examine the opinion of women entrepreneurs pertaining to their entrepreneurial work and about the qualities required for success in entrepreneurial activity.
- To let the women entrepreneur set or rest the objectives of this business and work individually and long with this growth for the realization of them
- To enable the women entrepreneurs to take strategic decisions
- To prepare a women entrepreneur for accepting totally unforeseen risks of business for a long time often training.

Methodology

Universe and Sample

The sample for the present study has been drawn from Visakhapatnam district. The district of Visakhapatnam consists of 43 mandals. The city of Visakha Municipal Corporation (which has attained the status of Greater Municipal Corporation) has 72 wards. As per the records of district industries center (DIC) there are only 50 women entrepreneurs spread over in 3 mandals of the district and 18 wards of the greater Visakha Municipal Corporation jurisdiction (limits). This women entrepreneurs who registered in DIC office as per DIC records became sample for the present study on purposive basis.

Tools

For the present evolution study on women entrepreneurs for primary data collection, a well structured schedule has been prepared and administered to women entrepreneurs in the study area by the researcher during the month of Oct 06—Jan 07 which was followed by pilot study. The secondary data has been collected from Census reports and DIC office.

Method

An interview method has been adopted to collect primary data from the women entrepreneurs, in the study area. Most of the interviews conducted individually. In some cases (about 5 percent of the cases) the interview of the women entrepreneurs was conducted in the presence of their husbands/parents/relatives/family members as per the request of the respondents. In about 15 percent of the cases, after the first meeting, the women entrepreneurs preferred to go over the interview schedule, and keep it over night with them. In some cases it was partially used as a questionnaire. Nevertheless, subseqntly, these entrepreneurs were also interviewed, and where necessary, the interviewer sought clarifications regarding the responses given. In a majority of the cases the researcher contacted each entrepreneur twice and on an average, the total time required to complete one interview was about one hundred and twenty minutes (two hours).

A majority strength of the interview schedule was that even the closed ended questions, in most cases, permitted a wide spectrum of responses, and further a variety of measurement techniques was used to elicit authentic responses and to measure certain attributes, aspects of the family situation vis-a- vis a typical general family having similar socio-economic background and having no working women.

Statistical Tools and Measures

The following statistical tools were used, as and when necessary, for the analysis of the data;

- Percentages
- measures of central tendency (mean, mode and median)
- measures of dispersion (standard deviation, index of qualitative variation)
- Analytical techniques varied across the one way ANOVA analysis, Mean, Standard deviation, Cross tabs. Universe F tests were used to further examine the data,

The Scaling of female entrepreneurs reasons for leaving were analyzed in several ways. The Eight reasons most frequently ranked as the first or second most influential reason for leaving to initiate a business were tabulated.

Summary Findings

Major findings of the study are:

- The mean age of the entrepreneurs is 42.42years and (74 percent) three fourths of (3/4) of them is in the age group of 36-50 years.
- Majority (96%percent) of the entrepreneurs are Hindus, while the proportion of Christians (4percent).
- A large proportion (100 percent) of the entrepreneurs has an urban background.
- the three fourths (3/4) of the entrepreneurs has professional or vocational qualifications (80 percent) of the respondents, either recognized or unrecognized by government. A majority if the entrepreneurs had a fairly high level of participation in curricular activities at the junior or senior college level.
- The mean 1.56 monthly family income (excluding the entrepreneur's income) of the married entrepreneurs (14 percent) of respondents the entrepreneur have a monthly income between Rs 30,000. Over (22percent) of the married entrepreneurs had got married in to family whose economic position was not very different from the position of their family.
- In large majority of the cases the enterprises are almost evenly functional throughout year.
- Have made the financial investment vis-à-vis the other partners in most cases, are making the largest time-energy investment for the business activity.
- In a vast majority of the enterprises covered by the study no diversification (in products or services) has been reported, since their inception. Where some sort of diversification has taken place it has been a strategy for survival.

- A large majority (86 percent) of the entrepreneurs who have employed one or more persons in or for their enterprises has shown a clear preference for female employees.
- About one fourth of the respondents have participated in EDP's for entry in to entrepreneurial activity. In all about (44 percent) of the entrepreneurs have sought the assistance of specialized agencies, external to their families for equipping themselves for entry in to entrepreneurial activity.
- A majority of the entrepreneurs (100 percent) had never tried to enter in to any job. Almost all the entrepreneurs who had tried to enter in to a job prior to their entry into entrepreneurial activity had managed to get a job. All such entrepreneurs have said that their work experience was extremely useful to them in the overall management of their entrepreneurial activity.
- Family income, educational qualifications as presence of working are not related to the phase of entry in to entrepreneurial activity.
- Psychological motives (4percent) of the cases and economic motives in (92 percent) of the cases and other motives in (4percent) of the respondents were the most important motives for entering in to entrepreneurial activity.
- Psychological motives were more dominant among entrepreneurs having higher educational qualifications, higher family income and background of business in their family.
- It is found that by and large, the women entrepreneurs report to be having a fairly high level of self confidence, prior to establish and run their enterprises. The level of such self confidence has been found to be strongly associated with the possession of professional/ vocational qualifications and with having a business background in the family.

Suggestions

- Providing support to the family, using one's own potentials and having an independent income (and a feeling of self-reliance) were perceived to be the important achievements by most of the women entrepreneurs. Further, a vast majority of the women entrepreneurs was satisfied with its achievements.
- Psychological achievements i..e -self actualization (use of one's own abilities, knowledge, skills and experience, and meaningful use of time) were rated as a higher achievement as compared to their economic achievement, by a majority of the women entrepreneurs.
- So they must be provided with market availability for this materials.
- So such type of overtaking must be controlled.
- This is to suggest that government must conduct work shops, seminars, etc.., to increase these management skills.
- They must have the availability of latest techniques.
- All the women entrepreneurs must have some network between them.
- They may form into a group so that they could discus their problems, their forthcoming programmes activities to take suggestions etc..,.
- The government has to check to regularly whether the loan that has been given to women entrepreneurs is properly by the women.

Chapter-14

Developing Women Entrepreneurship in India

D. Francis, R. Vijaya Krishna, D. Suseela

Introduction

Women community though almost equal to men in population, it is a subject of concern to note that, in this modern sophisticated world, she is treated as the second rated citizen or subordinate to men. Though various efforts are being made to improve the status of women, women folk could not take their maximum use and remained still backward. In almost all countries, the Governments are providing special provisions for women's development and efforts are being made to extract maximum use of women's talent.

In India, during Veda, Upanishad periods, women were given much respect and they enjoyed equal right with men in all fields. Slowly women's position deteriorated and now we can see that she is being exploited and harassed in all respects.

Though during British era steps were taken to improve the status of women in India it was only after the independence, she enjoyed privileged rights. As per constitution, she is given equal status with man and several special provisions are made for her upliftment. Yet it is sad to note that women could not utilize the legal advantages properly. Only a small percentage of women have taken maximum advantage of the legislations and facilities available to them and have shined in various fields. Now, we can see the ladies working not only in the Primary and Secondary sectors, but also being successful in the Military and Defence field as well. There are women Doctors, Lawyers, Scientists and Teachers and have shown that they are not less efficient to men, but are equally efficient, intelligent and hard working. In the field of business and commerce, women are lagging behind as compared to other fields. However, there are certain exceptions that a few ladies have shined in the industrial and commerce sectors also, and earned name and fame outside the country too. Due to increased cost of living, it becomes necessary for women also to undertake economic activity and support their families. Now the attitude of the society has also changed and working women is not seen with suspicious eyes as in the past. She is more liberated now and the modern woman leads a very happy and peaceful family life with her husband and family.

Again the modern woman has realized her values. She wants to make use of her intelligence, knowledge and education. She wants to make her children more efficient than earlier through her prestigious role. Even the time has changed so much that, the lady having a job or profession will get easily married. She can enjoy all the comforts and luxuries of life being economically independent. Throughout the world, women's participation in economic activities is increasing. The role of women entrepreneurship is also increasing. In India too, women are participating in large number in almost all the spheres of economic activity. From village to city, we can see large number of women workers and entrepreneurs contributing towards the national income of the country.

During the early decades of planning, women's role in economic activity was not given much importance and only the Draft of Sixth Five-Year plan (1980-85) had stressed for special emphasis on the issues of women entrepreneurship and the steps were undertaken in that direction. The Eighth Five-Year Plan (1992-97) promised to ensure that benefits of development from different sectors do not bypass women. The

Rashtriiya Mahila Kosh was set up in 1993 to meet the credit needs of poor and asset less women. The Ninth Five-Year Plan (1997-2002) made two significant changes in the strategy of planning for women. Firstly, "empowerment of women" became a primary objective and secondly the plan attempted "convergence of existing services" available in both women-specific and women related sectors. The Tenth Five-Year Plan (2002-2007) has made a major commitment towards "empowering women as the agent of socio-economic change and development". Based on the recommendation of National Policy for Empowerment of Women, the Tenth Five-Year Plan suggests a three-fold strategy for empowering women, through social empowerment, economic empowerment and gender justice.

The Concept of Entrepreneurship

Websters' Dictionary defines the term 'entrepreneur' as 'one who undertakes an enterprise' and becomes employer. An 'enterprise' has been defined as a bold or dangerous undertaking or an adventure. Various experts on entrepreneurship have defined the terms 'entrepreneur' and 'entrepreneurship' in different words. But most acceptable definition of the term 'entrepreneur' may be a "person or group of persons who assume(s) risk and undertake(s) an economic activity and provides goods, services and employment to society". Similarly, the term 'entrepreneurship' may be defined as risk-bearing and innovativeness capacity, capability and activity of a person or group of persons leading to starting and managing self-employment oriented economic activity.

Characteristics of Entrepreneur

To be a successful entrepreneur, a person has to acquire and develop certain qualities, which can be included by training and motivation. The essential entrepreneurial traits/qualities are:

1. High achievement motivation
2. Insatiable drive and persistent enthusiasm
3. Readiness for challenge

4. Persistent problem solving
5. Goal setting
6. Dealing with failure
7. Technical background
8. Experience in the line
9. Willingness to introduce something new (Sprit of innovation)
10. Taking initiative and seeking personal responsibility
11. Competing against self imposed standards
12. Tolerance to ambiguity and uncertainty
13. Hard working
14. Regularity and dedication to work
15. Self control
16. Self confidence
17. Confidence in self capability
18. Use of feed back
19. Willingness to take advice
20. Time management
21. Money as a measure
22. Drive and energy
23. Long term involvement
24. Total commitment and immersion

Women Entrepreneurship: Indian Scenario

Traditionally it was believed that women are physically and mentally weak and, hence, they are not fit for hard, and hazardous and risky tasks. But with the increasing empowerment of women in the world, now no job, profession or enterprise is such which women cannot undertake. Contrary to it, it can be observed that in oriental societies the women are born-risk seekers. They grow up with the feeling of management of risk and adjustment/adaptation with the changing environment.

Women entrepreneurship is the process where women take lead and organise a business or industry and provide employment opportunities to others. Though women entrepreneurship is a recent phenomenon in India, which came into prominence in late 1970's, now we see that more and more women are venturing as entrepreneurs in all kinds of business and economic activities and service sector. Though at the initial stage women entrepreneurship developed only at urban areas, lately it has extended its wings to rural and semi-urban areas too.

Women industries mainly fall into informal sector where less than 10 persons with or without power and less than than 20 persons without power are engaged and they will be of labour intensive and rely on indigeneous resources, family ownership and only small scale skills are sufficient. Though earlier women concentrated much on traditional activities, due to the spread of education, favourable government policies towards development of women entrepreneurship, women have changed their attitudes and diverted towards non-traditional activities too. They show favourable response to changing situations and get adjusted to them and have improved their position.

The Government and Non-Government organizations are giving more prominence to promote self-employment among women and build women entrepreneurship. Special financial assistance is provided and training programmes are organized for women to start their ventures.

Women Entrepreneurs

There has been a rapid growth of women entrepreneurs all over the world. In the fields of fashion, beauty and career counseling, many fashion designers are women with their own labels. To name a few: Ritu Kumar, known as the queen of Indian textiles, Ritu Beri, who has had a stint in the French fashion industry and Rina Dhaka among others. The Indian fashion industry is now conscious of the opportunities available in this industry abroad and the need to be globally competitive. The world of beauty culture has opened up many opportunities for women entrepreneurs. Women are setting up successfully small establishments as beauticians and hair stylists. Apart from clothes, women are successful in producing design accessories as well. Indian women have established brands in the world. Virita Jain of Biotique and Shahnaz Husain of Shahnaz Herbals are global brands today. It is time to collate data on small and big business run by women. In the field of education, counsellors are mostly women, primarily because men did not see it as a lucrative sector. As disposable incomes increase with the opening up of the economy; women are taking to opening up restaurants as well.

Work Force Participation Rate (WFPR) in India

The Work Force Participation Rate (WFPR), also called Labour Force Participation Rate (LFPR) is the percentage of working population to total population of a country. It is an important factor which affects production, saving and capital formation. It helps in analysing the occupational structure of a country and thus its level of employment. WFPR depends up on the age and sex structure of the population, age of marriage, average size of family, education, health, attitude to work, availability of work, etc. The work force participation rates in India for the Census years 1901 to 2001 are shown in Table-1. WFPR in the pre-independence period from 1901-31 was higher than in the post-independence period from 1951-91, except for the Census year 1961. The reason being the use of different definition of the 'work force' in the censuses. In the pre-independence census, main workers were lumped with unpaid family workers. But in the 1951 Census, unpaid family workers were excluded from the main workers. That is why the WFPR in 1951 was 39.1 per cent as compared to more than 43 per cent in the pre-independence years (1901-1931). Again in 1961, WFPR increased to 43 per cent because persons whose main activity was not economic were included in the main workers. WFPR declined to 34.2 per cent in 1971 because persons engaged in part time activities were excluded from the category of the main workers. But since the Census of 1981, WFPR had risen to 36.7 per cent in1981 to 37.7 per cent in 1991 and to 39.3

per cent in 2001. This has been due to the adoption of a rigorous of "worker" in terms of main workers and marginal workers.

Table 1
Gender-Wise Work Force Participation Rate in India: 1901-2001

(in Percentage)

Year	*Females*	*Males*	*Persons*
1901	31.1	61.1	46.6
1911	33.7	61.9	48.1
1921	32.7	60.5	46.9
1931	27.6	58.3	43.3
1951	23.3	54.0	39.1
1961	28.0	57.1	43.0
1971	14.2	52.7	34.2
1981	19.7	52.6	36.7
1991	22.7	51.6	37.7
2001	25.7	51.9	39.3

Source: Census Reports for various years.

In the case of WFPR by sex, it had been much higher for males as compared to females. This is because of the social status of women. They are generally not allowed to undertake productive work outside home. But since 1971, their work participation rate has been on the increase. It rose from 14.2 per cent in 1971 to 25.7 per cent in 2001. This is due to increasing literacy and declining birth rate. Now more and more women are entering the industrial and service sectors. With urbanisation and expansion of dairy and poultry farming, fisheries, horticulture, etc., more women are participating in such activities. On the other hand, the work participation rate for men declined from 52.7 per cent in 1971 to 51.9 per cent in 2001. This again shows that more women are taking the place of men in productive activities.

Gender-Wise Rural, Urban and Total Work Participation Rates in India

The gender wise rural, urban and total work participation rates in India during 1971-2001 are shown in Table-2. It indicates that women have a lower participation rate than men. However, since 1971, there had been a slight increase in the participation rate of women. The work participation rates of women in the urban areas between 1971 and 1991 were 7.18 and 9.74 respectively, which increased to 11.15 in 2001. Compared to the urban areas, there had been a steady increase in the participation rate among women during 1971-2001 in rural areas. In 1971, it was 25.92 in the rural areas, which increased to 27.20 in 1991 and to 30.98 in 2001. Examining the gender wise work participation rates, one finds that during 1971-2001, the work participation rate of women was nearly half of that of men.

Table 2
Gender-Wise Work Participation Rates in Rural and Urban Areas in India: 1971-2001

(in Percentage)

Year	*Category*	*Females*	*Males*	*Persons*
1971	Total	14.22	52.75	34.17
	Rural	25.92	53.78	35.33
	Urban	7.18	48.88	29.61
1981	Total	19.67	52.62	36.70
	Rural	23.06	53.77	38.79
	Urban	8.31	49.06	29.99
1991	Total	22.73	51.56	37.68
	Rural	27.20	52.50	40.24
	Urban	9.74	48.95	30.44
2001	Total	25.68	51.93	39.26
	Rural	30.98	52.36	41.95
	Urban	11.55	50.85	32.23

Source: Registrar General of India.

Gender Wise Total Workers and Work Participation Rate According to 2001 Census

According to 2001 Census, out of total population of 1,025 million, 402.5 million persons were workers, of these 275.5 million are males and 127.0 million are females (See Table-3). In relative terms, the share of males in total work force was 68.4 per cent and that of females was 31.6 per cent. Out of total rural population of 740.2 million, workers accounted for 310.6 million with 199.2 million being males and 111.5 million being females. Among the rural workers, the share of males was of the order of 64.1 per cent and that of females was of the order of 35.9 per cent. In the urban population, out of a total of 285.0 million, 91.9 million persons constituted the urban work force. Among them, 76.3 million were males and 15.6 million were females. This implies that the share of males in urban work force was 83 per cent and that of females was 17 per cent. From the data is concerned, the conclusion emerges that rural women are more burdened; not only they participate in large numbers in economic activity, they have to return home from that activity to undertake domestic work like cooking, cleaning, tending of cattle, not to mention child bearing and child rearing. As against them, vast majority of the urban women have withdrawn from economic activity outside the home and look after only domestic work.

Table 3
Total Workers and Work Participation Rates in India: 2001

		Females	*Males*	*Persons*
Total	Population	494.8	530.4	1025.2
	Workers	127.0 (31.6)	275.5 (68.4)	402.5 (100)
	% of workers	25.7	51.9	39.2
Rural	Population	359.8	380.4	740.2
	Workers	111.5 (35.9)	199.2 (64.1)	310.6 (100)
	% of workers	31.0	52.4	42.0
Urban	Population	135.0	150.0	285.0
	Workers	15.6 (17)	76.3 (83)	91.9 (100)
	% of workers	11.6	50.9	32.2

Note: Figures in brackets indicate percentage of female and male workforce.
Source: Registrar General of India.

Discrimination Against Women

We naturally require a change in mindset to allow economic participation of women on an equal footing with men in society. Women need to move away to a certain extent from the traditional roles of homemakers and child-rearing to more progressive roles where their economic contribution to society is regarded in a positive light. The UN Convention on the Elimination of All Forms of Discrimination Against Women (CEDAW), that India has ratified, mentions that, "State parties shall take all appropriate measures to eliminate discrimination against women in the field of employment in order to ensure, on a basis of equality of men and women, the same rights, in particular (a) The right to work as an inalienable right of all human beings; (b) The right to the same employment opportunities, including the application of the same criteria for selection in matters of employment; (c) The right to free choice of profession and employment, the right to promotion, job security and all benefits and conditions of service and the right to receive vocational training and retraining, including apprenticeships, advanced vocational training and recurrent training; (d) The right to equal remuneration, including benefits and to equal treatment in respect of work of equal values, as well as equality of treatment in the evaluation of the equality of work..." Given this and given the fact that India has ratified the Convention, it is important to put these rights into practice. Of course, the Indian Constitution guarantees equality to all its citizens, but this remains largely on paper due to feudal mindset in most parts of the country.

Suggestions for Improving the Status of Women Workers

The problems of women workers in India are multifarious and multidimensional. These problems can be solved through changes in the attitude of family, society and nation towards the women. Some suggestions are given below:

- There shall be compulsory education for women. When she is educated, she can manage her dual responsibility of home and work.
- Women should be given vocational training in their work so that their efficiency increases. They should be trained to develop their capabilities of decision-making and individual thinking.
- Women should be made aware of their constitutional and legal rights both in their work and in the social sphere.
- The attitude of the husband and family members should be changed towards the working women. Husband should come forward to share her burden.

- She should be given adequate facilities.
- She should be given financial freedom.
- Baby care centre should be opened at the work place where she can leave her child.
- Maternity benefit schemes should be enhanced in private sectors.
- Wage gaps between men and women should be reduced. Better medical facilities and congenial atmosphere should be provided to them.
- Another suggestion is to increase part time jobs for women in various organizations, which will give a sense of dignity and identity to the women.
- Women should change their attitude about themselves. They should be self- confident in their approach.
- More seminars, conferences and workshops on women should be organized. They should be encouraged to participate in them and express their views.

Conclusions

Now working women have become a major part of labour market of India and hence their problem cannot be ignored. When they are engaged in gainful employment and contributing to the household and national economy, they should be given the due respect and status they deserve in the family and the society. In the changing socio-cultural environment of India, women are entering in a new era. But they are still over burdened with the household cores. So measures should be introduced to reduce their household burden. This requires a drastical change in the mind set of the men folk towards women in general and working women in particular.

References

Birley, S. (1989), "Female Entrepreneurs: Are they Really any Different", *Journal of Small Business Management,* 27 (1), pp.32-37.

Garg, R.B.L. (2004), "Women Entrepreneurs:Problems and Prospects", *Social Welfare,* 50 (12), March, pp.16-18.

Khurana, I.R. (1988): "Strategy for Rural Development", *Khadi Gram Udyog,* 34 (8), pp. 335-344.

Mohiuddin, A. (1987), "Entrepreneurship in Rural Women", *Kurukshetra,* 35 (12), pp. 22-25.

Nelson, R.E.(1985), "Entrepreneurship and Self Employment Training", *Asian Development Bank,* Manila.

Rao, S.K. (1976), "Entrepreneur Development in India-Is Achievement Training the Answer", *Laghu Udyog,* 4. pp 9-12.

Sinha, Poonam. (2003), "Women Entrepreneurship in the North East India: Motivation, Social Support and Constraints", *Indian Journal of Industrial Relations,* 28 (4), April, pp. 425-41.

Sundaram, I. Satya (2004), "Encouraging Women's Entrepreneurship", *Social Welfare,* 50 (12), March, pp15-19.

Vidyu Lata. (1990), *Developing Rural Women,* Discovery Publishing House, New Delhi.

Vitz, M.D. (1987), *Women Entrepreneurs in India,* Mittal Publications, New Delhi.

CHAPTER-15

Women Empowerment Through Dairy Cooperatives

B. Ratna kumari, M. Sridevi

In India, livestock plays a multi-faceted role in providing draught power for the farm, manure for crops, energy for cooking and food for household consumption as well as the market. Livestock are less influenced by rain failure, compared to crops, and are invaluable in sustaining family income during drought. Livestock development is now considered as an important tool for rural development vis-a vis poverty alleviation. Women, who are almost half of our total population and contribute monetary and non-monetary inputs towards national income, however, occupy low position in socio-economic index of India. In animal husbandry women accounted for 93 per cent of total employment in dairy production (World Bank, 1991). Though women play a significant role in livestock management and production, women's control over livestock and its products is negligible. The vast majority of the dairy cooperative membership is assumed by men, leaving only 14 per cent to women (MOA, 1991).

A Government report indicates that though 85 per cent of the rural women are engaged in livestock activities (Viswanathan, 1989), their share in income is not so high. In most systems, women provide labour for the various tasks related to livestock but may or may not control the process of decision-making, particularly over the disposal of animals and animal products. Similarly, women may be involved in production, but may or may not own the means of production: livestock, land, water, etc.

Despite their considerable involvement and contribution women's role in livestock production has often been under-estimated, or worse, ignored. Gender-blindness is partly the result of a paternalistic bias, but also of the attitude of women themselves, who may have been conditioned by their culture and society to undervalue the worth of the work they do. As a result, it is very difficult to obtain information on the role of women in livestock production from existing research and project reports. In addition, their work is rarely reflected in national statistics. It is instructive to note that women in the Developing world work for longer hours and for more years than men.

Women's contribution to productive and reproductive activities inside as well as outside the household is immense in terms of time used and energy spent. Ironmonger (1996) argues that there is a need for major change in our view of reality, what needs to be measured, and our thinking about the way in which families and households participate in economic activity. The reality of the huge unpaid contribution of household members to economic value needs to be accepted, adopted as a benchmark fact, it would change nearly all of our deliberations about economic and social policy. Development strategies have given very little attention to women in comparison to their active involvement in the economy. They have been under-recognized while formulating policies in regard to providing incentives including credit, forming co-operatives and inclusion in the training extension programmes.

According to the latest statistics, of 5.5 lakh cooperatives, there are 11,760 women cooperatives, which means only 2 per cent. And regarding the empowerment of women through cooperatives, 60 per cent to 70 per cent of the women in developing countries are in the informal sector. And if the women have to be brought in the mainstream of the cooperative movement the membership has to be increased.

Recognition of women as workers is only one aspect of women empowerment. Control over products and income is another. Despite women's extensive role in dairy activity, their control over proceeds, access to credit and other resources, access to training and technical assistance-main sources of knowledge of modern dairy-is limited. Membership of organisations, access to credit and information, role in decision-making regarding financial matters are some of the indicators of women's access and control over resources.

In the past two decades, the number of all-women dairy cooperatives has risen significantly in India pointing to NDDB's emphasis on the empowerment of women dairy farmers. In 2005, some 12.1 million dairy farmers, of which 2.9 million are women, are organised in 112,590 village-level dairy cooperatives, of which 18,500 are all-women dairy cooperatives, where women are not just members but also its elected leaders.

Against this background to assess the empowerment of women through cooperative dairies an attempt is made in this study to examine the socio-economic conditions of women dairy farmers in cooperative and non-cooperative dairy sector.

Objectives

- To analyse the socio-economic profile of the members of the cooperative and non-cooperative dairy farmers.
- To assess the empowerment levels of women in dairy sector.
- To suggest strategies for the empowerment of women.

Methodology

The study is based on the data collected from both primary and secondary sources. The primary data has been collected by canvassing pre-designed schedules. Two agriculturally predominant villages viz. Alamanda Bhimavaram and Medicharla of Kotapadu mandal of Visakhapatnam district have been selected purposefully. The selection of the two villages is on the basis of concentration of milk producers. One hundred schedules have been canvassed covering both cooperative and non-cooperative dairy farmers from these two villages. Out of which only thirteen members were women dairy farmers belonging to both the cooperative and non-cooperative sector.

Role of Livestock in the Indian Agrarian Economy

India being an agrarian economy, largely depends on agriculture and allied activities. The performance of agriculture and allied sectors reveals their importance to the national economy. The share of agriculture in GDP increased from Rs.425 billion in 1980-81 to Rs.5,215 billion by 2003-04. During the same period the share of livestock sector in GDP increased from Rs.59 billion to Rs.1,315 billion. The share of agriculture in GDP declined from 34.72 per cent in 1980-81 to 20.70 per cent by 2003-04. On the other hand, the share of livestock sector in GDP increased from 4.82 per cent in 1980-81 to 5.22 per cent by 2003-04 5

Growth of milk production generally depends on the growth of livestock in any country. The total livestock population is stagnated during the last decade while the total bovine population is found to be declining during the same period. The buffalo population has increased steadily with a tremendous growth during the last decade.

Socio-Economic Conditions of Sample Women Dairy Farmers

To analyse the socio-economic conditions of sample women dairy farmers regarding the literacy level, occupation, savings, household assets, education level of women dairy farmers, etc. are analysed and useful conclusions are presented.

Literacy Level

The data relating to the distribution of sample women dairy farmers by the type of savings are presented in Table 1. From the table it can be observed that out of the total women sample households 23 per cent are literates while 77 per cent are illiterates.

Table 1
Distribution of Sample Women Dairy Farmers by Literacy Level

Literacy Level	*No. of Respondents*	*Percentage of Respondents*
Total literates	3	23
Total Illiterates	10	77
Total	13	100.00

Occupation Type

The data relating to the distribution of sample dairy farmers by the type of occupation is presented in Table 2. From the table it can be observed that out of the total sample women households 61.5 % are having dairying as main occupation while 38.5% are having dairy as subsidiary occupation.

Table 2
Distribution of Sample Dairy Farmers by Occupation Type

Occupation	*No. of Respondents*	*Percentage of Respondents*
Dairy as main occupation	8	61.5
Dairy as subsidiary occupation	5	38.5
Total	13	100.00

Age of Respondents

The data relating to the distribution of sample dairy farmers by the age of the respondents are presented in the Table–3. From the table it can be observed that out of the total sample women dairy farmers 61.5 per cent belonged to the age group between 30-50 years while 38.5 per cent belonged to more than 50 years of age.

Table 3
Distribution of Sample Dairy Farmers by the Age of Respondents

Age	*No. of Respondents*	*Percentage of Women Dairy Farmers*
30-40	4	30.75
41-50	4	30.75
>50	5	38.50
Total	13	100.00

Marital Status

The data relating to the distribution of sample women dairy farmers by their marital status is presented in Table–4. From the data it can be observed that out of the total sample women dairy farmers 76.9 per cent were widowed, while 15.4 per cent were married and 7.7 per cent were divorced. This indicates that most of the sample women dairy farmers were widowed women.

Table 4
Distribution of Sample Dairy Farmers by their Marital Status

Marital Status	*No. of Respondents*	*Percentage of Women Dairy Farmers*
Married	12	15.4
Widowed	10	76.9
Divorced	1	7.7
Total	13	100

Income from Dairying

The data relating to the distribution of sample dairy farmers by the size and source of income are presented in Table 5. From the table it may be observed that the income from dairying is less than Rs.1500 for 92.3% of the respondents while income from dairying is more than Rs.1500 for only 7.7%.

Table 5
Distribution of Sample Dairy Farmers by the Income from Dairying

Avg. Monthly Income from Dairying	*No. of Respondents*	*Percentage of Women Dairy Farmers*
>1500 from Dairying	1	7.7
< 1500 from Dairying	12	92.3
Total	13	100.00
>1500 from other sources	4	30.7
<1500 from other sources	9	69.3
Total	13	100.00

Land Holdings

The data relating to the distribution of sample dairy farmers by the size of land holdings are presented in Table 6. From the below table it can be observed that out of the total sample women dairy farmers 30.8% of the women dairy farmers are landless, while 61.5% have land holdings between 1 to 3 acres and only 7.7% have land holdings of more than 3 acres. This indicates that most of women have land between 1- 3 acres.

Table 6
Distribution of Sample Women Dairy Farmers by Land Holdings

Land Particulars	*No. of Respondents*	*Percentage of Women Dairy Farmers*
Landless	4	30.8
1 - 3 acres	8	61.5
>3 acres	1	7.7
Total	13	100.00

Savings

The data relating to the distribution of sample dairy farmers are presented in Table 7. From the table it can be observed that out of the total women dairy farmers 46 per cent are saving less than Rs.500 while 54 per cent are saving more than Rs.500. Most of the respondents are also saving in liquidity form.

Table 7
Distribution of Sample Dairy Farmers by the Type of Savings

Saving Per Month	*No. of Respondents*	*Percentage of Women Dairy Farmers*
<500	7	46
>500	6	54
Total	13	100.00
No. of respondents saving in liquidity form	11	84.61

Household Assets

The data relating to the distribution of sample dairy farmers by the type of house is given in Table–8. Out of the women sample dairy farmers 23.1% are having pucca houses, 61.5 per cent are having thatched houses and 15.4 per cent are having semi-pucca houses. This indicates that majority of the sample women dairy farmers are living in thatched houses.

Table 8
Distribution of Sample Dairy Farmers by the Type of House

Type of House	*No. of Respondents*	*Percentage of Women*
Pucca House	3	23.1
Thatched House	8	61.5
Semi-pucca house	2	15.4
Total	13	100.00

Cattle Wealth

The data relating to the distribution of sample women dairy farmers by the no. of milch animals is presented in Table 9. From the data it can be observed that out of the total sample women dairy farmers, majority i.e. 84.6 per cent are having only one milch animal while 15.4 per cent are having 2 milch animals. From this it can be observed that women dairy farmers are having only one or two milch animals.

Table 9
Distribution of Women Sample Dairy Farmers by Cattle Wealth

No. of Milch Animals	*No. of Women Dairy Farmers*	*Percentage of Women Dairy Farmers*
1 animal	11	84.6
2 animals	2	15.4
> 2 animals	0	0
Total	13	100.00

Comparative Study of the Cooperative and Non-Cooperative Dairy Farmers

- Our analysis of the socio-economic conditions of the sample dairy farmers brings out that the literacy level is high among the women cooperative dairy farmers when compared to the non-cooperative women dairy farmers. And from this it is inferred that the literacy level is having positive impact on the cooperative women dairy farmers.

- The analysis of the distribution of sample dairy farmer by size and source of income shows that the non-cooperative women dairy farmers main occupation is dairying while the cooperative women dairy farmers main occupation is cultivation indicating that the cooperative women dairy farmers are financially better off than the non- cooperative women dairy farmers.
- The analysis of the distribution of sample dairy farmers by size of land holdings reveals that out of the sample dairy farmers who did not own any land, 30.8% are landless while 61.5% are having land between 1-3 acres while only 7.7% are having more than 3 acres of land.
- The sample dairy farmers in the cooperative sector are capable of spending more on education than those in the non-cooperative sector, as the children of cooperative dairy farmers are provided with educational facilities through scholarships and concessions in fees for higher education by the cooperative dairy.
- The cooperative women dairy farmers are able to spend more on buffaloes (for cattle sheds, health, insurance) etc as they are provided with credit facilities from the Visakha Cooperative dairy. And they are also allowed to repay loan amount in instalments by supplying milk.
- The sample cooperative dairy farmers are spending more on cattle feed and fodder, when compared to the non-cooperative sample dairy farmers as they are getting subsides from the cooperative dairy.
- The sample cooperative women dairy farmers are earning an annual income in the range of Rs. 10,000/- to Rs. 20,000/- through selling milk while the non-cooperative women dairy farmers are earning less than Rs.10,000/- per annum.
- The pricing of milk is based on the fat content in the milk in the cooperative sector ranging between Rs. 23 to Rs.

11. while the non-cooperative dairy farmers are getting Rs. 15 per litre of milk irrespective of the fat content.

- Our analysis of the employment opportunities provided by Visakha Dairy shows that VCD is encouraging the children of the milk producers by recruiting them in the Dairy basing on their qualifications. Such provision is not provided for the non-cooperative dairy farmers. From our study, it is found that 14% of the sample dairy farmer households have already received employment benefits from the cooperative dairy.

Opinions of Sample Dairy Farmers

Majority of the sample cooperative women dairy farmers have expressed the need for providing high yielding milch animals with subsidy, the need for reducing interest rates on borrowings for purchasing milch animals, to conduct regular awareness camps to improve the dairying activity in the rural areas and the need for extending health facilities even to the remote villages.

Policy Implications

To increase women's access and control commensurate to their participation in dairy work affirmative action is required in a number of areas.

- First of all, financial incentive schemes like credit for milch animals, etc. should be framed in such a way that women's hold over assets increases.
- Secondly, women membership of the cooperative societies should be made more effective by increasing their control over earnings and number of exclusive women societies should also be enhanced.
- Representation of women should be increased in administrative and field staff of the milk plants and Directorate of Dairy Development.
- One-third of the elected members of the Board of Directors of District Milk Union and state level milk Federation should be reserved for women dairy farmers.

- Gender sensitisation of both male and female staff of dairy related organisations is very important in achieving the desired results.
- All these efforts will not bring the desired results unless relentless struggle against patriarchy on the wider social level succeeds. Both the civil society womens' organisations, NGO's etc. and Government can play its role in this struggle.
- Improvements in dairy animals and provision of small plots of land for the landless can go a long way in solving the problems of employment and poverty.
- The promotion of improved technologies in animal husbandry to reduce drudgery and improve health, efficiency and safety of women dairy farmers.
- Technological interventions are to be made to make the farm women aware of new technologies available to assist them in performing their work efficiently in animal husbandry.
- Concerted efforts made through skill training, field demonstrations, constant technical support and motivation results in acquisition of knowledge and skills in handling various drudgery reducing technologies in animal husbandry.

References

S.B.Verma, S.K.Jiloka, K.J.Kushwah (2006), "Role of Women in Livestock Farming", *Rural Women Empowerment,* Deep and Deep Publications, New Delhi.

Rupinder Kaur (2008), "Gender and Social Analysis of Dairy Farming- A Case Study of Punjab, *Journal of Rural Development,* Vol.27, No.(1), pp. 129-147, NIRD, Hyd.

Lalitha Krishnaswamy(2008), "Empowerment of Women and Youth through Cooperatives", *The Cooperator,* Vol.45,No.9m March.

Michael J.Papa, Arvind Singhal, Wendy: "*Organising for social Change*", Sage Publications, New Delhi.

M.Sridevi, Dr.K. Sailaja (2007), Socio-Economic Conditions of Sample Dairy Farmers–A Case Study of Visakha Cooperative Dairy, *Unpublished Report,* Andhra University, Visakhapatnam.

Sandeep Kumar (2005), "A Growth Profile and Future of Livestock Sector in India", *Agricultural Situation in India,* Vol.LXII, No.2, May 2005

K.Elumalai and U.K Pandey (2003), *Agricultural Situation in India,* Vol.LX, No.6, Sep.

Suman Singh, Puja Mathur and Madhu Rathore: "Alleviating Drudgery of Indian Farm Women through Technology Interventions in Animal Husbandry, *Journal of Rural Development,* Vol.27, No.(2), pp. 311-322, NIRD, Hyderabad.

Chapter-16

Empowerment of Women in the Plan Period : An Overview

K. Somasekhar

In India, Women constitute almost half of the total Population in the country. According to 2001 census, Women are 495.7 million in number as against total population of 1027.01 million. Thus they constitute 48.26 per cent of the total population of the country. While women in general in the country are under privileged in terms of social status and economic participation, the plights of rural women is much worse. Low earnings and lower wages, low level of skills, limited access to factors of production, low literacy, malnutrition, poor standards of health and living, greater exposure to exploitation, domestic violence and vulnerability to sexual crimes characterize the life, of poverty and unemployment add to the miserable plight of the women. As per the estimation of UNDP 1.3 billion world population living in poverty of which more than 70 per cent are women. Further, poverty rate among the women has been steadily increasing when compared with men.

Empowerment of women has been the main concern of all the countries in the recent period. It is widely recognized that empowerment of women contributes significantly to the social Development which in turn leads to the economic Development of country. It is widely accepted that economic development of a country largely depends upon the participation of every citizen including women in the economic activities. The participation in productive activities will have tremendous impact on the literacy, health and other living condition of the families and eliminate gender discrimination which ultimately leads to the empowerment of the women.

Concept of Empowerment

Empowerment is an abstract and complex concept and it is interpreted in many ways. According to the Random House Dictionary, empowerment comes from the term empower which means "to give power or authority" and "to enable or permit". The Key elements in empowerment are "enabling" and "Providing Power" and they reinforce each other. In practical terms however, empowerment would mean the process of challenging exiting inequality power relations, and gaining greater control over sources of power by the under privileged. This naturally gets reflected in improved social political and cultural status of women. Self-confidence and self-esteem of women proceed simultaneously with their empowerment. In brief, all these indicators can be classified into two broad categories namely visible and invisible indicators.

Empowerment literacy means, "becoming Powerful". It is a Theory "concerned with how people may gain collective control over their lives, so as to attract their interests as a group and a method to enhance the power of people who back it". Empowerment is a process whereby women become able to organize themselves to increase their own self-reliance, to assert their independent right to make choices and control resources which will assist in challenging and eliminating their own subordination. Empowerment is a participatory process, which begins at the levels of home and community. Empowerment is also a process of awareness and capacity building leading to greater participation, to great decision making power and control and to transformative action which enables individuals or groups to change balances of power in social, economic and political relations in society.

Empowerment as 'Power'

The women in development perspective which has been predominated within thinking on women and development since 1970, is constructed on that "Power over" view of Power. Such a conceptualization of power implying an instrumentalist approach however does not involve a structural change in power relations, which is critical to bring about a long-term change.

Power can make various forms as "Power to" "power with" and "Power from with for all of which allow the construction of as different meaning of empowerment. Such notions of power are generative rather than controlling power, and according to her if the process is important then these kinds of power are not finite.

At the organizational level the principal source of an individual/group's power over an organization is its strength of resources that is valued by the organization or its strength of coping mechanism during organizational contingencies/ Problems. At the inter personal level, the primary source of power of an individual/group is its official position. Personal characteristics, expertise and opportunity to access specialized knowledge.

The following components can be useful to understand the level of power of an individual and group.

- Power to make decision at household
- Level of change in power relations with time (household and group level)
- Level of political activity in challenging basic power relations in society
- Level of control over sources of power
- Access to resources
- Control of resources and benefits.

Process of Empowerment

Empowerment is a multidimensional process, which enables an individual to realize his/her full identify and power in all spheres of life. The empowerment process begins with and is supported by the economic independence, which implies access to, and control over productive resources, knowledge and awareness, self image autonomy and decision making power inside and outside the home. In the present scenario, women in general and rural women who live in rural areas and that they are relatively more neglected and dis-empowered compared to their male counterparts.

Empowerment "The process by which people, organization or groups who are powerless a become aware of the power dynamics at work in their life context, (b) develop the skills and capacity for gaining some reasonable control over their lives (c) exercise this control. Without infringing upon the rights of others (d) support the empowerment of others in the community.

In fact empowerment process requires transformation of structures of subordination through radical changes in law, property and other institutions that reinforce and perpetrate male domination. Power accrues to those who control or are able to influence the distraction of material resources, knowledge and the ideology that governs social relations in both Public and Private life. The extent of power held by particular individuals or groups corresponds to the kinds of resources they can control and the extent to which they can shape prevailing ideology whether social, religions, or political. This control in turn confers the power of decision-making. The process of challenging existing power relations and of gaining greater control over the sources of power may be termed as Empowerment. The term Empowerment refers to the range of activity from individual self-assertion to collective mobilization that challenges the basic power relations.

Status of Women

Women in the Indian society had a distinct place of honour in ancient times. She was treated with great respect for her feminine virtues. Maitrayee, Gargi, Seetha, Savithri are still held in honour and they are symbols of intelligence, wisdom, purity and endurance. Ancient Indian History ascribes a divine status to women, Laxmi, Durga and Saraswathi are three great

Goddesses of Prosperity, power and wisdom respectively. The ancient scriptures declared that "God lives where women are worshipped". However, a multitude of derogatory attributes have been ascribed to women in the post-vedic, period. According to Manu, women must never be independent. In childhood, she must be subject to the father, in youth to her husband and when her lord is dead to her son". Yet after the invasion of alien forces, the condition of Indian women started worsening. They were deprived of their natural rights and social status.

A report prepared on the status of women on the eve of world conference on the UN decade for women pointed out that women and girls are half of the world population, do the thirds of the worlds work hours, receive one-fourth of worlds income and own less than a hundredth of the worlds property. This clearly shows that women are not involved in the decision-making that allocates the resources for development. They are not involved in the process that decides who gets what, they are not in a position where they can control the distribution of goods and services.

Need for Empowerment

Women empowerment is a global issue which has gained momentum in recent decades. In India, besides ratification of international conventions, there are provisions in the constitution and several Legislative Acts have been passed to ensure women empowerment. No country can achieve its potential without adequately investing in and developing the capabilities of women. In the interest of long-term development it is necessary to facilitate their women empowerment.

Empowerment of women contributes to social development. Economic progress in any country could be achieved through social development, women constitute equal share with men in total population of our country. Women's empowerment can not be ignored while devising various policies for socio economic development of the country. Women comprise half of the world's population and their role in development cannot be overlooked.

Policies and Programmes for Empowerment of Women During the Plan Period

The First Five Year Plan (1951-56) envisaged a number of welfare measures for women. Establishment of the Central Social Welfare Board (CSWB), organization of Mahila Mandals and the community Development Programme were a few steps in this direction. The Second Five Year Plan (1956-61) was closely linked with overall approach of intensive agricultural development. The Welfare approach persisted during this plan period as well.

The Third Five Year Plan (1961-66) Supported female education as major welfare measure. Rural welfare services and condensed courses of education had priority, besides provision of services for maternal and child welfare, health education, nutrition and family planning. Similarly, the Fourth Five Year Plan (1969-74) continued emphasis on women's education. Here the basic policy was to promote women welfare within the family. The outlay for family planning was stepped up and a high priority was accorded to immunization and supplementary feeding programme.

From the Fifth Five Year Plan (1974-79) onwards there has been a marked shift in the approach to women's issues from welfare to development. During this plan emphasis was given for their economic development through the skill development training and employment is the principal focus for their overall development. Functional literacy programme got priority. This plan coincided with International women's Decade and submission of Report of the committee on the status of women in India. In 1976 Women's Welfare and Development was set up under the Ministry of Social Welfare to act as a nodal point to coordinate policies, programmes, for women's development. It is during this plan the Integrated. Rural Development Programme (IRDP) was launched with a view to elimination of Poverty. In this programme it is envisaged that 40 per cent of the beneficiaries should be necessarily women.

During the Sixth Five Year Plan (1980-85) The Development of women and child in the Rural Areas, popularly called as

DWCRA Programme was launched to bring the deprived rural women into the mainstream of development. The main approach of DWCRA programme is a group strategy. The women members of DWCRA form groups of 10-15 members each for taking up certain economic activities suited to their skill, aptitude and the local conditions. The objectives of the group strategy are to motivate the rural women to come together cutting across the social barriers take up income operating activities and to enable them to participate in the organized socio-economic activities for the development of the country. One of the most important activities initiated under DWCRA Programme has been the promotion of Thrift and credit. The Self-Help Groups thrift Starts with fixed savings and then progresses to maximum savings. The members of the DWCRA are encouraged to make voluntary thrift on regular basis. The basic assumption is that the saving practice would help to provide easy access to credit for rural women to meet their personal needs.

Besides it, the Government of India was setup the department of women and children in the year 1985 as a part of the Ministry of Human Resource Development to give the much needed impetus to the holistic development of women and children.

The Seventh Five Year Plan (1985-90) operationalized the concern for equity and Empowerment. For the first time emphasis was laid on qualitative aspects such as inculcation of confidence, generation of awareness with regards to rights and training in skills, better employment.

During the Seventh Plan Period a number of programmes were envisaged such as i) Women's Development Corporation (WDCs), ii) Support to Training and Employment Programme (STEP), iii) Training and production centers for women, iv) Awareness generation camps for rural and poor Women v) Women training center or Institutions for rehabilitation of women in distress vi) Voluntary action bureau and family counseling centers, vii) Short stay homes for women and girls viii) Free legal aid and Para legal training and ix) working women's hostels. The thrust of all these programmes was on provision employment and income generation, educational training, support services, general awareness and legal support.

Eighth Five Year Plan (1992-97) makes a shift from 'development' to 'empowerment' of the women. The National Commission for women set up in 1992 covers issues relating to safeguarding women's rights and promotion; of their empowerment Mahila Samrudhi Yojana was launched in 1993 with a view to have a greater control over household resources, and to remove inequalities and gender discrimination in the development sphere. It also encourages the women to start own saving for helping themselves. Rashtriya Mahila Kosh (National credit fund for women) has been set up in 1993 with the aim of reaching the poor women who are in need of credit. The schemes introduced during this plan like Jawahar Rozgar Yojana (JRY) and Employment Assurance scheme (EAS) provides special provision to ensure greater participation of women. The scheme of Balika Samrudhi Yojana was launched in 1997 to bring attitudinal change in the society towards girl child.

Another important landmark in the history of women welfare in India is the enactment of 73rd Constitutional Amendment Act of 1992 during this plan period. The Act revolutionized the Panchayati Raj Institutions. They provide for the reservation of 33.3 Per cent of the political for women in Panchayat with a view to empower the women politically.

The Ninth Five Year Plan (1997-2002) adopted a strategy of women's component plan under which not less than 30 per cent of funds/benefits are earmarked for women specific programmes. The main thrust of this plan is "Empowerment of women" and the strategy used from individual beneficiary approach to a group and /or cluster approach and to facilitate this process Self-Help Group will formed. Swarnjayanthi Gram Swarozgar Yojana which was launched in 1999, in the guidelines it is envisaged that 50 per cent of Groups formed in each block should be exclusively for women who will account for at least 40 per cent of total Swarozgar's. Steps has been taken to nurture these Groups to enable them to function effectively as well as to choose their economic activity.

The Sampoorna Grameen Rozgar Yojana (SGRY) was launched in 2001 to provide additional and supplementary wage, employment, to provide food security and improve nutritional level in rural areas. It is stipulated in this scheme that 30 per cent of the employment opportunities should be reserved for women.

The Tenth Five Year Plan (2002-2007) made a special focus to empower women through translating the National Policy for Empowerment of women into action. During this plan period National Rural Employment Guarantee Scheme (NREGS) launched in 2006. In this scheme priority shall be given to women in such a way that at least one third of the beneficiaries shall be women who are registered and requested for work under the scheme.

The National Policy on women launched during this plan period to promote the advancement, development and empowerment of women through various means.

Goals and Objectives of this Policy;

1. Creating an environment through positive economic and Social Policies for the full development of women to enable them to recognize their full potential.
2. Equal access to participation and decision making of women in social, political and economic life of the nation.
3. Equal access in women to health care, quality education at all levels, career and vocational guidance, proceeding employment opportunities and public offices, equal remuneration, occupational health and safety, social security and Public Offices etc.
4. Strengthening of the legal systems also aims at elimination of all forms of discrimination against women.
5. Changing social attitudes and community practices by the active participation and involvement of both men and women.
6. Main streaming the gender perspective in the developments process.

7. Elimination of discrimination and all other forms of violence, against women and the girl child.
8. Building and strengthening partnerships with the Civil Society, Particularly the women's organizations.

Conclusion

Thus several policies and programmes have been introduced and implemented by the Government of India right from First Five Year Plan to Tenth Five Year Plan in order to empower the women. But, the status of women in India has not been improved in desired extent. This is due to the not reaching the programmes to all the women particularly who live in remote, inaccessible villages and slum areas of urban areas. Still the country is witnessing largest section of the women living in the absolute poverty gender differences, violence against women and so on. The empowerment of women can be attained only when all the women in country will be benefited through the policies and programmes. Hence, it is need of the hour to make serious attention during the Eleventh Plan period to device a mechanism to extend the benefits to all the women in the country.

References

Batilwala, Srilatha (1995), "The Meaning of Women's Empowerment", New Delhi, Women's World.

Dept. of Women and Child Welfare (2001), Report on the Working Group on Empowerment of Women, Tenth Plan (2002-07), New Delhi, Ministry of HRD.

Government of India (2007-08), Annual Report of Ministry of Rural Development, New Delhi.

Government of India (1951-2002), Ten Five Year Plans, Planning Commission of India, New Delhi.

Karnakar, K.G. (1999), *Rural Credit and Self Help Groups – Micro Finance Needs and Concepts in India,* New Delhi, Sage Publications.

Mira Seth (2001), *"Women and Development: The Indian Experience"*, New Delhi Sage Publications.

Manimekalai and Rajeswari (2001), Empowerment of Women Through Self Help Groups, Vol.32 Kuruksheria, New Delhi.

National Commission for Women–Moving into the 21st century Through A partnership of Men and Women.

Neeta Tapan (2000), Need for Women Empowerment", Rawat Publications, New Delhi.

Ramalakshmi, C.S. (2003), "Empowerment Through Self-Help Groups", *Andhra Pradesh Supplement,* May:21-22.

Suguna, B. (2002), "Strategies for Empowerment of Rural Women", in the *Journal of Social Welfare,* Vol.49, No.5, New Delhi.

Sushma Sahay (1988), "Women and Empowerment Approaches and Strategies", Discovery Publishing House, New Delhi.

Chapter-17

Economic Empowerment of Women: A Group Approach

D. Sunder Raj, R. Venkata Ravi

Introduction

Development is human-oriented and equal participation of both men and women is an important precondition for the attainment of meaningful development and well being of all people. Development is an integrated process for economic growth and social progress. The experiences of the planned development of the country suggest that benefits of development are not equally shared by all sections of the people. It is now widely recognized and increasingly emphasized that success of development efforts would be achieved only when women are included or given equal opportunity for participation in all developmental programmes. Any attempt at improving the economic performance of the economy, reducing poverty or slowing down population growth or even arresting environmental degradation requires sincere and sustained efforts to involve women in the process of empowerment.

As the women, right from the early days, are some how isolated and kept aside in the development drama, citing various reasons belonging to culture tradition and religion, in the patriarchal society. Centuries together the unvoiced sorrow that of negligence, dominance, oppression, suppression and violence continued. More so, their role and contribution to the development of family as well as to the nation, is often undermined, unnoticed rather ignored. The term empowerment stands for capacity building of people who are marginalised, socially out casted, economically backward, physically challenged and knowledge wise illiterate/ignorant in general; and capacity building of women in particular.

Empowering women economically means developing them as more aware individuals who are economically productive and independent, socially developed, politically active, and are able to make judicious choices and intelligent decisions in matters that affect them and their nation (Raj, D. Sunder, 2006). This helps individuals to be more aware of opportunities available for them to make their lives better. More so, economic empowerment also helps women to evolve, as workers, citizens and human beings. It serves as a powerful instrument for women to achieve upward social and economic mobility and achieve power and status in society. Gender development constitutes an important part of development in this context. It is important in this respect to bring women into the mainstream of development so that society in turn benefits from the women development.

Need of Empowerment

Women are an integral part of every economy. All round development and harmonious growth of a nation would be possible only when women are considered as equal partners in progress with men. However, in most developing countries, women have a low social and economic status. In such countries effective empowerment of women is essential to harness the women labor in the main stream of economic development. Empowerment of women is a holistic concept. It is multi-dimensional in its approach and covers social, political, economic and social aspects. Of all these facets of women's development, economic empowerment is of utmost significance in order to achieve a lasting and sustainable development of society.

The position of women and their role in the context of development are particularly important not because they contribute half of the human resources but more so because they have to bear the brut of the daily struggle for survival. Though they constitute nearly half of the population, often their contribution to development in society is undermined. The underlying causes of gender inequality are related to social and economic structure, which is based on informal and formal norms, and practices. Consequently, the access of women particularly those belonging to weaker sections including Scheduled Casts/Scheduled Tribes/Other backward Classes and minorities, who are in the rural areas and in the informal, unorganized sector–to education, health and productive resources, among others, is inadequate. Therefore, they remain largely marginalized, poor and socially excluded.

UN observed the year 2001 as women empowerment year. The National Policy for the empowerment of women was also formed/evolved in the same year. Underlining the need for mainstreaming gender perspective in the development process the National Policy recognizes the causes of gender inequality, which are related to social and economic structure. Besides empowering women to participate in decision making process the policy also visualized the means of economic and social empowerment of women. The following are the objectives of policy

- Creating an environment through positive economic and social policies for full development of women to enable them to realise their full potential
- The dejure and defacto enjoyment of all human rights by women on equal basis with men in all spheres - political, economic, social, cultural and civil
- Equal access to participate and decision making in social, political and economic life of the nation
- Equal access to healthcare, quality education at all levels, career and vocational guidance, employment and equal remunerative

- Strengthening of legal systems aimed at elimination of all forms of discrimination against women
- Changing societal attitudes and community practices by active participation and involvement of both men and women
- Mainstreaming a gender perspective in the development process
- Elimination of discrimination and all forms of violence against women and the girl child; and
- Building and strengthening partnerships with civil society, particularly women's organization

In the present day context women involvement and their contribution, is important because of the rapid changing scenario. Economic empowerment of women can serve as an essential input in the nation's development.

Efforts towards Women Development

According to National Policy of Women Empowerment (2001), in recent years, the empowerment of women has been recognized as the central issue in determining the status of women. The National Commission for Women was set up by an Act of Parliament in 1990 to safeguard the rights and legal entitlements of women. The 73rd and 74th Amendments (1993) to the Constitution of India have provided for reservation of seats in the local bodies of Panchayats and Municipalities for women, laying a strong foundation for their participation in decision making at the local levels.

However, there still exists a widespread network the goals enunciated in the Constitution, legislation, policies, plans, programmes, and related mechanisms on the one hand and the situational reality of the status of women in India, on the other. This has been analysed extensively in the Report of the Committee on the Status of Women in India, "Towards Equality", 1974 and highlighted in the National Perspective Plan for Women, 1988-2000, the Shramshakti Report, 1988 and the Platform for Action, Five Years after-An assessment.

The importance of women empowerment was realized a few decades ago, but serious implementation of various programmes empowering women apparently is a recent development. It involves a long term redesigning of policies, programmes and more importantly attitudes and approaches towards women empowerment. Government of India has initiated a variety of programmes for the welfare and empowerment of women. There are at least 82 such programmes.

Five-Year Plans and Women Development

The First Five Year Plan (1951-56) envisaged a number of welfare measures for women. Establishments of the Central Social Welfare Board (CSWB), organization of Mahila Mandals or Women's Clubs and the Community Development Programmes were a few steps in this direction. The Second Five Year Plan (1956-61) was closely linked with the overall approach of intensive agricultural development. The welfare approach persisted during this plan period as well.

The Third Five Year Plan (1961-66) supported female education as major welfare measure. Rural welfare services and condensed courses of education had priority besides provision of services for maternal and child welfare, health education, nutrition and family planning. Similarly, the Fourth Five Year Plan (1969-74) continued emphasis on women's education. Here the basic policy was to promote women's welfare within the family. The outlay for family planning was stepped up and a high priority was accorded to immunization and supplementary feeding programmes.

The Fifth Five Year Plan (1974-79) emphasized training women in need of income and protection. Functional Literacy Programme got priority. This plan coincided with International Women's Decade and submission of Report of the Committee on the Status of Women in India. In 1976 Women's Welfare and Development Bureau was set up under the Ministry of Social Welfare. It was to act as a nodal point to coordinate policies, programmes for women's development.

The Sixth Five Year Plan (1980 - 85) saw definite shift from welfare to development. It recognized women's lack of access to resources as a critical factor impending their growth. Seventh Five Year Plan (1985-90), operationalised the concern for equity and empowerment. For the first time emphasis was laid on qualitative aspects such as inculcation of confidence, generation of awareness with regards to rights and training in skills for better employment.

During Sixth and Seventh Plan period, a number of programmes ware envisaged such as (Yadav: 2000): i) Women's Development Corporation (WDCs). ii) Support to Training and Employment Programme (STEP). iii) Training-cum-production Centers for Women. iv) Awareness Generation camps for Rural and Poor Women. v) Women's Training Centers or Institutes for Rehabilitation of Women in distress. vi) Voluntary Action Bureau and Family Counseling Centers. vii) The Short Stay Homes for Women and Girls. viii) The Free legal aid and Para-legal training and ix) The Working Women's Hostels. The thrust of all these programmes was on provision of employment and income generation, educational training, support services, general awareness and legal support to the women.

The Eighth Five Year Plan (1990-95) has focused on empowering women, especially at the grassroots level, through Panchayat Raj institutions. The Ninth Five Year Plan adopted a strategy of Women's Component Plan, under which not less than 30 percent of funds / benefits are earmarked for women specific programmes. Review by the Planning Commission of progress of women's Component Plan during Ninth plan (1997 - 2000) has confirmed that nearly 42.9 percent of the gross budgetary support (GBS) aggregating a total amount of Rs.51.942, 53 crores, has been spent on women in 5 Ministries / Departments namely Family Welfare, Health, Education, Women and Child and Indian System of Medicine and Homeopathy.

The Tenth Plan approach aims at empowering women through translating the recently adopted National Policy for Empowerment of Women (2001) into action and ensuring

'Survival, Protection and Development of Children through Rights Based Approach'. The Annual Plan 2002-03, being the first of year of the Tenth Plan, has initiated and brought into effect the thrust areas outlined in the approach along with relevant policies and programmes. For Annual Plan 2002-03 a total outlay of Rs.2, 220 crore has been provided for the Women and Child Development as against Rs.1650 crores made available in 2001-02.

Economic Development of Women

In India, besides ratification of international conventions, there are provisions in the Constitution and several legislative Acts have been passed to ensure women empowerment. However, empowering women appears on this front the situation is far from satisfactory. Women as an independent target group, account for 495.74 million, as per the 2001 census. No country can achieve its potential without adequately investing in and developing the capabilities of women. In the interest of long-term development it is necessary to facilitate their empowerment. Empowerment in its simplest form means redistribution of power that challenges the male dominance in the society. This does not, however, mean that the empowerment process adopts an antagonists' approach. It is only to enable women to supplement and coordinate with fellow men.

Since independence and more particularly after seventies, the Govt. of India has been laying considerable emphasis on economic empowerment of women. Sole motive behind this endeavour is to bring them into the mainstream of development. The constitutional obligations as well as different plans, programmes and policies have laid emphasis on raising the economic status of women. The preamble of Indian Constitution seeks to ensure all its citizens: "Justice, social and economic and political and equality of status and opportunity and to promote among them all". Stress was more on Welfare in 70s, Development in 80s, Empowerment in 90s and now to Decision-making and participation (Pattnaik, 2001).

Improvement in economic status is a more visible indicator of women empowerment. This naturally gets reflected in improved social, political and cultural status of women. Self-confidence and self-esteem of women proceed simultaneously with their empowerment. In brief, all indicators can be classified into two broad categories namely visible and invisible indicators. Amongst visible indicators a mention could be made of women's representation in parliament.

For a country like India where 36% of the population is poor, poverty alleviation is not only important but also helps in optimizing their contributions to the growth of the national economy. The experience of the last several years particularly in respect of financing poverty alleviation programmes and creation of employment in rural areas does reveal that a number of factors prevent small borrowers and poor people from securing adequate credit from formal credit agencies, such as, (1) lack of awareness among beneficiaries in respect of development through credit and thereby making proper use of credit, (2) lack of effective coordination among officials concerned at village, block and district level for proper planning, implementing, monitoring, revising and evaluating the performance under the programmes (Laxmi R. Kulshrestha & Archana Gupta, 2001).

Rural women particularly from lower strata of the society are seldom decision-makers in the family as well as in the community in spite of being major contributors to the family income. More so, rural women are less endowed than men with education, health care or productive assets and financial resources. Finance, being an entry point to rural development, non-accessibility and non-availability of credit to rural women have been instrumental in aggravating gender inequalities in the rural areas. Financial resources, if effectively delivered to women can help them make a meaningful improvement in their economic and social life, which promotes their empowerment.

Women once considered "non-productive and non-asset worthy" are now regarded as "agents of change and economic development". Albeit slowly, by participating in SHGs, in many places, women are getting their due. Women have certainly, led to the opening of closed minds and improving the quality of life and their social status (Hindu, May 7, 2000). According to Suguna B., (2001) "empowerment is capacity building leading to greater participation to greater decision-making power and control, and transformation action".

Group Approach

Women are an integral part of every economy. All round development and harmonious growth of a nation would be possible only when women are considered as equal partners in progress with men. Empowerment of women is essential to harness the women labor in the main stream of economic development. Empowerment of women is a holistic concept. It is multi-dimensional in its approach and covers social, political, economic and social aspects. Of all these facets of women's development, economic empowerment is of utmost significance in order to achieve a lasting and sustainable development of society. Self- Help Groups are the voluntary organizations which disburse micro credit to the members and facilitate them to enter into entrepreneurial activities. In India, the Self-Help Groups are promoted by N.G.O.s, banks and co-operatives. The National Bank for Agriculture and Rural Development (NABARD) launched a pilot project for linking SHGs in February, 1992. The Reserve Bank of India advises the commercial banks to participate actively in the linkage programme. Normally, after six months of existence of SHGs and after collecting a sufficient thrift fund, the Group approaches the link banks (either commercial or co-operative) with its credit plan. The NABARD gives 100 per cent refinance to the Banks on their lending through the SHGs.

The Self Help Groups (SHGs) are viable alternative to achieve the objective of individual development and to involve community through participation in all rural development programmes. SHGs enhance the equality status of women as participants, decision makers and beneficiaries in the democratic, economic, social and cultural spheres of life. For example tribals from 84 villages in four blocks of Koraput district in Orissa are today totally transformed lot and enjoy a better standard of living because of SHGs (HINDU, October 13, 2000). In all stages of economic and social activities involvement of women becomes essential and these groups encourage women to take active part in the socio-economic progress of our nation.

The SHGs bring out the capacity of women in moulding the community in right perspective and explore the initiative of women in taking up entrepreneurial ventures. Women's contribution to national development is crucial. The process of economic development would be incomplete and lopsided unless women are fully involved in it. The SHGs empower women and train them to take active part in the socio economic progress of the nation and make them sensitized, self-made and self-disciplined. The SHGs inculcate a great confidence in the minds of rural women to succeed in their day-to-day life.

Empowerment of women through Self Help Groups would lead to benefits not only to the individual women and women groups but also for the family and community as a whole through collective action for development. Empowering is not just for meeting their economic needs but also through more holistic social development (Murgan and Dharma lingam, 2000). Women are getting their due through SHGs. They make decision not only in family matters, but also in the community, village and society.

According to Gurumoorthy (2000), empowering women contributes to social development. Economic progress in any country whether developed or underdeveloped could be achieved through social development. Where as, Shridharan, Damyanty (1997), observe that traditional grassroots groups, which are based on the principles of need and collective action, are now more commonly referred as SHGs provide self-reliance. Puhazhendi et. al. (1999) opine that, the informal group of rural poor with active intervention of NGOs adequately supported by training and financial assistance ensured and also significantly improved women's participation both from economic and social aspects. The group approach is becoming more and more important as evidence by the recognition accorded by the GOI in the ongoing income generation programmes. The SHGs have become the focal point of the development schemes under the Unified Poverty Alleviation Programme (SGSY) launched from April 1999. NABARD's commitment of empowering atleast 100 million rural poor through one million SHGs by the year 2008 would further increase the emphasis of group approach among the rural poor, especially women. There is a greater potential for the group approach in future while conceptualising and implementing any programme for the rural poor, particularly women, through stakeholder approach.

An informal arrangement for credit supply to the poor through self-help groups is fast emerging as a promising tool for promoting income generating enterprises (Nagayya, 2000). "Lack of capital is a serious constraint to the development of rural women. Often, the barriers like legal provision; loan policies and procedures make credit inaccessible to women. It is widely recognized that women as a group and poor women in particular, have been adversely affected. For the socio-economic development of women and rural areas, we have to encourage this novel innovative approach; the micro-finance says Laxmi R. Kulshrestha (2000).

Impact of Group Approach

The impact of economic development of women on social front could be assessed mainly in terms of improvement in economic, literacy level, health, quality of life and standard of living. "Having gained economic empowerment, the women are not only able to keep social evils - like drinking and dowry - at bay. Also involved in planting trees in common areas and mass mobilization programme for forest conservation" (HINDU, May 7, 2000). Empowerment of poor, particularly approach and social mobilization are the possible process for eradicating poverty. Poverty can be effectively eradicated only when the poor start contributing to the growth process through their active involvement. Voluntary organization, community-based self-help groups and local governmental organizations have a substantial role to play (Sivasubramanian, 1999).

Women are critical actors in the process of moving their families out of poverty. According to Agarwal, Deepti (2001), women need to be viewed not as beneficiaries but as active participants in the process of development and change. The group approach to poverty alleviation implies strengthening of collective self help capacities at the local level to enable the poor to plan, manage and monitor their access to assets more in line with their needs and views. Empowerment of women can be effectively achieved if poor women could organize into groups – for community participation as well as for assertion of their rights in various services related to their economic and social well being. Simultaneously micro-credit and SHGs are also key elements for the empowerment of the rural women and help them to improve their living conditions and acquire small capital assets. A systematic strategy seeking to change societal attitudes for women, improve women's self-perception, create an enabling policy, institutional and legal environment and faster economic empowerment through mobilization, thrift, easy credit, up gradation of services and improved income generation opportunities are essential for emancipation of women. Satya Sundaram (2001) opines organizing the poor is crucial for their upliftment. They do not have crucial inputs like credit; it is here the empowerment of women assumes importance. SHGs have emerged, in order to help the rural poor particularly women, in securing inputs like credit and other services.

The group leader Ms. T. Katchchyani says "before SHG was formed the people of the village were perpetually in debt. They borrowed small sums needed for unexpected expenditure like repair of boats and purchase of new nets. The people did not know what 'saving' meant". The SHG helped members to develop financial discipline and empowered them to identify the problems they were facing and find solutions. SHGs have also increased women participation in village gram sabhas (HINDU November 12, 1999). It is here the importance of the women and their potentiality are exhibited, where a few women together are rewriting their fate. Women power is known when she participates in all development matters.

Participation in SHG has emboldened women financially and mentally has set to the opening of closed minds and improving the quality of life and their social status.

Factors that affect empowerment of women are; education, training, conscious-raising campaigns and group approach and self-employment training are very affective means. Self-Help group model of self-employment generation seems to be a workable model. Initially, the members will start income generating activities with the help of bank finance; however, gradually they will become self-reliant in financing and future growth. Women's economic development is synonymous with the achievement of equality and equal minded-ness in society. Women's economic development will result in traditional female values being more respected in the society.

Conclusion

Women empowerment and gender equality is globally recognised as a key element to achieve progress in all areas. It is one of the, third listed goal mentioned among the eight identified Millennium Development Goals (2000). It is observed that women are often in situations of extreme poverty, which are further aggravated by household and social discrimination. Therefore economic policies micro and macro alike, and poverty eradication programmes will have to specially address the needs and solve the problem of such women. Equal access to education for women and girls has to be ensured, and special measures have to be taken to eliminate discrimination, universalise education, eradicate illiteracy, create a gender-sensitive educational system, increase enrolment and retention rates of girls and improve the quality of education to facilitate life-long learning as well as development of occupation/vocation/technical skills by women.

The economic development, of women lead to benefits not only to the individual woman and women groups but also for the family and community as a whole through collective action for development. They assume the role of decision makers in major aspects of the family and village. The informal groups of women significantly improve women's participation both from economic and social aspects. Hence, women have to be encouraged to participate in country's development process itself. It is not just an ideal for a welfare state but imperative for the growth of an economy. There is growing emphasis on human resource development on one hand, several economic variables like income, employment and health status etc. on the other.

Women need to be viewed not as beneficiaries but as active participants in the process of development and change. Women are critical actors in the process of moving their families out of poverty. Empowerment of women can be effectively achieved if poor women could organize into groups for community participation as well as for assertion of their rights in various services related to their economic and social well-being. Empowerment is a multidimensional process, which enables an individual to realize his/her full identity and power in all spheres of life. The empowerment process begins with and is supported by the economic independence, which implies access to, and control over productive resources, knowledge and awareness, self-image autonomy and decision-making power inside and outside the home. In the present scenario, women in general and rural women live in rural areas and that they are relatively more neglected and dis-empowered compared to their male counterparts.

References

Agarwal, Deepti (2001), "Empowerment of Rural Women in India", *Social Welfare*, Vol. 48, No. 4, July.

Bhagyalakshmi, J. (2004), "Women's Empowerment: Miles to Go", *Yojana*, Vol. 48, August.

Doodkey, M.D. (1999), "Sustaining Rural Women", *Social Welfare*, Vol. 45, No. 12.

Gurumoorthy, T.R. (2000), "Self Help Groups Empower Rural Women", *Kurukshetra*, Vol. 48, No. 5, February.

Laxmi R. Kulshrestha (2000), "Micro Finance: The New Development Paradigm for Poor Rural Women", *Kurukshetra*, Vol. 49, No. 2, November.

Laxmi R. Kulshrestha; Archana Gupta (2001), "Self Help Groups: Innovations in Financing the Poor", *Kurukshetra,* Vol. 50, No. 1, Nov.

Murugan Dr. K.R. & Dr. B. Dharmalingam (2000), "Self Help Groups–New Women's Movement in Tamil Nadu", *Social Welfare,* Vol. 47, No. 5, August.

Nagayya D. (2000), "Micro Finance for Self Help Groups", *Kurukshetra,* Vol. 48, No. 11, August .

Pamecha, Suman & Ankita Khatik (2005), " Empowerment of Rural Women", *Social Action,* Vol. 55, No. 4, Oct-Dec.

Pattnaik Dr. B.K. (2001), "Gender Economic Empowerment and Rural Poverty Alleviation", *Kurukshetra,* Vol. 50, No. 2, Dec.

Peerzade, Sayed Afzal & Prema Parande (2005), "Economic Empowerment of Women: Theory and Practice", *Southern Economist,* Vol. 43, No. 21, March.

Puhazhendhi, V and B. Jayaraman (1999), "Increasing Women's Participation and Employment Generation among Rural Poor: An Approach through Informal Groups", *Indian Journal of Agriculture Economics,* Vol. 54, No. 3, July-Sept.

Satya Sundaran, I. (2001), "Self-Help Groups: Challenges and Opportunities", *Social Welfare,* Vol. 48, No. 4.

Shridharan, Damyanty (1997), "Encourage Self Help Groups", *Social Welfare,* Vol. 44, No. 7, October.

Sivasubramanian, M.N. (1999), "Credit Based Poverty Alleviation Programme: Innovative Approach", *Kurukshetra,* Vol. 48, No. 2.

Sooryamoorthy, R. (2005), "Microfinance and Women SHGs in Kerala: Loans for Members or Others", *Social Action,* Vol. 55, No. 1, Jan-Mar.

Sudan, Falendra K. (2005), "Empowering Rural Women through Micro Enterprise Development" *Social Change and Development,* Vol. 3, July.

Suguna B. (2001), "Women's Empowerment: Concept and Frame Work", *Social Welfare,* Vol.48, No. 9, December .

Sundari, Dr. S. and Dr. N. Geeta (2000), "Poverty, Credit and Micro Enterprises: A Gender Study", *Kurukshetra,* Vol. 49, No. 2, November.

Sunny, Dolly (2005), "Issues Confronting Women in the Changed Economic Scenario: Challenges and Tasks Ahead", *Southern Economist,* Vol. 43, No. 21, March.

Tripathy, Trilochan (2005), "Microenterprise: A Step towards Rural Women Empowerment", *ICFAI Journal of Agriculture Economics,* Vol.11, No. 4, October.

V.M. Rao (2002), "Women Self Help Groups: Profiles from Andhra Pradesh & Karnataka", *Kurukshetra,* Vol. 50, No. 6, April.

Venkataramana. M, D. Sunder Raj (2006), "Empowering Women through Group Approach" article communicated to edited book for publication.

----- (2000), "Full Credit for the Women", T*he Hindu,* May 7, .

-----(2000), "Self-Help Groups in Orissa transform Tribals" Living Standards, *The Hindu,* October 13.

CHAPTER-18

Empowering Women for Economic Development

M. Syamala

"Education is a gateway for an empowerment of woman and to make them useful citizens and enhance their personality".

In the recent years, empowerment of women has become a central issue which determines the status of women in the society. Empowerment is a process and not an event. Empowerment of women covers aspects such as women's role in the family, society, control over the resources etc. Traditionally women in India were suppressed, but now the time has changed, they are proving their capabilities in all walks of life. They are working and proving themselves equal in par with the men. In the present world empowering women socially, politically, economically has become the need of the hour. Abolition of gender discrimination in all walks of life, encouraging the participation of women in all fields of life, encouraging women in participating in policy and decision making at domestic as well as public levels are some of the dimensions of empowering women.

The history of women is neither linear nor organized. The history of women is an integral part of the civilization. It is closely related to the culture, society, state and with the lives of the people. No doubt women can be defined in various forms, but a good woman is the one who is sweet at talk, gentle in behavior, loving, caring and of course ever sacrificing. For a woman to achieve success in life education is essential. Women no longer are permitted to the four walls of the house. They have become important contributors in the economic development of the country. This article mainly highlights what is the position of the women in the modern society and what problems they are facing to make their stand. It also brings into light as how women are helpful in the economic development activities.

A few important areas which calls for empowerment of women in India are –

- Women and their participation in economic actives
- Women in political, economic, social and cultural activities
- Women and their education
- Women and their health
- Women in animal husbandry
- Women in organized sectors
- Women as entrepreneurs

Participation of Women

There is need to empower the women as for a long time they were suppressed. Empowerment of women means giving them privilege to the women in economical, social, political and cultural areas. They must be encouraged to participate in all the sectors of the society. Women constitute half of the population and their development reflects the progress of the society. The status of the women in the society is measured in terms of the level of income, employment, education, health as well as role played by them in family, community and the society. Major percentage of women is found in the agriculture, unorganized small industrial units or home based workers or home based small scale work units.

According to the NSS figures in 1991 only 14.1% of women were employed. Of this 6.60 percent were in government jobs.

Women labour force in rural area is 33.1 percent and 16.2 percent in urban areas. 42.8 percent of women undertake household chores. According to the ILO report it is found that women work more hours than men but they earn comparatively less. Many programs and activities haven been done to uplift the income of women and provide them equal pay as men but they gave only lip service and not real service. The report of National Commission on Self- Employed women in India (1987) found that women are paid below subsistence level. Moreover, their employment is irregular, uncertain, seasonal and discretionary and characterized by malpractices in payment. Even through the Ninth plan has made on of its objective for empowerment of women nothing special could be done.

Women have to empower themselves both in ownership and management to develop the country economically especially in rural areas. If villages develop in India then whole country will develop. As India lives in villages. To empower women DRDA i.e. District Rural Development Agency was formed. 30% of loans were given to women under IRDP scheme. Women in general and rural women in particular have been excluded from governance despite their enormous social and economic contribution to the productive and reproductive spheres of their societies. The dichotomy of public and private created by the sexual division of labor that defines women's role in the private arena of the home and men's roles in the public arena has been instrumental in excluding women from politics which is seen as public realm thus a male preserve. With the increasing gender awareness created by women's movements, the artificial divide between public and private has been increasingly challenged across the globe. The assertion is that private and public spheres are interconnected, private matters such as sexuality, reproduction etc. are relevant for public sphere and public policies impacts on private matters, therefore, men and women's voices needs to be included in all decision-making processes in the public and private spheres.

Women constitute fifty percent of world population. No country in the world could truly claim itself democratic while keeping half of its female population out of decision making processes that directly impact on their lives. Women clearly have distinct perspectives on politics and governance. However, they have been historically excluded from the formal and informal governance structures and globally suffer from disadvantage in accessing opportunities, resources and power. They face socio-cultural economic and political barriers to enter in politics. The male domination and lack of democratic culture within political parties blocks women's entry in governance. In order to redress the gender gap in governance structures globally, women needs to be facilitated through affirmative action and measures to enter in governance structures co I isss. Their physical presence is a pre-condition for making a difference in governance. The reservation of 30% seats at the local government, regional or national level or at the party lists, recommended by CEDAW seems to be an effective strategy which has worked globally to narrow the gender gap in formal political structures. However, it is important to remember that women are not a homogenous group; they are also divided along the lines of class, religion, ethnicity, rural urban back ground. Therefore, quotas for women in governance structures should be cognizance of the difference among women and should be filled in a manner that provide equal opportunities to women belonging to different classes, rural and urban backgrounds.

The growing strength of the women's movement and their increasing assertion that women's political participation is a sine qua non for gender equality is a development that stands out. Achieving gender justice requires a strong gender focus in electoral, constitutional, legal and judicial frameworks and support to women to be actively involved in implementation at the national level. UNIFEM advocates for gender responsive legislation that create pathways for the empowerment of women and their organizations.

Education of Women

If a male member of the family is educated then only he is considered to be educated but if a women or the mother in the family is educated then it means the whole family is educated. Education is just like a key that opens the doors towards a developed life and developed nation. In 1958 the Government of India has appointed National Committee on Women's Education in order to recommend special measures to bridge the gap between the education of girls and boys at both primary and secondary level. National Policy on Education (NEP) 1986 has its main objective to remove illiteracy in women. The 1991 census show that women literacy in rural areas was 30.62 percent and that in urban areas was 60.05 percent. Women need to be taught how to efficiently utilize their time to raise their family income and quality of life. Vocational education that is-preparing toys, pickles, jams, jells, bags, knitting, tailoring, papad making, kitchen gardening, masala and candle making etc, with the locally available raw material are few major content areas for women. This process of "learning by doing and earning" would empower women not only with education but also with socially and economically useful productive work (SEUPW).

Health of Women

The physic and health of women is not as strong as the men. Though the mental stability is high but the body strength is comparatively less. The National Perspective Plan for Women (1988-2000) of Government of India has noted poor health of women due to synergistic effects of high level's of infections, malnutrition and uncontrolled fertility. Women are facing many health problems. Some of them are listed below -

- Low age of marriage leads to prolonged period of child bearing and rearing, which results in maternal mortality and morbidity. It is high in rural areas than in urban areas.
- Physical assaults like rape, burning, beating, hazards at work, etc.

- Malnutrition
- Because of poverty some rural women migrate to the urban areas and land up in sex trading, as a result become victims of sexually transmitted diseases which cannot be cured.
- They suffer from infections as they live in unhygienic conditions.

Healthy women can build up a healthy and wealthy nation. So, health of women must be upgraded to have a strong economy. Women must be empowered to take decisions about the number of children, use of family planning and other family based decisions. Further, the male members need to be accountable to the reproductive health care of women. Adequate women doctors must be posted in the hospitals to take care of the private health problems of the women. WHO expects that the maternal health care should ensure every expectant and nursing mother maintain good health, learn the art of child care, has normal delivery and bears healthy children.

Women's Participation in Politics

The Universal Declaration of Human Rights states that every one has the right to take part in the government of his or her country. In India the 1996 Lok Sabha has only 5.6% of women member (32 out of 544). But now it has increased only to 6% political empowerment of women does not imply just a right to vote silently but to discuss, share politics by knowing its pros and cons, thereby to influence policies of decision making. The 73rd & 74th constitutional amendments of India which introducede panchyat Raj Institution throughout the country and assured reservation of one third seats for women in panchyat of municipal bodies is a good example of women political empowerment at the grass root level. Not only is this, in parliament 30% of seats are to be reserved for the women. But the bill has not been passed. Women political leaders are needed to be legally empowered to deal with the physical and sexual abuse and curb the menace of wine and gambling.

Issues that need Attention

There are some issues that need some attention concerning the women empowerment. Women constitute the largest number among the literates, knowledge have- nots and under privileged of Indian society. Women are the back bone of the national development. The UNESCO report on "Women and the media" states: "the perspective of women reflected in the messages disseminated by the mass media express male concepts of women. The commercial produce message systems and symbols which create on structure prevailing images of social reality which show women as house wife, consumers and sex objects. Women in advertising are always young and attractive, they are frequently depicted as sexually objects, as in the home, and they are seldom shown as intelligent people. The mass media's role primarily re-enforce definitions and identities set in a frame work constructed for and by men."

Women in Animal Husbandry

The UN report laminated " Women constitute about half of the world's population, account for 60% of the working hours, contribute of course officially, up to 30 percent of labour force, yet receive only 10 percent of the income and own less than one percent of the world's property. In the same year a report was presented by the parliamentary committed on the status of women in India" Women are not weak but oppressed and powerless, not incapable but uninitiated, not inadequate but unacknowledged, unrecognized and rendered but helpless due to denial of opportunity, subjugation and suppression." Women were found to be solely responsible for the activities such as giving feed and water to the animals, clearing and bathing of animals, maintenance and cleaning of cattle shed, fodder collection, collection of cow dung and preparation cow dung cakes etc. Thy also participate in taking care of sick animals , care of pregnant animals, care of new born, milking and grazing of animals. Participation of women in selling of milk was found low. The level of involvement of women was quite low in breeding activities and sale and purchase of life stock and feed items. Women belonging to small farm holdings, lower caste with lower socio-economic status, with less education, with less material possessions, having less urban contact as well as having conservation values involve themselves more in animal husbandry activities.

Time spent on animal husbandry activities by women vary from 2-5 hours per day. Although the contribution of women in animal husbandry sector is quite enormous, they have not been actively involved in the main stream of development and there is hardly any appreciation and recognition of their extensive contribution. Training of women in animal husbandry was found to be totally neglected aspect. Cooperative sector show that the women make up hardly 17 percent of the total countrywide membership and constitute less than 3 percent of the dairy cooperative societies board members.

Participation of Women in Industrial Activities

To strengthen their efforts towards self-employment, the Commission motivated them and formed them into a co-operative Society under the banner "Creative Women Textile Co-operative Society" with 26 members. With the guidance of the Commission these young entrepreneurs, under their banner of Creative Women Textile Co-operative Society, have participated in Exhibitions organized by other prestigious institutions viz., 1. Lepakshi Handicrafts on the Necklace road; 2. in the exhibition organized by Rural Development Department, Government of India at Pingali Venkatarama Reddi Hall near Tank-bund. On their own efforts, they organised a Textile Products Exhibition-cum sale as Business Mela inviting other women entrepreneurs as well, at T.T.D. Kalyana Mandapam, Himayathnagar, Hyderabad, from 4-8-2000 to 8-8-2000.

Several women, though trained in different crafts and vocational training are not able to find a footing in commercial market. Women trained in Fashion Technology and Dress Designing and Fabric Printing are one such category. By virtue of their training in these vocational courses, in their efforts for self-employment, these women have been designing textile products and selling them in a limited market, namely to their neighbors, relatives and friends. Thus they were not having any access to the wider concept of marketing. In order to display their creative talents and to provide exposure to them and to the society and access to the marketing concept and to build up self-confidence in them, the Commission has organized an Exhibition-cum-sale of their products exclusively designed by them. This concept of Exhibition-cum-sale was very well received and they made good business and developed self confidence in themselves.

The contribution of women in Khadi village industries is depicted in a table below-

Table 1
Women's Participation in KVI Activities

Industry	*Activity*	*Women's% in KVI Employment*
Cotton khadi	spinning	7.98
Muslin Khadi	spinning	0.17
Silk Khadi	spinning	0.30
Wollen Khadi	spinning	1.38
Leathers	Embroidery works	0.51
Other village industries	Papad, agarbathi, bamboo and cane work etc.	11.90
Total		22.24

KVI annual report 1999.

Participation of Women as Entrepreneur

Entrepreneurship is a more suitable profession for women than regular employment in any sector of the society as they have to play dual role. Entrepreneur has to either have or develop aptitude towards innovation, organization, creation of wealth and risk taking. The risks here are financial, psychological, social and managerial for an entrepreneur. The risks are even more for the woman entrepreneur as she has to work in a male dominated area. A large number of Indian women are slowly emerging out of a system that had oppressed and exploited for centuries. Women are becoming self reliant in many fields. They are the vehicles of silent socio-economic revolution. As per the census of India 2001, statistics show that out of the total of 32.62 crores of economically active female population, only 6.03 crores, that is, almost 18.5 percent are employed, where as out of 34.97 crores of economically active males, 23.63 crores, that is, 67.6 percent are employed in paid jobs. The number of women job seekers are the employment exchanges rose from 36.64 lakhs in 1988 to 5.9 million in 1995 and now it has increased to 9.39 million in the recent past. Women play a crucial role in all walks of life and they contribute to the national economy both for GNP and GDP. The women participation rate in the productive economic activities has increased from 22.73 in 1991 to 28.6 in 2001. Women work force in the service sector is very meager when compared to the total employable population of women. Hence it is necessary to encourage and guide women to organize business and services in large number. When a survey was done as to why many women want to become entrepreneur, the answer was based on fine reasons they are-

- Job frustration
- Low income
- Desire to be independent
- Desire to have self employment
- To satisfy their ambition and interest

Areas which are very favourable for the women to work are–tailoring, embroidery, designing, papad, pickle making, beauty parlors, health clubs, various shops, weaving, knitting, crocheting, boutiques, advertising, industrial activities, engineering and electronics, trading, construction, furniture etc. Though they are many areas for them to work they find many constraints like -Social prejudice, low education, lack of awareness, technological constraints, personal constraints, socio-psycho constraints, lack of infrastructure, lack of planning, lack of information, lack of subsidies, etc. Many steps have been taken to train women in this field. Many schemes and training programmes were introduced to encourage women entrepreneurs. Some of them are IRDP, TRYSEM, SEP, STEP, DWC, etc. A study was made in Andhra Pradesh for

200 women to find as how many of them from various age groups were involved in various productive activities. The following table shows the age groups of the women entrepreneurs.

Table 2
Age group of Women Entrepreneurs

Age Group	*No. of Women Entrepreneurs*
20-24	20
25-29	31
30-34	39
35-39	63
40-44	21
45-49	19
50 and above	10
Total	200

It is found from the table that the age group of 35-39 is maximum in various productive activities and the least we find in the age group of above 50 years. Out of these 200 women 164 were married, 19 were widows, 13 were divorced and 8 unmarried. Many of them were encouraged by–village leaders, husbands, family, friends, welfare institutions. Only 6.3 percent of women were self motivated among them.

Conclusion

It is very difficult to make any conclusion regarding this topic. But the fact is that now women are in very field of life. They are at par with the men. They are trying to make their existence in this male dominating world. Many of them are encouraged uplifted by the men folk. The women empowerment will definitely lead to economic development and well being of not only a family, village, city state but the whole nation.

References

Akhouri, M.M.P. (1990), "Entrepreneurship for Women in India", NIESBUD, New Delhi.

Social Welfare, Vol. 38, No.2, May 1991

Social Welfare, Vol. 33, No.12, March 1987

Social Welfare, Vol. 52, No6, September 2005

Social Welfare, Vol. 45, No.12, March 1999

Social Welfare, various other volumes of 2002 and 2005

Yojana 2003 and 2005

Kurshetra 2006 , KVI annual report 1999.

CHAPTER-19

Problems of Women Entrepreneurship in India

L.K. Mohana Rao

Introduction

Women community though equal to men in population, is subject to a lot of deprivations even in this modern sophisticated world. Women are still treated as the second rate citizen or subordinate to men in all major fields of life i.e., social, economic and political. Though various efforts are being made to improve the status of women, women folk could not make maximum use of them and hence remained backward. In almost all countries, the Governments are providing special provisions for women's development and efforts are being made to extract maximum use of women's talent. It has been clear for decades that women in many parts of the world make key contributions in areas of development such as agriculture, health, education, water resources management etc.

In India, the shift from "welfare" to "development" of women took place in the Sixth Five Year Plan (1980-85). The Eighth Five-Year Plan (1992-97) promised to ensure that the benefits of development from different sectors do not bypass women. The Rashtriiya Mahila Kosh was set up in 1993 to meet the credit needs of the poor and the assetgless women. The

Ninth Five-Year Plan (1997-2002) made two significant changes in the strategy of planning for women. Firstly, "empowerment of women" became a primary objective and secondly, the plan attempted "convergence of existing services" available in both women-specific and women related sectors. The Tenth Five-Year Plan (2002-2007) has made a major commitment towards "empowering women as the agent of socio-economic change and development". Based on the recommendation of National Policy for Empowerment of Women, the Tenth Five-Year Plan suggests a three- fold strategy for empowering women, through social empowerment, economic empowerment and gender justice.

The Concept of Entrepreneurship

Entrepreneurship is the creative and innovative response to the environment, which can take place in variety of fields of social endeavour-business, industry, Agriculture, Education, Social work and the like and it is the potent limiting factor in economic development.

It is an act of assuming risk of business ownership. In fact, it is the mental urge to take risk in the face of uncertainties and an initiation and capacity of seeing things in a way afterwards proves to be true. And it is an individual set-up of managing things in a proper manner. It is multidimensional encompassing financial, managerial and functional aspects.

Empowerment of Women

In India, females head only 10 per cent of the total households and the ownership of land and other properties are mainly in the name of the male members of the family. Hence, women have hardly any ownership of resources and autonomy to take decision.

However, the participation of women in income generating activities of the family has been increasing over time. Female work participation not only increases their family income but also brings economic independence among women in the household. This helps them to participate more effectively in intra-household decision-making and have better access to information. Moreover, where women are economically active, female children are perceived as potential wage earners and they receive a higher share of household resources than where women are economically unproductive. But female work participation alone cannot ensure true economic empowerment as the ownership of resources may still lie in the hands of the male members. Thus, female work participation rate is a necessary condition but is not a sufficient condition for economic empowerment of women. Economic empowerment of women is possible only when women have full autonomy to spend their income and also control resources.

Entrepreneurship development among women can be considered a possible approach to economic empowerment of women. A woman as an entrepreneur is economically more powerful than as a mere worker because ownership not only confers control over assets (and liabilities) but also gives her the freedom to take decisions. This will also uplift her social status significantly. Through entrepreneurship development a woman will not only generate income for herself but also will generate employment for other women in the locality. This will act as an employment in the women sector.

Women Entrepreneur

In India, very few women entrepreneurs are in the big enterprises. They are mainly concentrated in the Small Scale Sectors (SSIs).

In the SSI sector the participation of women can be classified into three types.

- Women as the owners of enterprises.
- Women as managers of enterprises, and
- Women as employees.

With regard to ownership an SSI managed by one or more women entrepreneurs in propriety concerns or in which she/ they individually or jointly have a share capital of not less than 51 per cent as partners/shareholders/Directors of private Limited Company/Member of cooperative Society is called a women enterprise.

The share of the units managed by women in terms of employment was 7.14. The employment generated per Rs. one lakh investment is the units managed by women was 2.49.

Women in India are still less likely to start a new business than men, although the gap seems to be declining. The share of female entrepreneurs (10 per cent) is still significantly low when compared to their work participation rate (25.7 per cent). Hence, it is very important to know the impediment to growth of women entrepreneurship.

Women Entrepreneurship: Indian Scenario

Traditionally, it was believed that women are physically and mentally weak and, hence, they are not fit for hard, hazardous and risky tasks. But with the increasing empowerment of women in the world, now no job, profession or enterprise is such which women cannot undertake. Contrary to it, it can be observed that in oriental societies the women are born-risk seekers. They grow up with the feeling of management of risk and adjustment/adaptation with the changing environment.

Women entrepreneurship is the process where women take lead and organise a business or industry and provide employment opportunities to others. Though women entrepreneurship is a recent phenomenon in India, which came into prominence in late 1970's, now we see that more and more women are venturing as entrepreneurs in all kinds of business and economic activities and service sector. Though at the initial stage women entrepreneurship developed only at urban areas, lately it has extended its wings to rural and semi-urban areas too.

Women industries mainly fall into informal sector where less than 10 persons with or without power and less than than 20 persons without power are engaged and they will be of labour intensive and rely on indigeneous resources, family ownership and only small scale skills are sufficient. Though earlier women concentrated much on traditional activities, due to the spread of education, favourable government policies towards development of women entrepreneurship, women have changed their attitudes and diverted towards non-traditional activities too. They show favourable response to changing situations and get adjusted to them and have improved their position.

The Government and Non-Government organizations are giving more prominence to promote self-employment among women and build women entrepreneurship. Special financial assistance is provided and training programmes are organized for women to start their ventures.

Work Force Participation Rate (WFPR) in India

The Work Force Participation Rate (WFPR), also called Labour Force Participation Rate (LFPR) is the percentage of working population to total population of a country. It is an important factor which affects production, saving and capital formation. It helps in analysing the occupational structure of a country and thus its level of employment. WFPR depends up on the age and sex structure of the population, age of marriage, average size of family, education, health, attitude to work, availability of work, etc. The work force participation rates in India for the Census years 1901 to 2001 are shown in Table-1. WFPR in the pre-independence period from 1901-31 was higher than in the post-independence period from 1951-91, except for the Census year 1961. The reason being the use of different definition of the 'work force' in the censuses. In the pre-independence census, main workers were lumped with unpaid family workers. But in the 1951 Census, unpaid family workers were excluded from the main workers. That is why the WFPR in 1951 was 39.1 per cent as compared to more than 43 per cent in the pre-independence years (1901-1931). Again in 1961, WFPR increased to 43 per cent because persons whose main activity was not economic were included in the main workers. WFPR declined to 34.2 per cent in 1971 because persons engaged in part time activities were excluded from the category of the main workers. But since the Census of 1981, WFPR had risen to 36.7 per cent in1981 to 37.7 per cent in 1991 and to 39.3 per cent in 2001. This has been due to the adoption of a rigorous of "worker" in terms of main workers and marginal workers.

In the case of WFPR by sex, it had been much higher for males as compared to females. This is because of the social status of women. They are generally not allowed to undertake productive work outside home. But since 1971, their work participation rate has been on the increase. It rose from 14.2 per cent in 1971 to 25.7 per cent in 2001. This is due to increasing literacy and declining birth rate. Now more and more women are entering the industrial and service sectors. With urbanisation and expansion of dairy and poultry farming, fisheries, horticulture, etc., more women are participating in such activities. On the other hand, the work participation rate for men declined from 52.7 per cent in 1971 to 51.9 per cent in 2001. This again shows that more women are taking the place of men in productive activities.

Table 1

Gender-Wise Work Force Participation Rate in India: 1901-2001

(in Percentage)

Year	*Females*	*Males*	*Persons*
1901	31.1	61.1	46.6
1911	33.7	61.9	48.1
1921	32.7	60.5	46.9
1931	27.6	58.3	43.3
1951	23.3	54.0	39.1
1961	28.0	57.1	43.0
1971	14.2	52.7	34.2
1981	19.7	52.6	36.7
1991	22.7	51.6	37.7
2001	25.7	51.9	39.3

Source: Census Reports for various years.

Employment of Women

Women contribute greatly to the economy. They are pioneers in various professions. Women are working in different sectors of the economy as agricultural labourers, road construction workers, domestic helpers, petty crafts women, self-employed women, doctors, engineers, lecturers and white collared executives.

Employment of women is an index of their status in society. According to census data the work participation rate of women is steadily arising from 14.22 per cent in 1971 to 19.67 per cent in 1981. The rise in work participation of women has been even steeper from 37.81 lakhs in 1991 to 47.74 lakhs in 1998. Table-2 shows male and female work force in public and private sectors.

The U N Statistics on women indicate that a majority of the female work force is involved in unpaid family work. Only a few of them work as employees, very few were self-employed or employers. An overall representation of women in the labour force still remains low. It reflects a higher capacity of the population. Globalisation and liberalization and privatization have adverse effect on women employment. They are loosing employment due to technological changes, substitution of women labour and deskilling of women's work.

Table 2
Employment of Women in Organized Public and Private Sectors: 1971-2001

	Public Sector		*Private Sector*		*Total*	
Year	*Male*	*Female*	*Male*	*Female*	*Male*	*Female*
1971	98.70	8.60	56.80	10.80	155.50	19.30
1981	139.80	14.90	61.00	12.90	200.50	27.93
1991	167.10	23.40	62.40	14.30	229.50	37.81
1997	168.66	27.28	67.77	19.09	236.08	46.37
1999	166.04	52.11	66.80	20.18	232.84	48.29
2000	164.57	28.57	65.80	20.66	230.37	49.23
2001	162.79	28.59	65.62	20.90	228.40	49.49

Source: Ministry of Labour, (DGE&T).

Major Areas of Women Entrepreneurship

Agriculture, Horticulture, Sericulture, Dairying and Animal Husbandry, Fisheries, Home based industries like handicrafts, Beedi Industry, Agrbati making, Tailoring and Garment industry, Pottery and Black smithy industry, Doll making, fancy items, bee keeping, Jewellery, Beauty Parlour, Printing, Textiles. Electronics chemicals, food processing, nursery and baby crèche centers, Stationary etc.

Thus women entrepreneurs can take a lead in both un-organized and organized sectors.

Major Problems of Women Entrepreneur

In India women entrepreneurship is facing so many problems. The major problems are:

- *Family Discouragement:* As women in India have to work amidst social taboos, restrictions etc., they are not supported much to undertake entrepreneurship by their family members.
- *Social Barriers:* Women entrepreneurs in India are always seen with suspicious eyes, particularly in rural areas, they face more social barriers.
- *Caste and Religion:* Though India is a secular country, in practice, castes and religious systems dominate with one another and it hinders women entrepreneurs.
- *Lack of Self-Confidence and Risk bearing Capacity:* Women lack self–confidence and always feel that they may not be successful and hence hesitate to take risks.
- *Psychological Factors:* Always woman feel that she is 'women' and less efficient than man and hesitates to take risks. As she has to play a dual role if she is employed or engaged in work. She has to strive hard to balance her family life with care and hence feels better to be housewife.
- *Lack of Practical Knowledge:* Though women may be educated and have qualified knowledge, she lacks practical knowledge and hence hesitates to establish her own venture.
- *Problem of Finance:* Women entrepreneurs lack property in their own name and hence banks and financial institutions may hesitate to finance women based projects.
- *Problem of Marketing:* As generally women entrepreneurs will have small-scale business they have to strive hard to sell their products in the modern competitive world. Their marketing knowledge will be less and lack marketing skills as compared to men.

- *Problems of Middlemen:* Women entrepreneurs have to face the problems of middlemen more, as they generally depend, more on them. Their margin of profit will be more and hence cause for higher selling price, which affects consumer's attraction towards women's products.
- *Lack of Information:* Women entrepreneurs' lack knowledge of availability of raw materials, financial facilities and Government help and subsidy etc.; they lack knowledge of advanced technology also and hence cannot widen their markets.

Hence, it becomes necessary for the society and Government to find remedies for the problems of women entrepreneurship. Already the Central and State Governments and non-governments organizations have taken so many steps to solve the problems of women entrepreneurs, yet they have to provide special incentives and subsidy. As entrepreneurship opportunities will be more in small and medium scale industries, the sector should be given prominence and proper marketing strategy of such products should be planned and implemented, which will give scope for women entrepreneurs. If Indian women's talent will be utilized properly, one day India will become an ideal country to others.

References

Birley, S. (1989), "Female Entrepreneurs: Are they Really any Different", *Journal of Small Business Management,* 27 (1), pp.32-37.

Garg, R.B.L. (2004), "Women Entrepreneurs: Problems and Prospects", *Social Welfare,* 50 (12), March, pp.16-18.

Khurana, I.R. (1988), "Strategy for Rural Development", *Khadi Gram Udyog,* 34 (8), pp.335-344.

Mohiuddin, A. (1987): "Entrepreneurship in Rural Women", *Kurukshetra,* 35 (12), pp.22-25.

Nelson, R.E.(1985), *Entrepreneurship and Self Employment Training,* Asian Development Bank, Manila.

Rao, S.K. (1976), Entrepreneur Development in India- Is Achievement Training the Answer, *Laghu Udyog,* 4. pp. 9-12.

Sinha, Poonam (2003), "Women Entrepreneurship in the North East India: Motivation, Social Support and Constraints", *Indian Journal of Industrial Relations,* 28 (4), April, pp. 425-41.

Sundaram, I. Satya. (2004), "Encouraging Women's Entrepreneurship", *Social Welfare,* 50 (12), March, pp.15-19.

Vidyu Lata. (1990), *Developing Rural Women,* Discovery Publishing House, New Delhi.

Vitz, M.D. (1987), *Women Entrepreneurs in India,* Mittal Publications, New Delhi.

CHAPTER-20

Micro Finance Towards Empowerment of Rural Women: A Study of Tekkali Mandal in Srikakulam District of Andhra Pradesh

M. Sundara Rao, D. Pulla Rao

Introduction

In India over the centuries, a very large number of women in the rural regions, have been carrying the burden of poverty, ignorance, outmoded customs and traditional women have been laying down and surrendering all their comforts for the welfare of the children. Rather than rural men, the rural women performs a hope of activities and these activities range from child rearing to house hold affairs and farm operations. In terms of economics benefits many of these activities are not visible and flexible, even then rural women pay a crucial role in the rural economy. To leave about the extent of knowledge, the women participation can be solicited in the Indian economy. Such activities are so needed to the rural life and the women. Collecting fuel and fodder gathering seed from forests, fetching drinking water, cooking for the house hold, child rearing, a host of household and form operation have been performed by women because of the traditions, customs and usage which have insisted the women to assume responsibility and compared men, these are all markedly different.

Against this background the Indian Government have been vigorously working for the empowerment of women in general, rural women in particular by launching various developmental programmes of which Development of Women and Children in Rural Area (DWCRA) is prominent one. Therefore an attempt has been made to look through the impact of the above said scheme on alleviation of poverty of rural women. One such effort is the DWCRA scheme which was introduced in 1982 as a subcomponent of IRDP to accelerate the integration of women with the rural development programmes. The primary objectives of the DWCRA scheme is to focus attention on the women members of rural families below the poverty line with a view to providing them with opportunities of self employment as sustained. The SHG programme in India is initially introduced in 50 selected districts. Later, it was extended to more districts in a phased manner.

In this regard the study of Venkata Ramana, M. (1995) comparatively studied the functioning and performance of DWCRA groups, by way of observing two successful groups and failed groups. Hemalatha Prasad, C. (1995) has carefully examined the socio-economic factors that make a DWCRA group successful in a case study undertaken in Gurgoan Dist. of Haryana. Manimekala and Rajeswari (2000) examined the empowerment of women through SHGs in rural micro enterprises in Tiruchinapalli district of Tamil Nadu.

Based on both primary and secondary data, Datta and Raman (2001) studies SHGs under Rastriya Seva samithi (RASS) at Tirupati. From these studies it is revealed that the Self Help Groups (SHGs) are viable alternatives to achieve the objectives of rural development and to get community participation in all the rural development programmes. SHG is a viable organisation set up to disburse micro credit to the rural women for the purpose of making them enterprising women and encouraging them to enter into entrepreneurial activities. The women led SHG and DWCRA have successfully demonstrated how to mobilise and mange thrift, appraise credit needs, maintain linkages with the bank and enforce financial self-discipline.

These studies also reveal that an in depth analysis of DWCRA scheme is very essential to find out whether such programme is contributing for women enlistment economically and socially. There is also a need to identify the loopholes in the scheme for making them operationally successful. The above analysis shows that SHG is on of the important programme to rural women and it is a boon to the rural women-folk. The studies in the context of working patterns of SHGs in Srikakulam district are very few. On the other side the earlier studies have more gaps and not covered the determinants of productive activities, various independent and appropriate statistical tools to analyze the study. The need for rural development programmes specifically for the development of rural women is much imperative in a backward region like Srikakulam District. Hence an attempt is made in this study to evaluate the SHG programme in Tekkali Mandal of Srikakulam District.

Methodology

This study is based on both primary as well as secondary date sources. The Tekkali mandal of Srikakulam district is selected for the study because it is one of the most backward areas in the state. The selected mandal has high poverty, lowest female literacy rate, high birth and infant mortality rates, poor health status and large socially disadvantaged sections of population (SC, ST& BC). Thus the Tekkali mandal is a typical case for analyzing the social dynamic operating against the emancipation of women through social mobilization and economic support and self-employment programmes. Secondary data on status of SHG programme in the Tekkali mandal have been collected from annual reports of IRDP, district year books published by Chief Planning Officer and women and child development offices, Srikakulam. T h e study is limited to Tekkali mandal of Srikakulam district of Andhra Pradesh.

To select the sample Multi Stage Random Sampling technique is applied in sample selection. The process of selection involves stage-I selection of village, stage-II selection of Self Help Groups and stage-III selection house hold. In stage-I from Tekkali mandal three villages Ravi Valasa, Lingala Valasa and Seetha Puram selected. At stage -II from each village 6 SHGs are selected. At stage-III from each selected SHG ten member house holds are selected. Totally 18 SHGs from Tekkali mandal are selected for evaluating the functioning of SHGs at group levels. For purpose of studying the impact of SHG on socio economic conditions of the SHG members 10 members from each SHG, a total of 180 households are selected by following the Multi stage, Probability Proportionate Sampling (PPS). Data was ascertained from each selected SHG member with the help of a structured questionnaire by Personal Interview method.

Functioning of Selected SHGs

The center and state Governments have been implementing the DWCRA scheme with a sacred objective of alleviating the poverty among downtrodden sections and women section of the society. In this study an attempt has been made to evaluate the performance of DWCRA scheme. More specifically an attempt has been made to study to what extent the scheme is helpful to increase the awareness of the rural women in the Tekkali mandal of Srikakulam district.

SHGs Participation in Developmental Activities

At the outset to assess the functioning of selected SHGs important aspects like participation of SHG members in various developmental activities, the level of, matching/grant/revolving fund drawn and amount fertilization particulars, amount repaid by the SHG members in the study area have been discussed. Along with thrift, the SHG/DWCRA has been giving priority to health, family welfare, literacy, and social awareness activities like convergence activities as a basic determinant of the families' economic development and welfare. These activities also recognized by SHGs of Tekkali mandal in Srikakulam District. Table 1 shows the active role played by SHG members in various developmental activities like participation in Mahila Mandal meetings, craft centers, thrift movement, health and family camp, prohibition literacy complain, and Pallebata etc. in the study area.

Table 1
SHG Members' Participation In Developmental Activities

Topic	*R.Valasa*	*L.Valasa*	*S.Puram*	*Total*
Mahila mandal activities	51(65.00)	43(71.67)	30(50.0)	124(68.89)
Craft centre	30(50.0)	14(23.33)	8(13.33)	52(28.89)
Health and family welfare campaign camp	55(91.67)	26(43.33)	14(23.33)	85(47.22)
Literacy campaign	50(83.33)	30(50.0)	24(40.0)	104(57.78)
Thrift	60(100.0)	44(73.33)	32(55.67)	132(73.33)
Praja padam/Pallebata	40(66.67)	30(50.0)	21(35.0)	81(45.00)
Total	60	60	60	180

Note: figures in the parenthesis are percentage to column total

It is found from the Table 1 that, a majority of respondents participated in thrift (73.33 percent), family welfare and health campaign and Mahila mandal activities (68.69 %), Prajapadam, pallebata (45%) and literacy aspects (57.78 %) respectively. Among the three villages SHGs the proportion is relatively higher in Ravi Valasa groups ranging from 65 per cent in Mahila Mandal and in thrift (100 %). In the case of Lingala Valasa groups the selected SHG members ranging from 23.33 per cent in literacy aspects and 73.33 per cent in thrift. Across the Seetha Puram groups they are ranging from craft centers (13.33 %) and in thrift (53.32 %). It is observed from the table that, the thrift activities have occupied a good position in all aspects of SHGs. Thrift concepts linked with bank linkage and bank loans. So it may be a reason behind well performance of the SHG members in thrift activities rather than in other activities. As a whole it is observed that, a major number of the respondents have participated in village development activities for the free of cost and they consist of 61.17 per cent of the total respondent. It is so because everybody wants to keep his/her village in a good position. It may not be continues process. In the leisure time every one ready to participate in the village development programme.

SHGs Participation in Different Activities

The selected SHG members of all the selected three villages participating in different programmes. The information relating to their participation in different activities and programmes are presented in Table 2.

Table 2
SHG Members Participation in Different Programmes

Topic	*R.Valasa*	*L.Valasa*	*S.Puram*	*Total*
Mahila mandal activities	50(83.33)	20(33.33)	8(8.87)	78(43.33)
Thrift	60(100.0)	45(75.0)	28(46.67)	133(73.89)
Family planning	52(86.87)	38(63.33)	18(30.0)	108(60.00)
Health aspects	58(96.97)	30(50.0)	14(23.33)	102(56.67)
Literacy aspects	42(70.0)	23(38.33)	13(21.67)	78(43.33)
Praja padam/Pallebata	40(66.67)	29(48.33)	19(31.67)	88(48.89)
Total	60	60	60	180

Note: Figures in the parenthesis are percentage to column total

From the Table 2 it can be noticed that, the selected SHG members are participating in the discussion on various developmental aspects to be organized by them. Among the SHG members, majority of respondents discussed about thrift (73.89 percent), followed by family planning and health (60 percent), participating in the programmes like pallebata to place their problems before the administration (48.89 percent) ,literacy aspects (43.33 percent) and Mahila Mandal activities (43.33 percent). From the above table it is revealed that the Self Help Groups (SHGs) are viable alternatives to achieve the objectives of rural development and to get community participation in all the rural development programmes.

Financial Assistance Received by Selected SHGs from Different Sources

SHG is a viable organisation set up to disburse micro credit to the rural women for the purpose of making them enterprising women and encouraging them to enter into entrepreneurial activities. The women led SHG and DWCRA have successfully demonstrated how to mobilize and manage thrift, appraise credit needs, maintain linkages with the bank and enforce financial self-discipline. The theoretical aspects of protection are necessary to built the sector or at gross root level. In this regard an attempt is made to analyze the revolving fund utilization sanctioned by Government .through DRDA. Matching/revolving fund is the amount provided by Government as the simple payment worth of Rs. 10,000 to 15,000 per group. The amount to be drawn for two purposes viz. economic or productive purpose and unproductive purpose or daily transaction. The SHGs are also attempt to the demand for money for the above purposes. But they are living in poor economic conditions. Hence they may depend on financial support which they were created them selves called Self-Help Groups fund (SGHGR). These fund may includes, matching grant, SHG Fund, financial recovery of debts, interest on borrowing saving, Government special grants, special grant from NGOs, profits from SHG activities, in some cases donations to the groups, in centres etc. SHG is a right organization to provide money when they need for money.

Table 3

Amount drawn from Matching Grant Fund by the Selected SHGs

No. of Times Drawn	*R. Valasa*	*L. Valasa*	*S. Puram*	*Total*
1st time	30,000(75.0)	24000(60.0)	20000(50.0)	53000(44.17)
2nd time	33000(82)	21000(52.50)	15000(37.50)	69000(57.50)
3rd time	39000(97.50)	26000(65.0)	14000(35.0)	84000(70.0)
4th time	40000(100.0)	15000(37.50)	-	55000(45.83)
Total	40000	40000	40000.	120000

Note: figures in parenthesis are percentage to column totals.

The drawn money by the SHGs may be used for productive and non-productive purposes. In rural areas the families are very poor and they are unable to reach their daily transactions. They needed money for, health, marriages, functions, cloth, education, house repairs, unforeseen distress, deliveries and maintenance of old age people, child care etc. These people are depending more on moneylenders. SHGs attacking the situation and releasing money to their own needs taking into consideration the needs of respondents pushed them to draw funds from the financial institutions. In this context the details pertaining to the amount drawn by the selected SHG members has presented in Table 3.

From the Table 3 it can be observed that the selected SHGs are able to tap Government support. The selected SHGs raised their resources to the tune of Rs. 88.235 as matching grant from DRDA, Srikakulam. But the above grant was kept with the concerned banks in the form of fixed deposits according to the Government rules. In recent months, by the pressure of SHGs releasing the money basing on the rate of saving and matching grant to income generating activities to eradicate middle men and bogus group formation in field, the DRDA made a policy. They released matching grant in the name of groups and kept with Banking institutions as the group avail credit linkage with the bank. Total amount of matching grant of SHGs is Rs. 1, 20,000 and drawn in 4 times. The drawn amount utilized for productive purposes and little portion of amount is also used to un-productive activities like family maintenance expenditure. The pattern of matching grant drawn during 1st to 4th times is registered as 44.71 per cent, 57.50%, 70% and 45.83 percent respectively by unanimous decision of all SHG members. In the case of three villages, the proportion of the amount drawn during the said period, Ravi Valasa groups drawn higher compared to the two categories. It is ranging from 75 to 100 per cent. Regarding Lingala Valasa groups the percentages indicating a fluctuating trend in the drawn position. The highest amount is drawn in the third time and later it is recorded to 35.50 per cent. On the other hand the amount drawn by Seetha Puram groups in each time has shown a declining trend from 50 to 35 percent.

Utilisation Patterns

The concerned Banks have not able to release or accept to draw amount if the saving position of SHGs are not in good position and if they are not able to fulfill the required ratio with matching grant. It is found that Ravi Valasa groups are better in saving position in the study area. In addition to the matching grant, SHGs have bank linkage facilities. The concerned branches extended their support to SHGs in the form of credit advance. The three selected villages SHGs have receive the bank facilities but Ravi Valasa village stood in first place in utilizing the amount to income generating productive activities. The utilization patterns of bank finance towards productive and other purposes are presented in Table 4.

From the Table- 4 it can be noticed that the total amount sanctioned to SHGs is recorded at Rs. 1371000, but only 67.91 per cent of amount is utilized in various income generating productive activities viz; sheep rearing, vegetable cultivation and vegetable vending, jute based products, dairy, petty trade and agarbathi production. The proportion of amount utilized on the above-mentioned productive economic activities is 67.91 percent. Out of which 16.65 percentage of amount utilized on sheep raring, petty trade has occupied 9.56 percent of amount. The remaining amount is utilized for vegetable cultivation and vegetable vending (18.26), Jute based products (16.22%), Agarbathi Production (11.28%) and Dairy (4.83%). Among the three village SHG members, large proportion of amount is utilized in Ravi Valasa (80.0%) and second place got by Lingala Valasa followed by Seetha Puram (54.68). Except Seetha Puram groups remaining groups have taken 4th time bank linkage.

Repayment Position

The repayment patterns of selected SHGs are presented in the following Table 5.

Amount repaid by SHG members of bank loans including, Bank linkages, bank micro- enterprises credit loan. presented in the above Table-5 shows that the loan repayment performance of the SHG members out of the total amount taken by the groups is quite satisfactory, as a whole the proportion of amount repaid is 88.83 percent and the remaining 11.17 per cent is recorded as out standing registered with the institutions. Among the selected villages SHG members, the proportion of amount repaid is cent percent in case of Ravi Valasa village

Table 4

Amount utilization on Productive and Consumption Purposes by SHGs

Productive and Consumption	*R. Valasa*	*L. Valasa*	*S. Puram*	*Total*
Sheep rearing	75000(18.34)	80000(26.14)	-	155000(16.65)
Vegetable Cultivation and vending	60000(14.67)	45000 (14.71)	65000(30.01)	170000(18.26)
Jute based products	86000(21.03)	65000(21.24)	-	151000(16.22)
Dairy	45000(11.0)	-	-	45000(4.83)
Petty trade	28000(6.85)	-	61000(28.24)	89000(9.56)
Agar batti production	55000(13.0)	50000(16.34)	-	105000(11.28)
Consumption purpose	60000(15.0)	66000(21.57)	90000(41.67)	216000(23.20)
Total amount utilization	409000(80.0)	306000(65.81)	216000(54.68)	931000(67.91)
Total amount sanctioned	511000	465000	395000	1371000

Note: figures in parenthesis are percentage to column totals.

groups, the repayment of Lingala Valasa groups is recorded as 87.91 percent and 68.98 percent is recorded in case of Seetha Puram groups. Similarly the amount out standing is recorded as zero in case of Ravi Valasa groups, 12.09 percent in case of Lingala Valasa groups and 31.02 percent in case of Seetha Puram Groups. This situation explains that the proportion of amount out standing is different from one village to village. Low level of incomes, returns, high consumption may be attributed as the reasons behind the poor recoveries of loans in the Seetha Puram and Lingala Valasa villages.

Table 5

Amount Repaid by Selected SHG Members

Particulars	*R.Valasa (N=60)*	*L.Valasa (N=60)*	*S.Purim (N=60)*	*Total*
Amount taken	409000	261000	216,000	931,000
Amount repaid	409000(100.00)	269.00(87.91)	149,000(68.98)	8,27,000(88.83)
Out standing	-	37,000(12.09)	67,000(31.02)	1,04,000(11.17)

Note: Figures in parenthesis are percentage to column totals

It is observed from this study that the amount drawn by different SHGs in different villages shows that, the SHGs in Seetha Puram village drawn finance from the banks on the name of productive activities and the amount are utilized for consumption purposes. The SHGs in Seetha Puram are spending the loan amounts received by them for consumption purposes. Hence this study suggests the need for providing proper guidance and supervision to all the SHGs in the adoption of productive and income generating activities.

Conclusion

There are several benefits being bestowed by the different activities under the DWCRA scheme. According to the study, the women respondents are receiving both the employment opportunities and the income under the scheme in the study villages. Among the villages, the respondents of Ravi Valasa are able to get more employment opportunities and incomes as the resources are available at cheaper rate for their activities when compared to other villages. Regarding activities, the vegetable marketing activity, kirana business activity and dairy activity under this scheme are providing more employment opportunities and incomes to the rural women in the study area. The findings of this study ultimately indicate that micro finance is playing very vital role in the upbringing of the living conditions of rural women. The findings of this study ultimately suggests that, In view of fast changing scenario in rural areas, a vision for self reliance and urge for development has to be inculcated in rural societies especially in the women folk. These vital changes can be accomplished by establishing thrift and credit societies. Adult literacy centers, DWACRA groups have to be established in al the interior rural villages. The local organisations have to be empowered and guided properly in functioning and maintenance by women liaison workers and community coordinators.

References

Agarwal. B. (1998), Patriarchy and the Modernizing State: An Introduction; in Bina Agarwal(ed) *Structures of Patriarchy: State Community and house hold in Modernizing Asia,* New Delhi, Kalifor women, pp.1-28.

Batliwala Srilatha (1997), "Empowerment Women", *Seminar No:* 449, New Delhi, p.89.

GOI (1974), Towards Equality New Delhi.

GOI (1989), *National Perspective Plan for Women,* New Delhi.

GOI (1999), *9Th Five Year Plan Document,* New Delhi.

Government of Andhra Pradesh (2001), 'Strategy paper on Women's Empowerment', Department of Women Development and Child welfare, Hyderabad.

Hall C.M. (1992), *Women and Empowerment: Strategies for Increasing Autonomy,* Hemisphere Publishing Corporation, Washington.

Hasan Zoya (ed) (1994), *Forging Identities: Gender Communities and the State,* New Delhi, Kalifor Women.

Jet Buss maker and keep van Kersbergan (1994), "Gender and Welfare States: Some Theoretical Reflection"in *Gendering Welfare States,* ed. by Diane Sainsbury, London, says Publication.

Kate young (1993), *Planning Development with Women: Making a World of Difference,* MacMillian, p.157.

Kosambi Meera (1997), "Gender Reform and Competing State Controls over Women: The Rakhmabai lax (1884–1988) in *Social Reform, Sexuality and the State* (ed. by) Patricia Uberoi, New Delhi, Sage Publications.

Marilee Karl (1995), *Women and Empowerment: Participation and Decision Making,* London, Zed Books Ltd.

Maithreyi Krishna Raj (2000), *Public Policy: An Agenda,* IAWS, Hyderabad.

Patricia Uberoi (1996) (ed), *Social Reform, Sexuality and the State,* New Delhi, Safe Publication, pp.6.

Sangari.K and Vaid.S. (Eds) (1999), Recasting women: An Introduction is Recasting women: *Essays in Colonial History* New Delhi, Kalifor, Women, pp.1-26.

Stephen.F. (1997), Women's Empowerment: A Process of Restricting Power Relations, "Search Bulletin, XII pp.4-13., Quoted by B.V.Jaya Lakshmi (2001) *Women's Empowerment* Published by IDPS, Visakhapatnam.

Chapter-21

Women Participation in National Rural Employment Guarantee Scheme (NREGS) In Vizianagaram District of Andhra Pradesh

—— Ch. Appa Rao, G. Ramachandrudu, S. Prasada Rao, A. Venu ——

Introduction

There are number of employment programmes implemented by the Government of India namely The National Rural Employment Programme (NREP); The Rural Land Less Employment Guarantee Programme (RLEGP); The Integrated Rural Development Programme (IRDP); The Scheme of Training Rural Youth for Self-Employment (TRYSEM); Jawahar Rozgar Yojana (JRY); The Employment Assurance Scheme (EAS); Swarnajayanthi Gram Swarojgar Yojana (SGSY); Sampoorna Grameena Rozgar Yojana (SGRY) and Swarna Jayanti Shahari Rozgar Yojana (SJSRY). In recent years no programme for rural areas has received as much attention as the employment guarantee.

The National Rural Employment Guarantee Scheme (NREGS) should be viewed as a demand driven programme but not a supply oriented one. The government has a statutory obligation to provide employment to every household, or, if unable to do so, to provide an unemployment allowance. The mute question is whether rural poor, unorganized, exploited, on the fringes of hunger, disillusioned by government schemes and unfulfilled promises will be able to assert their right in the existing scenario of politico- bureaucratic nexus. National Rural Employment Guarantee Act (NREGA) being passed in September, 2005, the NREGS was implemented from February2, 2006 in 200 identified districts of the country with the objective of providing 100 days of wage employment, unskilled manual work, livelihood security to rural households and creation of durable community assets.

Review of Literature

Sudha Narayanan (2008) conducted a survey in Tamil Nadu on "Employment Guarantee, Women's Work and Childcare". The study covered 11 villages and 15 NREGA worksites located in two blocks of Viluppuram District in Tamil Nadu. She finds that the National Rural Employment Guarantee Act has brought about major changes in the lives of women. However, the Act overlooks the fact that child care is a problem for many of the working women, especially for young mothers. He interviewed around 70 per cent of the women and find that there were no child care facilities at the work site. Finally, she suggest that the provision of effective child care facilities at NREGS worksite is important for the improving the programme.

Shah. M and P. Ambasta (2008) in their article in THE HINDU (Dt. 08-09-2008) highlighted the success of Andhra Pradesh, NREGS particularly the social audit system. The success in Andhra Pradesh is unfavourable and achievement is due to an extraordinary support of top echelons of the political and the beaurocratic leadership. According to the authors the noval features of Andhra Pradesh NREGS are (a) the use of Information Technology (IT) and (b) role of civil society (NGOs). The use of IT system enables the programme managers to send the measurement sheets and muster rolls of entire week are closed and reach the Mandal Computer Centre, on day 8th the pay orders are generated and checks are prepared. The second novel features of Andhra Pradesh

NREGS is the involvement of the civil society the organizations like Mazdoor Kisan Shakti Sangathan(SKSS) which have been actively involved in conducting social auditing. In every village the District Resource Person (DRP) identified a few energetic literate youth who usually belong to NREGS workers themselves. After being trained in the social auditing process, these youth form teams, which go from door to door authenticating muster rolls, checkout work sites, record written statements of workers and conduct series of meetings in each village. There are about 30,000 trained village youth who are conducting social audit that they have already covered 12 million people. Nearly Rs 1.25 crore of misappropriate funds are recovered. The authors however pointed out that the following weaknesses in Andhra Pradesh NREGS. (a) The most important is the quality of assets created and (b) The government has not paid adequate attention to strengthening the process of people's planning and implementation of works. The immense potential of NREGS for transforming rural livelihoods thus remains completely unrealized. The Andhra Pradesh Cabinet promises full support to any independent initiative of wage seekers to carry out additional social audit.

Lalit Mathur (2007) clearly explains that the National Rural Employment Guarantee Act (NREGA) is now in its second year. Argentina had introduced a job creation scheme, the Plan Jefesy de Hogar, in 2002. The NREGA is the first tangible commitment to the poor that they can expect to earn a living wage, without loss of dignity, and demand this as a right. The NREGA will be extended to the entire country from 2008-09, the Act itself was enacted after considerable opposition from within the government itself. The employment guarantee already covers more than half the country-over three lakh villages and 1.5 lakh gram panchayats in the most arid and drought-prone regions; tribal and forest areas where many villages are still not accessible – in its vastness, reach and scope, it is truly huge. It is certainly not easy of implementation. Out of 2.16 crore households who sought employment, 2.10 crore households (97 per cent) were provided work of 90 crore person days, an average of 45 days in the year. The participation of

Women (41 per cent), Scheduled Castes (25 per cent) and Scheduled Tribes (36 per cent) was high; equally significantly, unskilled wages comprised 67 per cent of the total expenditure, and 94 per cent of the expenditure on wages. About 8.41 lakh works were taken up of which 3.97 lakhs were completed, and out of the Rs. 12,073 crore available for the programme, Rs. 8,823 core (73 per cent) was utilized. This trend has continued during 2007-08. The utilization per district was more than Rs 100 crore in Rajasthan (115) and Madhya Pradesh (103) and high also in Chattisgarh (61) and Assam (85); on the other hand this was less than Rs. 25 crore in Gujarat (14), Maharashtra (18) and Tamil Nadu (25).

The objective of 100 days of employment was not achieved in any state. However, the per district person days of employment and households provided employment were comparatively high in Madhya Pradesh (1.6 lakh households, 68 days), Orissa (0.7 lakh households, 57 days), Chattisgarh (1.7 lakh households, 54 days) and Rajasthan (two lakh households, 83 days). In West Bengal and Tamil Nadu although three lakh and 1.2 lakh households, respectively worked under the NREGA, they could do so only for 14 and 26 days, respectively. In such programmes there will inevitably be some leakages and imperfections, with reports from districts of things going wrong, of delays, of corruption, and so on. The NREGA has impacted the poor: large numbers of unlettered households have made the effort to come forward to register; migration has reduced in several villages in Andhra Pradesh, Chattisgarh, Orissa and Rajasthan; wages less than the minimum wage were raised in many states; the participation of women increased significantly even in the districts of Rajasthan and eastern UP; unemployment allowances were sought and actually paid in Madhya Pradesh and Orissa; the maintenance of muster rolls has become a feature in several districts. The Employment Guarantee has evidently begun well. A system of regular and continuous flow of authoritative information is essential more than just sporadic reports and studies, as at present, dependent on the initiative of individuals and groups. Government could take up concurrent evaluations.

More effective monitoring, time-series studies, and focused reports on critical as-pacts like minimum wages and muster rolls. Not just by the centre, but also by the states; not by the departments of rural development alone, but by others as well-labour, agriculture, forests, planning, the NSSO and its network. This is an important period for the NREGA for it is one of learning as well. The number of "facilitators" who are involved with the NREGA is staggering several lakh government officials, panchayat functionaries, elected representatives, NGOs and community groups. They play a critical role but have had little preparation for the challenge.

Mihir Shah (2007) argued that the enactment of NREGA is the fruition of a long and hard struggle over many years. The NREGA is best seen as an attempt to provide a big push in India's regions of distress. For it promises the largest ever employment programme in human history. As this programme extends to cover the whole country within the next few years, the government will need to allocate over Rs. 30,000 crore every year for NREGA. In order to minimize village people have to be involved in all aspects of the work, including in site selection, cost estimation and the way work will be measured and paid. Corruption in employment programmes is not merely a matter of preventing fudges muster rolls. The much more creative dimensions of corruption arise from the way the Schedule of Rates (SOR) is deployed both to embroider estimates and cheat labour. People are paid according to the value placed on their work by the SOR. How the rates in the SORs are arrived at and how the SORs are used is neither very well known nor easily amenable to popular understanding. On the basis of a careful study of SORs of nine NREGA states, Vijaya Shankar et al (2006) have shown that SORs currently in use make mechanization and the use of contactors almost inevitable. NREGA could well degenerate into a contractor-run, non-participatory programme. The process of arriving at these rates needs to be made much more transparent and participatory. Under NREGA, a working group should be set up in each district to carry out this exercise. The role of this group should be to prepare and revise the District Schedule of

Rates based on fresh time and motion studies. A powerful tool to check corruption is Information Technology (IT) that must also be a key component of NREGA reforms. As Andhra Pradesh has shown best, all stages of NREGA work, from registration of workers to issue of job cards, preparation of work estimates of muster rolls can be very effectively computerized. Since each job card issued, each work undertaken and every payment made anywhere in the state has a unique identification code, and since all this information is just a click away on the web anyone interested can access this information and field-check to see whether or not what is reported is true. The 100 days restriction is causing all manner of problems in NREGA implementation. At times the number of job card holders in a village restricted to 100 days, are unable to complete works crucial for the village. In the high migration districts of Orissa, it is being felt that a mere 100 days per family is not enough to halt people leaving their villages in search of work. If people feel this is not enough work, they will migrate irrespective of NREGA. The enactment of the NREGA is classic success story of civil society in India. What the activists, who worked for the passage of NREGA, need to appreciate is that this is perhaps the last chance of pushing for an agenda of enlightened state action in favour of India's marginalized. The weaknesses need to be pointed out. But not in the spirit of debunking the programme. We must recognize that the NREGA architecture, if actually put into place, could potentially herald a revolution in rural governance, through its unprecedented mechanisms for transparency, social audit and e-governance-a truly participatory and empowered democracy at the rural grassroots. The support structure to enable Gram Panchayats to implement NREGA is utterly inadequate. Most states only provide, if at all, for a gram rozgar sewak. It is in the open assembly of the gram sabha that NREGA plans will have to be presented, explained and approved. In many parts of India, this vital institution is still in its infancy. CSOs will provide the missing support structure that PRIs require to effectively implement NREGA. These CSOs have all been formally invited by the PRIs to help them plan, implement and social audit NREGA work.

Objectives

The objectives of the paper are:

1. To analyse the socio-economic features of the sample respondents.
2. To measure the impact of NREGS on Employment, Income, Assets and Consumption Pattern of sample respondents.
3. To suggest policy measures for further strengthening of the programme in rural areas.

Methodology

Vizianagaram District is selected for intensive study. The district is one of themost backward and socially disadvantage sections of the people with lowest female literacy, high poverty levels and highest out-migration from the district. The study covers six mandals five villages in each mandal and from each village 50 sample households in Vizianagaram district. The total sample beneficiaries are 1500 (803 are Males and 697 are Females).

Findings of the Study are

Information extracted from the sample respondents relating to socio-economic features like caste, age, literacy status, type of house, occupational structure, number of workers in family etc. These details are shown in Table-1.

Caste

The female and male respondents represent 47 and 53 per cent respectively. While 68 per cent belong to female respondents. In case of forward caste female respondents are higher whereas the male respondents are higher among Schedule Castes. The table clearly shows that female workers among forward caste is higher than that of all other castes.

Age

Among female respondents 38 per cent are less than 30 years of age group and it is 22 per cent in male respondents between 31-50 age group. The male respondent is significantly higher

Table 1
Socio -Economic Background Characteristics of the Sample Respondents

	Male		*Female*		*Total*	
Caste:	No.	%	No.	%	No	%
Forward Caste	30	3.7	108	15.5	138	9.2
Backward Classes	582	72.5	477	68.4	1059	70.6
Scheduled Caste	131	16.3	69	9.9	200	13.3
Scheduled Tribe	60	7.5	43	6.2	103	6.9
Total	803	100.0	697	100.0	1500	100.0
Age						
<30	178	22.2	267	38.3	445	29.7
31-40	268	33.4	217	31.1	485	32.3
41-50	196	24.4	152	21.8	348	23.2
51-60	124	15.4	53	7.6	177	11.8
>61	37	4.6	8	1.1	45	3.0
Total	803	100.0	697	100.0	1500	100.0
Literacy Status:						
1-5	86	10.7	153	22.0	239	15.9
6-8	41	5.1	24	3.4	65	4.3
9-10	56	7.0	9	1.3	65	4.3
>11	27	3.4	4	.6	31	2.1
Illiterate	593	73.8	507	72.7	1100	73.3
Total	803	100.0	697	100.0	1500	100.0

Contd.

Caste:	*Male*		*Female*		*Total*	
	No.	%	No.	%	No	%
Type of House						
Kutcha	322	40.1	235	33.7	557	37.1
semi Pucca	167	20.8	156	22.4	323	21.5
Pucca	309	38.5	304	43.6	613	40.9
No house	5	0.6	2	0.3	7	0.5
Total	803	100.0	697	100.0	1500	100.0
Occupational Structure						
Cultivation	52	6.5	31	4.4	83	5.5
Labour	751	93.5	663	95.1	1414	94.3
Business			1	0.1	1	0.1
Others			2	0.3	2	0.1
Total	803	100.0	697	100.0	1500	100.0
No. of Workers in Family						
Below 2	488	60.8	529	75.9	1017	67.8
3-5	298	37.1	162	23.2	460	30.7
Above 6	17	2.1	6	0.9	23	1.5
Total	803	100.0	697	100.0	1500	100.0

when compared to the female respondents. More than half of the per cent of the male respondents is higher in the age group of 51-60 years.

Literacy Status

Education is an important social indicator, which improves not only social status but also its impact on the future development perspectives. The illiteracy rates among male and female respondents are more or less similar.

Type of House

Housing is one of the important social indicator its shows the quality life of the people. The table clearly evidence that 44 per cent of female respondents and 39 per cent of male respondents living in Pucca houses. The male respondents are having kuccha and semi-pucca houses constitute 40 and 21 percent respectively, while corresponding figures are 34 and 22 per cent among female respondents respectively.

Occupational Structure

Occupation wise agricultural labourer among female respondents accounted for 95 per cent which 94 per cent in male respondents. Among female respondents agriculture labourer are marginally higher and in case cultivators marginally lower when compared to male respondents.

No. of Workers in Family

The extent of workers less than 2 in the family is significantly higher among female respondents (76 per cent) compared to male respondents (61 per cent). This is the reverse the case 3 to 5 and above 6 workers in the family.

Impact of NREGS on Employment

The details on the impact of NREGS on employment are presented in Table-2. The average number of working days of a worker is marginally higher among male at 214 days and it is 208 days for female.

Table 2

Source	Male		Female	
	No. of Days (Average)	%	No. of Days (Average)	%
Own farm	33.09	15.44	30.34	14.56
Agricultural labour	42.26	19.72	41.58	19.96
Non-agricultural labour	56.93	26.57	56.01	26.89
NREGS works	82.01	38.27	80.38	38.59
Total Working Days	214.30	100.00	208.31	100.00

Impact of NREGS on Income

Information extracted from the sample respondents on income in different sources. The details are shown in Table-3. Various sources of income received by the sample respondents, the extent of income received from NREGS is considerly higher (Rs. 6146), followed by income from own farm (Rs. 4786), non-agricultural labour (Rs. 4462) and agricultural labour (Rs. 3036) among male respondents while the corresponding figures for female respondents are Rs. 5775, 4028, 4480 and 2630 respectively. The table clearly indicates that income from NREGS is higher in both male and female respondents. Next to NREGS female respondents reported that their income is high in non-agricultural labour whereas male participants received income from their own farm.

Table 3
Impact on Income 2007-08 (Average income in Rs.)

Source of Income	Male	%	Female	%
Own farm	4785.65	25.97	4028.48	23.82
Agricultural labour	3035.72	16.47	2629.77	15.55
Non agricultural labour	4462.48	24.21	4480.60	26.49
NREGS	6146.64	33.35	5775.00	34.14
Total	18430.49	100.00	16913.86	100.00

Impact of NREGS on Assets

Information elicited from the sample respondent on farm assets and household durables. The details are shown in Table-4. In case of durable goods increased to the extent of 40, 37, and 28

Table 4

Assets	Male			Female			Total		
	Before	*After*	*% change*	*Before*	*After*	*% change*	*Before*	*After*	*% change*
Farm Assets									
1. Land (acres)	120736.5	128814	6.69	110228.2	111149	0.83	116708.3	121024	3.70
2. Type of House:									
a) Pucca	113289	116009	2.40	115491.1	115979	0.42	114384.1	115994	1.41
b) Semi-Pucca	51076	62252	21.88	52797.2	62714.29	18.78	51893.69	62476.34	20.39
c) Kutcha	23561.08	24062.46	2.13	20817.47	22327.35	7.25	22372.62	23330.9	4.28
3. Bullock Cart	9898.46	10455	5.63	11032.26	14455	31.02	10647.31	11432.65	7.38
4. Plough	1056.52	1057	0	2582.82	2764	7.05	1550	1608.82	3.79
5. Buffaloes	16920	17825	5.35	14632.75	15160	3.6	15931.89	16610.2	4.26
6. Bullocks	15839	17164.06	8.37	17137.25	17846.15	4.14	16424.78	17469.83	6.36
7. Cows	11458	11995.33	4.69	9125	10210.34	11.54	11049.15	11214.29	1.49
8. Sheep & Goat	5546	6533	17.80	4069.75	5595.59	37.5	4883.18	6129.07	25.51
9. Poultry	427	614	43.79	359.5	466	29.8	385.45	543.33	40.96
10. Others	5000	5500	10.00	5200	5800	11.54	5000	5200	4.00
Durable Assets									
11. Cycle	1646.26	1677	1.89	1421.19	1384.44	-2.6	1526	1500.21	-1.69
12. Radio/Tape recorder	3409.46	4679	37.25	2598.56	2855.45	9.89	3256.67	3078.26	-5.48
13. T.V.	5083.53	7121.15	40.01	4682.42	8072.31	72.4	4865.84	4538.46	-6.73
14. Sewing machine	10000	10000	0	15000	18500	23.33	12500	7650	-38.8
15. Scooter	47500	50000	5.26	—	—	—	47500	35000	-26.32
16. Motor cycle	32500	41667	28.21	43250	44333.33	2.5	39666.67	43000	8.40
17. Gold/Silver	24389	25333.33	3.87	18378.05	2000	8.83	20211.86	19957.63	-1.26
18. Others	2950	3050	3.31	39125	40268	2.92	39125	10850	-72.27

for T.V, Radio/ Tape recorder and Motor Cycle among male respondents and among female respondents the changes are more manifest items like TV and Sewing machines.

Impact of NREGS on Consumption Pattern

The details on consumption pattern of the sample respondents are presented in Table-5. The impact of NREGS on consumption patterns vary between male and female respondents. The expenditure on food items among female respondents is much higher on items like milk (40%), followed by non-vegetarian (31%), tea - coffee (27%), pulses (26%) and oil (25%). The lowest expenditure on cereals accounted for (11%) among female respondents. While the male respondents the expenditure on food items are more on milk (45%), tea–coffee (33%), non-vegetarian (31%) and sugar (28%).

Conclusions

The NREGS is now in its third year. There are 5.2 crore households (2.1 in 2006-07 and 3.1 in 2007-08), provided 220 crore person-days of employment, in which the participation by Scheduled Castes, Scheduled Tribes and women has been high. The major proportions of both male and female respondents belong to backward classes. About 73 per cent of male respondents belong to backward classes. Among female respondents have completed primary school education (22 per cent); in case of secondary, high school and college education female respondents is lagging behind male respondents. Female respondents have more Pucca houses and less of kutcha and semi-pucca houses. A high proportion is contributed through NREG works 82 days for male and 80 days for female. Both the respondents received highest income through NREG works excited in the study area. The impact of NREGS on farm assets is higher on poultry, housing, sheep, goat and bullock cart among male and female respondents. The changes in expenditure on non–food items are more striking on the items viz. health care (58%) followed by alcohol (54%), education (49%) and smoking (37%) in males. Among the female respondents the expenditure non–food items are more manifest the items

Table 5
Average Impact of NREGS on Consumption Patterns

(Value in Rs.)

Source	*Male*			*Female*			*Total*		
	Before	*After*	*% change*	*Before*	*After*	*% change*	*Before*	*After*	*% change*
Food Items (per week)									
1 Cereals	189.92	213.25	12.00	180.78	201.73	11.60	185.68	207.90	12.00
2 Pulses	49.71	62.38	24.00	50.35	62.83	26.00	50.01	62.59	24.00
3 Milk (litres)	29.34	41.50	44.83	29.78	42.47	40.00	29.55	41.95	44.83
4 Tea/Coffee	32.94	44.09	33.33	32.51	42.46	27.27	32.74	43.32	33.33
5 Sugar	21.49	26.95	28.57	21.52	26.19	18.18	21.51	26.60	28.57
6 Vegetables	100.65	124.15	22.28	95.02	116.36	22.18	98.04	120.54	22.28
7 Non-vegetarian	84.39	109.99	30.95	85.40	111.46	30.59	84.85	110.67	30.95
8 Oil	71.74	86.00	19.44	67.80	85.07	25.00	69.92	85.57	19.44
9 Others	564.08	737.11	30.67	406.18	498.61	22.91	491.53	626.25	30.67
Non Food Items (one year)									
1 Cloth	2328.06	2916.62	25.30	2395.73	2926.45	22.12	2359.36	2921.15	25.30
2 Cosmetics	441.15	508.80	15.42	441.22	533.17	20.86	441.18	519.54	15.42
3 Entertainment	215.54	315.57	46.29	274.56	390.27	41.82	241.26	348.09	46.29
4 Education	2138.66	3182.31	48.76	2629.93	3468.45	31.86	2377.64	3319.59	48.76
5 Healthcare	1632.49	2580.37	58.09	1826.67	2787.67	52.60	1727.66	2680.17	58.09
6 Ceremonies/Functions	2008.89	6773.91	237.18	1202.38	3051.49	153.82	1538.43	4940.07	237.18
7 Firewood/Fuel	502.50	480.86	-4.37	621.43	1444.44	132.53	566.54	1022.88	- 4.37
8 Smoking	1406.47	1932.85	37.48	1407.78	1814.56	28.98	1407.07	1878.51	37.48
9 Alcohol	2658.68	4089.26	53.84	3230.39	4436.32	37.34	2917.55	4242.82	53.84

like social ceremonies/functions (154%), fire wood/fuel (132%), health care (53%) and entertainment (42%).

Since large number of women in the reproductive age are coming forward to work in NREGS, the worst hits are infants and young children who are left in the houses, The "Aaya" facility is not popular nor there facilities at the worksite. Perhaps strengthening anganwadi centres is one alternative and they should be converted into crèches. Undoubtedly, programme like NREGS proper planning, effective implementation, close monitoring and independent evaluation are the key instruments for delivering maximum benefits to the target groups. NREGS may be creating Social awareness about literacy, health care, AIDS, Sanitation, drinking water, balanced nutritional diet, anti liquor and care of the aged. The success of any programme largely depends on monitoring, evaluation and constant help and efficient administration.

References

Sudha Narayanan (2008), "Employment Guarantee, Women's Work and Childcare", *Economic and Political Weekly*, pp. 10-13.

Mihar Shah and P.Ambsata (2008), "NREGA Andhra Pradesh shows the Way", *The Hindu* News Paper, Sep 08.

Lalit Mathur (2007), "Employment Guarantee: Progress So Far", *Economic and Political Weekly*, Vol.XLII (52), pp. 17-20.

Mihir shah (2007), 'Employment Guarantee, Civil Society and India Democracy'; *Economic and Political Weekly*, Vol.XLII (45and46), pp. 43-51.

CHAPTER-22

Women Entrepreneurship–The Road Ahead

— A.V. Naga Varma, Y. Rama Krishna, J. Chandra Prasad —

It is imperative to note the participation of women in economic activities as self-employed individuals. Many of the traditional occupations open to women were mainly based on caste and creed and the nature of self-employment was based on the standard of living. Presently, not only are women generating employment for themselves in the unorganized sector, they are also providing employment to others. The country needs to mobilize and utilize fully all its resources including human resources. The participation of women in economic activities is necessary not only from a human resource point of view but is essential even for the objective of raising the status of women in society. The economic status of women is now accepted as an indicator of a society's stage of development.

Therefore, it becomes imperative for the Government to frame policies for the development of entrepreneurship among women. The long-term objectives of the development programmes for women should aim at raising their economic and social status in order to bring them into the mainstream of national life and development. For this, due recognition has to be accorded to the role and contribution of women in the various social, economic, political and cultural activities.

The following are the major factors influencing women entrepreneurs.

The emergence of women entrepreneurs and women-owned firms and their significant contributions to the economy is visible in India. These businesses are ready for continued growth in the future.

The number of women entrepreneurs has increased, especially during the 1990s. The new generation of women-owned enterprises is actively seeking capital for their businesses, using modern technology to find and create a niche in both the domestic and export markets. While women-owned businesses possesses the potential and are capable of contributing much more, it is essential to formulate strategic support and sustain their efforts in the right direction.

Surveys demonstrate that women's primary entrepreneurial activity is focused on the small and medium enterprise (SME) sector. Approximately 60 per cent are small-scale entrepreneurs, 15 per cent are large-scale manufacturers, and the remainder consists of cottage and micro-entrepreneurs. They work in a wide range of sectors from trade and services, to tailoring, beauty parlours, and printing. However, the involvement of women entrepreneurs in the production sector is minimal and the development of this sector is rather slow. Empirical evidence shows that women contribute significantly to the running of family businesses mostly in the form of unpaid effort and skills.

Women with small families are more likely to become entrepreneurs. A majority of women entrepreneurs are married. Unmarried women face difficulties in getting financial support to launch their enterprises. Many women entrepreneurs belong to the low-in-come group. A large number of women with little or no education enter into business without undergoing any training. Most of these practicing women entrepreneurs lack vocational education. Working capital is limited and profit margins are low. Women from the low-income group exercise greater freedom in making the decision to start business as compared to middle class women who suffer from cultural constraints.

Many women become entrepreneurs out of economic necessity. Women's hard work is generally responsible for the launch and sustainability of the business. Support systems do not effectively handle their important need for vision and confidence building and also for developing better business orientation and skills. Gender discrimination is encountered at every stage of business development. Women entrepreneurs are security oriented rather than growth oriented. Women prefer diversification to specialization. Women prefer stabilization of income and minimization of risk over maximization of income. Though the trend is changing. It is not uncommon to find enterprises owned by women but run by men. In the field of technology women have made a conscious decision to set up technology-based enterprises.

Many have ventured into hi-tech areas such as manufacturing solar thermals, vacuum reactors, television boosters, air compressors, voltage stabilizers, and amplifiers as reflected in the data collected about women entrepreneurs (Poornima M. Charantimath, Entrepreneurship Development Small Business Enterprises, Person Education M. Charantimath, New Delhi, 2006, p. 103) However, for most women their businesses remain micro enterprises.

Since the turn of the century, the status of women in India has been changing due to growing industrialization and urbanization, spatial mobility, and social legislation. Over the years, more and more of women are going in for higher education, technical and professional education. Their proportion in the labour force has also increased.

With the spread of education and awareness, women have shifted from the extended kitchen, handicrafts and traditional cottage industries to non-traditional higher levels of activities. During the 1970s, the decade of the International Women's Year, efforts to promote self-employment among women received greater attention from the government and private agencies. The new industrial policy of the Government of India has laid special emphasis on the need to conduct special entrepreneurial training programmes for women to enable them to start their own ventures.

Financial institutions and banks have also set up special cells to assist women entrepreneurs. The result has been the emergence of more women entrepreneurs on the economic scene in recent years, though the number is still quite low. Women entrepreneurship, on the whole, still remains a much neglected field.

While almost half the population of India comprises women, the businesses owned and operated by them constitute less than 5 per cent. This is a reflection of social, cultural as well as economic distortions in the decades of development. However, women's contribution and participation in economic activity and production of goods and services is much greater than statistics reveal, since much of it takes place in the informal sector and also in households.

As education has spread and compulsions for earning have grown, more and more women have started to go out of the homes and opt for employment-for a wage, or for an entrepreneurial career. The problems and constraints experienced by women entrepreneurs have resulted in restricting the expansion of women entrepreneurship. The major barriers encountered by women entrepreneurs are as follows.

Women generally lack confidence in their own capabilities. Having accepted a subordinate status for long, even at home, members of their family do not appear to have total confidence in their abilities and on their decision-making. Society in general also lacks confidence in a women's strength, traits, and competence.

Another problem faced by women entrepreneurs is lack of access to funds because they do not possess any tangible security and credit in the market. Since women do not enjoy right over property of any form, they have limited access over external sources of funds.

Socio-Cultural Barriers: A woman has a perform her family duties irrespective of her career as a working woman or an entrepreneur. In our society, more importance is given to educating the male child as compared to the female child. This results in lack of schooling and vocational training of women, their lack of attaining technical skills and thereby lack of awareness of opportunities available.

Production in a manufacturing enterprise involves coordination of a number of activities. While some of these activities are in the control of the entrepreneur, there are others over which she has little control. Improper coordination and delay in execution of any activity cause production problems in industry. The inability of women entrepreneurs to keep pace with the latest advances in technology and lack of technical know-how results in high cost of technology acquisition and machinery utilization. These problems result in increasing the cost of production and adversely affecting the profitability of the unit.

Heavy competition in the market, and their lack of mobility makes the women entrepreneurs dependent on middlemen. For marketing their products, women entrepreneurs are at the mercy of middleman who pocket a major chunk of profit. Further, women entrepreneurs also find it difficult to capture the market and make their products popular. They lack information on the changing market. In addition, women entrepreneurs, face difficulty in collection of payments.

To overcome the resistance from husband and members of the family at the time of setting up of their venture, prospective women entrepreneurs are advised to maintain their cool and persistently convince them, without confronting them, regarding the benefits of setting up of an enterprise. The woman requires to have a strong will power under the circumstances. The inflow of money will eventually solve this problem.

Shouldering the dual responsibilities of an entrepreneur and a homemaker can be effectively undertaken by a women entrepreneur through better time management. The members of the family can also be involved in the business, which will help in sharing the burden of entrepreneurial work.

A woman can start her business when her children are grown up enough to take care of their own small needs. This gives the women enough time enough to manage her enterprise.

For marketing her products, a women entrepreneur must establish her credibility in terms of quality and competitiveness of product or service. She should acquire relevant techniques and skills to win customer's loyalty. E-commerce business will also help greatly in this regard.

Workshop and seminars should be organized frequently for the officials of financial and support agencies and for women entrepreneurs to make their relations more cordial.

It has been observed that there is a tendency to project a higher value of sales, production, and profits in project reports to impress the bankers. Such a project profile is not appropriate from a financial management point of view. So, women entrepreneurs need to undertake training in various aspects of financial management to understand its finer implications.

Banks and financial institutions must maintain a minimum target of loan to be disbursed to women entrepreneurs. Collateral security should be dispensed with in the case of women entrepreneurs because many women hardly have any property or other assets in their name to keep as guarantee.

Women entrepreneurs should acquire relevant training in technology and in details of their plant and machinery. They should be knowledgeable about the functioning of machines and processes. They should be more assertive with their employees. Group entrepreneurship is a viable option for the weaker sections of the society and it helps woman to overcome their poverty.

In olden days, due to shyness and fear, women were not ready to come forward to undertake any work, job and business in the society. They concentrated only in family affairs. But nowadays women have more awareness about the society, problems, circumstances and opportunities available before them. They are ready to take any risk to come forward economically as they have more responsibility to take care of their children and more interest in the development of their family. If there is an income to a woman in the family, surely it will be spent only for the development of the family not for themselves.

There is a proverb i.e., "anything is possible with a help of women. Similarly anything can be demolished by a woman". But nowadays most of the women concentrate in developing the family both in the case of nuclear and joint family. So both the Government and men should encourage the women to become entrepreneurs in all fields. They must be motivated to establish business concerns which will help to develop their family income and the standard of income of the particular region and a considerable contribution towards national income as whole and women will lead to make our nation to become a super power in the world.

References

Kausal, Rachana (2000), *Women and Human Rights in India;* Kaveri Books, New Delhi.

Serageldin, Ismail (1991), "Culture, Empowerment and the Development Paradigm," *Development 1*, pp. 88-90.

Arja P.P. (1991), "Hurdles to Women Entrepreneurs", *'Financial Express'*, September 18th, p. 7.

Employment News (2005), "Women Entrepreneurship for Self-employment", *www.employmentnews.com.*

Kamala Singh (1992), *"Women Entrepreneurs"*, Ashish Publishing House, New Delhi.

UNDP (2005), *Human Development Report,* Oxford University Press.

Chapter-23

Development of Women Entrepreneurs: An Overview

— Jagannath B. Kukkudi, Ramesh B. Agadi, Veershetty Rathod —

"most women want to be prompted as quickly as men.
most women want their talents recognized.
most women don't want to act like men"

Introduction

During the past decade, the environment for multinational corporations has been quite volatile, with numerous challenges for the firms operating in this arena. However, throughout this period there have emerged a number of executive leaders who have been recognized for their contributions to organizational excellence and leadership despite the environmental fluctuations. But invariably even few years back women power was not so welcome to hold and glorify the top positions of different corporate houses. Several myths were there and so women employees used to face barriers while climbing up the corporate ladder. But time and again women power have proved them, succeeded over those imposed barriers and made major contribution towards organizational excellence.

The role of women worldwide is undergoing a dramatic change. Women today share the podium with men in almost all fields, be it kitchen or in defense. Working women are no longer a rarity and are now accepted as an integral part of the working force. Indian organization has experienced a steady increase in the number of women employees and this pattern is bound to continue in the future as well. Women recently began to join the ranks of managers in large numbers. But women at the top management positions are still a rare species. Globally, they comprise only 10 percent of senior managers in Fortune 500 companies, less than 4% are in the uppermost ranks of CEO, president, executive vice-president and COO and less than 3% of them are top corporate earners. In India too, it is no different. May be the situation is worse.

Women Entrepreneurs may be defined as the women or a group of women who initiate, organize and operate a business enterprise. Government of India has defined women entrepreneurs as an enterprise owned and controlled by a women having a minimum financial interest of 51% of the capital and giving at least 51% of employment generated in the enterprise to women. Like a male entrepreneurs a women entrepreneur has many functions. They should explore the prospects of starting new enterprise; undertake risks, introduction of new innovations, coordination administration and control of business and providing effective leadership in all aspects of business.

Role of Women as an Entrepreneur

Imaginative

It refers to the imaginative approach or original ideas with competitive market. Well-planned approach is needed to examine the existing situation and to identify the entrepreneurial opportunities. It further implies that women entrepreneur's have association with knowledgeable people and contracting the right organization offering support and services.

Attribute to Work Hard

Enterprising women have further ability to work hard. The imaginative ideas have to come to a fair play. Hard work is needed to build up an enterprise.

Persistence

Women entrepreneurs must have an intention to fulfill their dreams. They have to make a dream transferred into an idea enterprise; Studies show that successful women work hard.

Ability and Desire to take Risk

The desire refers to the willingness to take risk and ability to the proficiency in planning, making forecast estimates and calculations.

Profit Earning Capacity

She should have a capacity to get maximum return out of invested capital.

Hindrances of Women Entrepreneurs

Women in India are faced many problems to get ahead their life in business. A few problems can be detailed as;

Socio-Personal Problems

The greatest deterrent to women entrepreneurs is that they are women. A kind of patriarchal-male dominant social order is the building block to them in their way towards business success. Male members think it a big risk financing the ventures run by women.

Economic Problems

The financial institutions are skeptical about the entrepreneurial abilities of women. The bankers consider women loonies as higher risk than men loonies. The bankers put unrealistic and unreasonable securities to get loan to women entrepreneurs.

Marketing Problems

Marketing is another area, which very often proves to be the graveyard of many small-scale women entrepreneurs. It has been found that the small-scale entrepreneurs, owing to their high achievement orientation, generally set higher goals in terms of marketing of their products or services but later on find them difficult to achieve.

Occupational Mobility Problems

Occupational mobility, such as shifting from one product line to another is an area where women entrepreneurs are generally found to be more at a disadvantageous position than their male counterparts.

Family Obligations

Women's family obligations also bar them from becoming successful entrepreneurs in both developed and developing nations. "Having primary responsibility for children, home and older dependent family members, few women can devote all their time and energies to their business.

Government Assistance Problems

The women entrepreneurs were exasperated by the indifferent attitude of government officials of all the small industry related departments like taxation, labour, power, etc. i.e. when the authorities come to know that the unit is being run by a woman, they discourage allotting sales tax number and giving electricity connection.

Personnel Problems

The women entrepreneurs also expressed their inability to change the negative attitude of labour force while some of them complained of unionism amongst them. Moreover the women entrepreneurs admitted the lack of experience and self-confidence on their part to deal with personnel working in their organizations.

Problems of Technological Knowledge

Knowledge of latest technological changes, know how, and education level of the person are significant factor that affect business. The literacy rate of women in India is found at low level compared to male population. Many women in developing nations lack the education needed to spur successful entrepreneurship.

Attitude Towards Risk

Low-level risk taking attitude is another factor affecting women folk decision to get into business. Low-level education provides low-level self-confidence and self-reliance to the women folk to engage in business, which is continuous risk taking and strategic cession making profession.

Lack of Motivation

Achievement motivation of the women folk is less compared to male members. The low level of education and confidence leads to low level achievement and advancement of motivation among women folk to engage in business operations and running a business concern.

Cost of Production

High production cost of some business operations adversely affects the development of women entrepreneurs. The installation of new machineries during expansion of the productive capacity and like similar factors dissuades the women entrepreneurs from venturing into new areas.

Development of Women Entrepreneurs–Recent Trends

All women who have accomplished great things have had a great aim have fixed their gaze on a goal which was so high. This is the secret behind the success of every women entrepreneur who had thrown away the fear in their thought and transpires out with thundering spirit. Several national and international organizations and agencies have appreciated the need for and importance of developing women entrepreneurs in recent years. A brief review of it is given here.

The *United Nations* declared the decade 1975-85 as the *Decade for Women.* The World Conference of the United Nations Decade for Women held at Copenhagen in Denmark on 30th June 1980 adopted a programme aimed at promoting full and equal opportunities and treatment of women in employment and their access to non-traditional skilled trades.

The *First National Conference* of Women Entrepreneurs held at New Delhi in November 1981 advocated the need for developing women entrepreneurs for the overall development of the country. It called for priority to women in allotment of land, sheds, sanction of power, licensing etc.

The *Second International Conference* of Women Entrepreneurs organized by the National Alliance of Young Entrepreneurs (NAYE) held in 1989 at New Delhi also adopted certain declarations involving women's participation in industry.

The *Government of India* has been assigning increasing importance to the development of women entrepreneurs in the country in recent years. The *Sixth Five Year Plan*, for example, proposed for promoting female employment in women-owned industries. The Government moved a step forward in the *Seventh Five Year Plan* by including a special chapter on Integration of Women in Development. The chapter suggested.

- To treat women as specific target groups in all development programmes and involve them in decision making process.
- To devise and diversify vocational training facilities for women to suit their varied needs and skills.
- To promote appropriate technologies to improve their efficiency and productivity.
- To provide assistance for marketing their products.

Ranks of Business Opportunities for Women Entrepreneurs

Areas	*Rank*
Cosmetics and Beauty Parlors	01
Garments and Textile Items	02
Education and Training	03
Interior Decoration	04
Nursery and Creches	05
Handicrafts	06
3P's (Pickles, Powder [spices] and Papad)	07
Consultancy Services	08
Medicare (Medical and Paramedical)	09
Engineering Goods	10

The percentage of business started and operated by women in the U.S. is less than those started by men. However, the number is increasing at a rapid rate. For example, the number of female sole proprietors was 3,104,029 or 22% of all sole proprietors, according to the *Internal Revenue Service, U.S.* Women entrepreneurs can also hire professionals, trained under Small Industry Management Assistant's Programme (SIMAP) of Small Industries Development Bank of India (SIDBI).

First Woman Entrepreneur in the World

Rita Singh, founder of the *M'escos (Mid-east Shipping Company)* group, is one of the first woman entrepreneurs in the business world. Starting from scratch about 20 years ago, she now exports trendy M'escos shoes, owns a fleet of state-of-the-art-helicopters and ships, and Rs.450 crore steel plant. The M'escos group with an annual turnover of over Rs.1500 crore, employs more than 7,000 peoples

Tips for Development of Women Entrepreneurs

Right efforts from all areas are required in the development of women entrepreneurs and their greater participation in the entrepreneurial activities. Following efforts can be taken into account for effective development of women entrepreneurs.

1. Consider women as specific target group for all developmental programmes.
2. Better educational facilities and schemes should be extended to women folk from government part.
3. Encourage women's participation in decision-making.
4. Vocational training to be extended to women community that enables them to understand the production process and production management.
5. Skill development to be done in women's polytechnics and industrial training institutes. Skills are put to work in training-cum-production workshops.
6. Training on professional competence and leadership skill to be extended to women entrepreneurs.

7. Training and counselling on a large scale of existing women entrepreneurs to remove psychological causes like lack of self-confidence and fear of success.
8. Activities in which women are trained should focus on their marketability and profitability.
9. To encourage more passive women entrepreneurs the Women training programme should be organized that taught to recognize her own psychological needs and express them.
10. State finance corporations and financing institutions should permit by statute to extend purely trade related finance to women entrepreneurs.
11. Women's development corporations have to gain access to open-ended financing.
12. The financial institutions should provide more working capital assistance both for small scale venture and large scale ventures.
13. Repeated gender sensitization programmes should be held to train financiers to treat women with dignity and respect as persons in their own right.
14. A Women Entrepreneur's Guidance Cell set up to handle the various problems of women entrepreneurs all over the state.
15. Programmes for encouraging entrepreneurship among women are to be extended at local level.

Women in World Business

Women recently started playing a vital role in international business. However the role of women is not equal to that of men even today. The role of women in economic activities varies from country to country. The women in the middle management position seem to age around 34 years or below. Rarely can married women in such a position be found. Motivation paves way to some women to make their foot prints in all types of business including industrial goods and high technology. Thus hardly can any business be found without a women competing with a man to reach the specific career goal.

In recent years the Global Entrepreneurship Monitor has shown an increase in women's participation in enterprise in the world. However, a gap still remains between the number of men and women engaged in entrepreneurial activity, and women continue to be the largest under-represented group. There is enormous benefit to be realized for our economy if more women are encouraged to maximize the use of their skills in an existing business or new business start-up. The role of women in different countries is exhibited as below:

Country	*Role of Women Entreprenuers*
Saudi Arabia	Restrictions on women's freedom.E.g. they are not permitted to drive, to travel on an airplane alone or to stay in a hotel without a male family member.
Japan	Japan women seldom work after marriage;Consequently, women are unlikely to progress far within organizations.
U.S	Women have attained a degree of equality in business, but they are seldom found in top management.
Ireland	The constitution has been interpreted to mean that women should only the work force if her husband is not able to look after the family economically.
China (the Govt provided extensive educational facilities for women)	Women hold many of same positions as men, but they are required to retire at an earlier age.
Hong Kong	They are effective in doing business, so mostly they are in secretarial positions.
Malaysia	Equal opportunity is given to women, they do not enter business.
Canada	Majority of nurses and secretaries are women while the majority of fire fighters, construction workers and foresters are men.
Singapore	Employment is quite common. 80% of women work force is in the age of 10 to 24 years. Professional women are in government service.
Bahrain	They are educated and are given opportunity, but they are discouraged from seeking employment.
South Korea	They rarely enter business.
Thailand	Women are seen as "the hind legs of the elephant" - powerful but following - and are in subordinate positions. Some women hold top positions in government and private business.
Denmark	Women get 32 weeks of maternity leave.
Greece	Women get 15 weeks
Spain	Women get 16 weeks
Most of the European countries	They are attempting to promote equal opportunities for women
U.S.A and Canada	It is better compared to women employment in almost all the other countries in the world. However , women work in jobs subordinate to men in the U.S.A and Canada.
Africa	They mostly confine to domestic activities
West Indies	The minimum wage for women is lower than for men , regardless of the work performed.
India	Employment is quite common. 80% of women work force is in the age of 10 to 24 years. Professional women are in government service.

Source: http://www.woman.ch.

Five Fredrick Harbiscon Functions of a Women Entrepreneur

- Exploration of the prospects of starting a new business enterprise.
- Undertaking a risk and handling of economic uncertainties involved in business.
- Introduction of innovations, imitations of innovations.
- Co ordination, administration and control.
- Supervision and leadership.

Conclusion

Independence brought promise of equality of opportunity in all sphere to the Indian women and laws guaranteeing for their equal rights of participation in political process and equal opportunities and rights in education and employment were enacted. But unfortunately, the government sponsored development activities have benefited only a small section of women. The large majority of them are still unaffected by change and development activities, have benefited only a small section of women i.e. the urban middle class women. The large majority of them are still unaffected by change and development.

Women have made great workers over the part- decade. Women achieved a lot in many fields. Now-a-days, thus there is no a field with out a women's contribution. The growth their after have also increased to the high level. But it has not yet reached the highest level. Even the current scenario, the women are portioned at the level below to that of men. Still socialism, take of political awareness and tokenism play a vital role in preventing the women's growth.

References

Medha Dubhashi Vinze (1987), *Women Entrepreneurs in India: A Socio-Economic Study of Delhi* - 1975-76, Mittal Publications, New Delhi.

Renuka V. (2001), "Opportunities and Challenges for Women in Business", *India Together, Online Report,* Civil Society Information Exchange Pvt. Ltd.

Meena, N.L. (1991), 'National Policy and Programs for Women in India' in Papers and Proceedings of the *Regional Conference on Gender Issues in Agriculture, ADB and UNIFEM.* (Manila, 5-6 December, 1990).

Jose P., Ajith Kumar. & Paul T.M. (1994), *Entrepreneurship Development,* Himalaya Publishing.

Starcher, D.C. (1996), *Women Entrepreneurs: Catalysts for Transformation.* Retrieved July 6, 2001: http:// www.ebbf.org/woman.htm[10] (c20012695[11])

"The Female Poverty Trap" (2001, May 8). *The Economist.* Retrieved March 14, 2001: *http://www.economist.com*

Amarnath, Nischinta; Ghosh, Debashish (2005), *The Voyage to Excellence: The Ascent of 21 Women Leaders of India Inc.,* Pustak Mahal.

Robbins, P. Stephens (1999), *Organizational Behavior – Concepts, Controversies, Applications,* Prentice Hall of India Private Limited, 8th Edition.

Sekharan, Uma (2004), *Organisational Behavior – Text and Cases,* Tata McGraw-Hill Publishing Company Limited, New Delhi, 2nd Edition.

CHAPTER-24

Woman Empowerment through Microenterprises–A Case Study of Orissa

Sanjeeb Kumar Jena, Jayanta K. Parida

During the 1990s, Micro-Finance Programmes (MFPs) and Microenterprises (MEs) programmes have emerged as a mainstream development intervention for addressing poverty alleviation and women's empowerment (Dichter, 1999; Wright, 1999; Rahman, 1999; Mayoux, 1998b; Amin *et al.*, 1998; Kabeer, 1998; Johnson and Roglay, 1997; Hulme and Mosley, 1997; Hashemi *et al.*, 1996). These programmes have become a much-favoured intervention among international development agencies, providing a 'new paradigm for thinking about economic and social development' (Mordouch, 1997:1 in Rahman, 1999). There is almost a global consensus that micro-lending to the poor to set up microenterprises, individually or collectively, focusing on achieving equitable and sustainable gain which is considered as the key element for economic and social development in the twenty-first century (Mayoux, 1999b; Micro-Credit Summit, 1997).

Some have described this preoccupation with credit as the 'missing piece strategy' to poverty alleviation (McKee, 1989:1003), with Roglay (1996:100) calling it the 'hard-selling of a new anti-poverty formula by the 'micro-finance evangelists.'

Successive evaluations attesting to substantial developmental benefits (Amin *et al.*, 1998; Kabeer, 1998; Hashemi *et al.*, 1996) have over the past decade led to an increase in funding for MFPs, which according to Mayoux (1998b) is likely to further increase. There is no doubt that MFPs and MEs have been successful in reaching women, particularly given the challenging socio-cultural conditions in which they live. However, in the context of these programme interventions being increasingly promoted as a mechanism for women's empowerment, it becomes essential to analyze and determine the nature and extent of empowerment promoted by them.

Purpose of the Study

This study aims at to examine the extent of women's empowerment being promoted by MEs in a most under-developed district of India- Malkanagiri, situated in the state of Orissa (last ranked according to India Human Resource Development Index 2007). The underlying assumption is that participation in MEs have been accelerating the pace of development in form of developing personal, social, economic and political empowerment of women.

The study is anchored on the premise that issues of empowerment and transformation need to be located within the individual subjects' social, cultural and historical context. In other words, it takes cognizance of the way women actively transform their reality within the social constraints of their lives. By doing so, it recognizes the plurality of voices and multiple realities that such an exploration leads to. The idea is not to resolve or dissolve the paradoxes, uncertainties and contradictions that emerge from the study, but in fact to recognize the issues involved in analyzing emerging factors relating to women's empowerment.

Methodology

The study is a literature review of the microenterprise sector. It analyses and synthesizes the current debates and trends within the sector from a global perspective. It also looks at the theoretical debates on empowerment as propounded by development practitioners and academicians, to facilitate a better understanding of the conceptual frameworks on the various concepts of empowerment.

The present study is based on primary as well as secondary data. The primary data has been collected from the 60 women artisans engaged in bamboo crafts. The district was specifically selected keeping in view of its rich craft traditions, high demand of artifacts, poverty dominated and unutilized human resources. A broad analytical framework has been devised on the basis of open-ended interview schedule to collect primary data. Field visits, physical observation and in depth interviews with them so also with their dependants in two phases; one in the year 2000, i.e., just when the Craft Village Scheme was introduced and second in the year 2008 have been collected and analysed by applying different statistical techniques.

Limitations of the Study

Analyzing the impact of credit on women's empowerment is a stupendous task. The concept of empowerment is itself a multi-dimensional indicator of change, difficult to define, identify or measure. It refers to a variety of attitudes and attributes, which are likely to vary across class, time, and space (Mayoux, 1998a; Hulme, 1998; Schuler *et al.*, 1997; Ackerely, 1995). The social, political and cultural dimensions of empowerment are inherently interconnected, qualitative and subjective, making impact assessment an even more complex and dynamic a task (Hulme, 1998; Goetz and Sen Gupta, 1996).

Apart from the limitations posed by conceptualizing empowerment, credit impact studies also pose problems of proving causality and attribution. It is difficult to attribute an empowered state to credit intervention alone, as there may be other factors in a woman's life contributing to such changes. In fact, most research studies make linear and deterministic linkages between credit interventions and women's empowerment, failing to consider other factors which may have contributed to the empowered state.

Micro-Finance/Micro-enterprise Programs

There is no doubt, poverty is one of the biggest problem and the greatest task facing world over. When estimating poverty, the same reference poverty line has to be used, and expressed in a common unit across countries. Therefore, for the purpose of global aggregation and comparison, the World Bank uses reference lines set at $1 per day for the *"poorest"* or *"very poor"* people (or those in the extreme economic poverty) and $2 per day for the *"poor"* people who are living in the upper half of those living below their nation's poverty line* (more precisely $1.08 and $2.15 in 1993 Purchasing Power Parity terms).

Traditional finance systems have long history and countless variations. In fact, in most countries they continue to flourish despite the emergence of formal finance systems (Rutherford, 2000; Ardener and Burman, 1995; Christesen, 1993). Broadly, these can be seen as ranging from traditional institutions such as local money lending and self-finance from relatives and friends, to more formal sources of credit such as trade credit and group-based MFPs promoted by Non-government Organisations (NGOs) (Bastelaer, 1999; Johnson and Roglay 1997). Perhaps the most common source of informal finance is loans from family and friends, characterized by uncollateralized credit that carries little or no interest. They are usually intended to meet the consumption and contingency needs of households, rather than to build investment capability.

A commercial variation of such loans is the traditional moneylender. Moneylenders directly draw on traditional patron-client relationships or a set of hierarchical social interactions that are reminiscent of the vertical dimensions of Coleman's (1990) definition of social capital. These relationships are exploitative in nature, as interest rates are set in such a way that full repayment is unlikely (Bastelaer, 1999; Johnson and Roglay, 1997).

These informal sources have played a vital role in meeting the financial, social and safety net needs of the poor in urban and rural areas. Their services are easily accessible, flexible and responsive to clients' specific needs more efficiently, as they can handle small sums of money without complex procedures or documentation.

Amid the dispiriting news, excitement is building about a set of unusual financial institutions prospering in distant corners of the world. The hope is that much poverty can be alleviated—and that economic and social structures can be transformed fundamentally—by providing financial services to low-income households. These institutions, united under the banner of *microfinance for micro-enterprise,* share a commitment to serving poor that have been excluded from the formal banking sector.

The Underlying Rationale

MEs through MFPs operate on the principle of group-based lending, commonly referred to as 'solidarity groups' (Reinke, 1998). They consist of self-selected, small and homogeneous borrower groups, jointly liable for loans, with varying degrees of participation in program management. Joint responsibility and liability for loans enhance accountability and result in a higher rate of repayment than the standard bilateral loan agreements of formal financial systems. Credit disbursement is organized on the principle of 'social collateral,' where borrowers' reputation or the social networks to which they belong take the place of traditional physical or financial collateral (Bastelaer, 1999).

In this sense, MEs operate through existing stocks of social capital. The group processes strengthen existing social relations, institutions and shared values and in the process create an environment supportive for the emergence of fresh social capital (Narayan, 2000; Mayoux, 1999a; Bastelaer, 1999). They transform 'beneficiaries' into 'clients' through the development and enforcement of contracts between lenders and borrowers and by supporting the ownership and control of resources by the poorest.

Group-based credit programmes promoted by NGOs allow poor people access to financial services that they have historically been denied. In this sense, they address the market failures of formal financial institutions (Khandker, 1998;

Mayoux, 1998b; Wood and Sharif, 1997). MFPs, by extending loans for production, support a virtuous cycle of investment, savings and further investments. In fact, credit is seen as a mechanism for generating self-employment opportunities for the poor and/or improving the productivity of existing enterprises, referred to as the 'promotional' strategy by Hulme and Mosley (1996:106). This leads to economic empowerment, which is assumed to promote a 'virtuous spiral' of broader social and political change by women (Mayoux, 1998b, 1999b; Ebdon, 1995). By making consumption credit available during periods of cyclical or unexpected crisis, MEs also play a social protection role (Edgcomb and Barton, 1998:1; Hulme and Mosley, 1996:106).

Women's Empowerment

Empowerment is central to the issues of equality, liberation and justice, with the concept of power being fundamental to its understanding. The concept of empowerment is used in many ways and in a wide range of contexts, and is applied by organizations of differing world views and political persuasions. There has been increasing global recognition of the vital importance of empowerment in developing responses to underdevelopment and the increasing poverty (Craig and Mayo, 1995).

Commonly, empowerment is described as 'a process whereby women become able to organize themselves to increase their own self-reliance, to assert their independent right to make choices and to control resources which will assist in challenging and eliminating their own subordination' (Rowlands, 1997:17). Women's empowerment is seen as entailing a shift from positions of powerlessness towards strategic social, economic and political participation. This implies taking on power both at the individual and social levels (Kabeer, 1994, 1999; Nelson and Wright, 1995; Moser, 1993; Friedmann, 1992).

All the conceptualizations of empowerment emphasize four main dimensions-individual or personal, economic, collective/social group and political. Most see the empowerment process as addressing a combination of these dimensions and affecting different domains: household, community, national and international. These views of empowerment are grounded within different concepts of power, the root concept within which empowerment is located, leading to different mechanisms for social change and transformation. They can broadly be organized along a continuum, with personal and political empowerment forming the two ends.

Personal End of the Empowerment Continnum

Rowlands (1997) identified four different forms that power can take. 'Power over' is controlling power; 'power to' is generative or productive power creating new possibilities and actions without domination; 'power with' is relational and exists only in its exercise; 'power within' is seen in terms of self-reliance and self-esteem without any significant negative effects upon the power of the powerful. Once empowered, they can share the fruits of development, become agents of their own development and in the process achieving self-reliance (Craig and Mayo 1995).

Personal empowerment for Rowlands (1997) is key to the entire empowerment process, and involves fundamental psychological and psychosocial processes and changes. She views empowerment processes as dynamic, aimed at finding 'more spaces for control' and encompassing changes at the personal, relational and collective levels. At the personal level these processes involve developing confidence and abilities, while undoing the effects of internalized oppression. Her understanding of personal empowerment is based on the concept of 'power-within.' It sees women as confronting gender conditioning and their own internalized oppression, and re-negotiating their roles within the household.

Empowerment within close relationships is associated with, and to a large extent dependent upon, self-confidence, self-esteem and a sense of agency. According to Rowlands, this is not an invariable consequence of personal empowerment, though personal empowerment is a necessary precondition for negotiating and influencing close relationships. In many respects, altering close relationships seems to be the most difficult area of change for women. Oakley *et al.* (1997:18) goes beyond close relationships and views empowerment as 'power in terms of increasing relations which people establish with other organizations.'

Political End of the Empowerment Continuum

In their respective conceptualizations of empowerment, Price (1992), Friedmann (1992), Johnson (1992) and Young (1993), the notion of empowerment signifies 'power-over,' which conceptualizes power in zero-sum terms. It is seen as a 'capacity to act' and is conceived as a quantitative phenomenon that is used as an instrument for domination (Rowlands, 1997; Hindess, 1996; Elshtain, 1992). Increasing the power of one group implies, by definition, decreasing the power of others. Such a concept of power involves relationships between those who have more of it and those who have less.

Women's empowerment according to Johnson (1992 in Rowlands, 1997:18) involves 'gaining voice, having mobility and establishing a public presence'. She associates empowerment with collective public action that challenges existing power structures and identifies different development priorities. Johnson's conceptualization emphasizes individual and political empowerment, with the former not necessarily seen as leading to the latter. This makes concerted, planned and strategic effort to increase the effective participation of women in the political arena imperative.

For Young (1993: 159), empowerment allows women 'to take control of their own lives, to set their own agendas, to organize to help each other and make demands on the state for support and on society itself for change.' It implies the radical alteration of the processes and structures which reproduce women's subordinate position as a gender. In other words, empowerment is premised on a 'transformatory potential' relating to the '...need to transform women's position in such a way that the advance will be sustained'..

Women's Economic Empowerment through Microenterprises

According to UNIFEM, "gaining the ability to generate choices and exercise bargaining power," "developing a sense of self-worth, a belief in one's ability to secure desired changes, and the right to control one's life" are important elements of women's empowerment. Empowerment is an implicit, if not explicit, goal of a great number of microfinance institutions around the world. Empowerment is about change, choice, and power. It is a process of change by which individuals or groups with little or no power gain the power and ability to make choices that affect their lives. The structures of power—who has it, what its sources are, and how it is exercised—directly affect the choices that women are able to make in their lives.

Microfinance (MF) / microenterprise (ME) programs have the potential to transform power relations and empower the poor—both men and women. In well-run ME programs, there is a relationship of respect between the provider and the client that is inherently empowering. This is true regardless of the methodology or approach (whether the institution takes a minimalist approach of delivering financial services only or a more holistic or integrated approach). As a consequence, microfinance and microenterprise have become a central component of many donor agencies' and national governments' gender, poverty alleviation, and community development strategies.

Why to Target Women?

Many different rationales can be offered for placing a priority on increasing women's access to microfinance services.

Gender and Development: Research done by UNDP, UNIFEM, and the World Bank, among others, indicates that gender inequalities in developing societies inhibit economic growth and development. For example, a recent World Bank report confirms that societies that discriminate on the basis of gender pay the cost of greater poverty, slower economic growth, weaker governance, and a lower living standard of their people. Microfinance has come to play a major role in many of these donors' gender and development strategies because of its direct relationship to both poverty alleviation and women.." As part of its poverty reduction priority, CIDA supports programs that provide "increased access to productive assets (especially land, capital, and credit), processing, and marketing for women." By giving women access to working capital and training, microfinance helps mobilize women's productive capacity to alleviate poverty and maximize economic output. In this case, women's entitlement to financial services, development aid, and equal rights rests primarily on their potential contribution to society rather than on their intrinsic rights as human beings and members of that society.

Women are the Poorest of the Poor: It is generally accepted that women are disproportionately represented among the world's poorest people. Women have a higher unemployment rate than men in virtually every country. In general women also make up the majority of the lower paid, unorganized informal sector of most economies. By providing access to financing for income-generating activities, microfinance institutions can significantly reduce women's vulnerability to poverty. A reduction in women's vulnerability can sometimes also translate into empowerment if greater financial security allows the women to become more assertive in household and community affairs.

Women spend more of their Income on their Families: Women have been shown to spend more of their income on their households; therefore, when women are helped to increase their incomes, the welfare of the whole family is improved. Assisting women, therefore, generates a multiplier effect that enlarges the impact of the institutions' activities. Women who are empowered will have the power to make the life choices that are best for them.

Efficiency and Sustainability: Arguments have been made for and against targeting women on the grounds of efficiency and sustainability. Proponents of targeting women on the grounds of sustainability cite women's repayment records and cooperativeness. A collective wisdom has emerged that women's repayment rates are typically far superior to those of men. Lower arrears and loan loss rates have an important effect on the efficiency and sustainability of the institution. Many programs have also found women to be more cooperative and prefer to work with them for that reason as well.

Women's Rights Perspective: Women's equal access to financial resources is a human rights issue. This is so because access to credit is an important mechanism for reducing women's poverty. It has been an explicit focus of a variety of human rights instruments.

Empowering Women: Last, but not least, one of the often articulated rationales for supporting microfinance and the targeting of women by microfinance programs is that microfinance is an effective means or entry point for empowering women. By putting financial resources in the hands of women, microfinance institutions help level the playing field and promote gender equality.

Access to Credit and Empowerment

The basic theory is that microenterprise empowers women by putting capital in their hands and allowing them to earn an independent income and contribute financially to their households and communities. This economic empowerment is expected to generate increased self-esteem, respect, and other forms of empowerment for women beneficiaries. Involvement in successful income-generating activities should translate into greater control and empowerment.

Microenterprises and Malkangiri District

Malakangiri, a part of the undivided Koraput district is characterized by its unparallel natural beauty–high mountains, deep valleys, perennial streams, dark forests, green fields and unadulterated tribal life and their culture. The district is divided into two different physical divisions. The eastern part is covered with steep ghats, platues, valleys sparsely inhabited by primitive tribes notable among whom are bondas, koyas, porajas, and didayis.. Almost the whole of the district is a vast dense jungle. Potteru, Saberi, Kolab and Machhakunda are the main rivers flowing in the district. This district is very rich in minerals and also has a lot of potential in agriculture particularly in plantation and horticulture. But majority of the population lives below the poverty line and their socio-economic condition is beyond imagination. In order to overcome from the clutch of the poverty the available natural resources need to be exploited to achieve the desired goal of poverty alleviation and self-employment. Crafts like tribal jewelry, terracotta, dhokra casting, bamboo works, brass and bell metal products, golden grass products have the potential to grow into serious commercial venture. The Bamboo craft sector in Malkangiri district operates with the following strengths, weaknesses, opportunities and threats.

Strength

Availability of a major cross-section of craftsmen with desired level of skill and competencies

- Low level of investment with little gestation period
- Generation of self-employment
- No/less power utilization in production process
- High level of value addition to investment
- Economic empowerment of women
- Utilization of local resources
- Easy adaptation of appropriate technology
- Eco-friendly
- Products having adequate demand in domestic and foreign market

Weakness

- Highly unorganized and widely dispersed sector
- Lack of opportunity/willingness for adaptation to
    - Market oriented designs.
    - Production diversification.
    - Cross-culture innovation.
    - Advanced technology.

- Lack of exposure to different market segments.
- Lack of enterprising and marketing skill.
- In-adequate market intelligence.
- Non-conducive policies on utilization of forest based raw materials.
- Inadequate institutional credit flow leading to exploitative lending.
- Inability of timely execution of large orders.
- Lack of proper branding of products resulting in duplication.
- Lack of awareness and measures for quality assurance.

Opportunity

- Availability of large Manpower and Labor force.
- Ample scope of Govt schematic support for artisans under various schemes
- High export potential.
- Least impact of WTO in this sector.
- Availability of traditional skill.

Threat

- Imitation by other States due to lack of patenting.
- Frequent occurrence of natural calamity.
- Seasonal availability of raw materials needing huge fund for due time procurement.
- Seasonal employment in Crafts like Terracotta.
- High illiteracy rate to adjust with the changed scenario

The bamboo craft sector in Malkangiri has been one of the sun rising sector of that area. It has got enough scope for the development in small and tiny sector. Though the craft is a traditional art-form mingled with traditional values and culture, due to lack of income generating abilities throughout the year, the craftsmanship is going to be vanished from these areas. However, the cluster development program for handicraft sector initiated in KBK districts in the year 2001 by the Director of Handicraft and Cottage Industries (DH&CI) has brought some improvement in the development of these crafts.

All the bamboo craft involves traditional skill and a traditional market approach fulfilling the household utility need of the local communities in the past. The artisans possess traditional skill to take up the bamboo craft as an entrepreneurial venture. Thus they formed the SHGs to be grouped together to set up microenterprises to earn their livelihood. Whatever schemes and programmes implemented in the past for the development of these craft artisans was less significant in providing them a sustainable livelihood. The major limitations are the lack of marketing avenues and an all round the year employment.

After the intervention of Director of Handicraft and Cottage Industries, through implementation of Craft Village Scheme in the year 2000, there has been a significant improvement of craft sector and the artisans improved their income and sustainability. The limitations of the previous schemes have been eliminated by appointing a NGO as Cluster Development Agency (CDA) in collaboration with District Industries Center. The CDAs not only give training to the artisans but also they provide marketing, technical and financial support to the microenterprises set up by the artisans in the form of Self Help Groups.

Microenterprise Programs and Women's Empowerment- The Malkangiri Experience

Analysis of the data for both rounds of the survey, before (2000) and after (2008) the intervention given by the DH&CI under Craft Village Scheme, followed the core AIMS data analysis plan. This called for a set of descriptive tables for data from Rounds 1 and 2, plus statistical analysis ANOVA.

The quantitative analysis tested the core AIMS hypotheses about impact at the household, enterprise, and individual levels. For each of these hypotheses, a quantitative measure (impact variable) was defined. The most potent statistical test undertaken, the analysis of variation (ANOVA) took into account the possibility that the relationship might be influenced by other factors, known as moderating variables.

This study suggests that it is simplistic to assume that merely providing women with their own financial resources will directly lead to a virtuous cycle of personal, social and political empowerment. In other words, it rejects the 'magic bullet' belief that economic empowerment, through single strategic interventions will lead to a reversal in gender relationships. However, the analysis indicates that MEs operating from either the minimalist or the integrated approaches create empowerment-promoting conditions for women by providing opportunities for strengthening the personal, social, economic and political dimensions. Furthermore, MEs operating from the integrated framework create conditions that have wider social and political effects, having a positive impact on women's status.

Women's Empowerment: An Analysis of the Different Dimensions

Personal empowerment is core to the entire empowerment process. Evidence suggests that the social aspects of credit programmes and the manner in which these aspects are organized contribute to personal empowerment of women by strengthening 'power-within.' The analysis had shown that the women respondents have shown a marked increase in their interaction with different persons in the society like family members, with members of husband's family, neighbours, personal friends outside family, and with outsiders like strangers, community leaders and government officials. The Table-1 shows a significant difference in the statistics collected before and after the ME intervention on position of the women with respect to their interaction.

Table 1
ANOVA
Interact Freely With Different Persons in the Society

Source of Variation	*SS*	*df*	*MS*	*F*	*F critical*
Between Groups	2044.9	1	2044.9	18.523	5.317
Within Groups	883.2	8	110.4	2928.1	9
Total	2928.1	9			

The Table-2 also supports the above result, a significant difference in the interaction patterns of the women entrepreneurs of the MEs at the time of trading, i.e., interaction with the employer, employees, traders, suppliers, buyers and customers, police personnel and medical staff.

Table 2
ANOVA
Commonly Accepted Views for the Trade

Source of Variation	*d.f.*	*SS*	*MS*	*F*	*F critical*
Between Groups	1	1849.6	1849.6	16.147	5.317
Within Groups	8	916.4	114.55		
Total	9	2766			

The group-based weekly credit meetings, an aspect common to most MEs, draw women out of their homes and give them an opportunity to be part of larger social processes. In many cases, this is the only significant group outside the family to which the woman has ever belongs, allowing them to develop a sense of identity. These group-based meetings also promote social empowerment by providing an opportunity for instilling a greater sense of awareness of social and political issues.The awareness level of the respondents had shown a tremendous change. Table-3 shows a significant difference in the awareness level of the respondents with respect to their rights, so to discard the null hypothesis of no change in awareness level among the women respondents after ME intervention.

Table 3
ANOVA
Awareness Towards Various Rights

Source of Variation	*SS*	*df*	*MS*	*F*	*F critical*
Between Groups	1512.9	1	1512.9	8.202	5.317
Within Groups	1475.6	8	184.45		
Total	2988.5	9			

By providing opportunities for frequent interaction with programme staff and other members of the social network, such meetings expose women to new ideas and values. This increases their self-confidence and makes them more assertive of their rights than women who have not had similar exposure. More specifically, it has been noted that when women members play leadership roles, as group leaders and/or centre leaders, they experience an increased sense of self-confidence and self-worth. Similarly, in programmes where credit groups are federated at a spatially higher level, group meetings are significantly more empowering for women as they provide an enhanced status and greater bargaining power in local communities. But, the Table-4 depicts the insignificant difference in making bargaining with the traders as the women in these regions are highly dependent on the male communities. The change is seen but seems to be very slow and steady and the trend shows that the respondents are in the way of a transition take up the higher responsibilities as expected.

Table 4
ANOVA
Independent Negotiation in Trade

Source of Variation	*df*	*SS*	*MS*	*F*	*F crit*
Between Groups	1	42.667	42.667	0.441	7.708
Within Groups	4	386.667	96.667		
Total	5	429.334			

MEs, especially those operating from an integrated perspective and as part of larger programmes, occasionally involve training programmes and related activities. These provide women with opportunities to travel outside the village and expand their knowledge beyond the four walls of their household and immediate community. The increased mobility leads to a greater sense of self-confidence, and is empowering in its own right, In this sense, MEs can become a mechanism for promoting the inclusion of women into broader social processes. The same may be evidenced in the Table–5. This clearly evidenced of the fact that in Malkanagiri district women after their involvement through SHG managed in broadening their outlook and attitude to a greater extent.

Table 5
ANOVA
Independent Mobility

Source of Variation	*df*	*SS*	*MS*	*F*	*F crit*
Between Groups	1	66.25	66.25	4.731	4.600
Within Groups	14	4388.75	313.482		
Total	15	4731			

Table 6
Paired Samples Test for Change in the Earnings of the Women Artisans of Bamboo Crafts

Paired Differences							
			95% Confidence Interval of the Difference				
Mean	*Std. Deviation*	*Std. Error Mean*	*Lower*	*Upper*	*t*	*df*	*Significance (2-tailed)*
28.683	4.789	.618	27.446	29.920	46.396	59	.000

The above Table-6 shows a marked difference in the earnings of the women entrepreneurs due to the micro-enterprises. The timely intervention of NGOs and GOs in developing their skill level and proper marketing of the products have brought a miracle of change in their earning capacity. The opening of various marketing avenues for the trade and change in the designs and aesthetic of the end products, the traders have got increased revenue, leads to increase in sustainability in income and expenditure patterns. The statistics showed that the entrepreneurs have spend more money on food (an increase of 210%), child education (260%), medical care and child care (330%), sanitation and water (500%). The saving habits are also improved with the increase in the earnings as all the respondents are having bank accounts and the average saving per year per respondent found to be a minimum of Rs.2500/= per annum apart from the savings through SHGs. A significant change is also experienced in the expenditure pattern of the respondents as shown in Table-6.

Table 6
ANOVA
Change in the Average Monthly Expenses

Source of Variation	*SS*	*df*	*MS*	*F*	*F crit*
Between Groups	8642857.14	1	8642857.14	5.0947	4.747
Within Groups	20357142.8571429	12	1696428.57		
Total	29000000	13			

Another interesting factor which is observed during the interaction with the respondents is that the confidence level of the respondent to diversify to other trades is not so high as expected, and evidenced from Table-7. The tribal society has common characteristics of not changing the trade so frequently as seen in other areas. This may be due to the conservative attitude of the population to adhere to the changes. Lack of change agents, and the alienation to their culture may the reasons for such debacles.

Table 7
ANOVA
Capacity to Earning through Diversification of Trade

Source of Variation	*df*	*SS*	*MS*	*F*	*F crit*
Between Groups	1	12.5	12.5	0.0560	5.9873
Within Groups	6	1337	222.833		
Total	7	1349.5			

The effect of increased intra-household bargaining power can take on an even greater significance when credit programmes are made part of larger social mobilization effort, such as consciousness-raising and functional literacy (Amin *et al.*, 1998). Families associated in the process are attracted by the education system of the state and coming out slowly from the superstition against the education of their wards.This can be very well marked from the Table-8.

Economic contributions by women made possible through credit access, results in an increase in the security and welfare of the entire household. Such contributions can change the socio economic position of women and their families.. Evidence suggests that over time these results in shifting their spending pattern and more resources being spent on women's clothing and the household's health needs.

Table 8
ANOVA
Physical Attainment of Education, Skill etc.

Source of Variation	*df*	*SS*	*MS*	*F*	*F crit*
Between Groups	1	392	392	0.734	5.987
Within Groups	6	3204	534		
Total	7	3596			

Table 9
ANOVA
Contribution to Household

Source of Variation	*SS*	*df*	*MS*	*F*	*F crit*
Between Groups	930.125	1	930.125	6.301	5.987
Within Groups	885.75	6	147.625		
Total	1815.875	7			

While fitting the data of two different periods with respect to the contribution of the women entrepreneurs to their household in terms of ability to feed the family, to educate the children, earning at par with other male members of the family, working longer than other members of the family and the ability to take the burden of the family independently, it is noted a significant difference in nominal values (Table–9). The women respondents are also now recognize their potentiality of being a respectable part of the community, particularly in their village. Some of the members of the SHGs are also being elected as the Gram panchayat members and Sarapanach also. When the status of the women was compared before and after the micro-enterprise interventions, a significance difference has been noticed (Table–10) while the attributes are helping neighbors (physically and financially), helping in resolving conflicts, taking the demands of the community to the appropriate authorities, protest against any bad action against the community, and playing role of a leader and being a role model for others.

Table 10
ANOVA
Contribution to Community

Source of Variation	*SS*	*df*	*MS*	*F*	*F crit*
Between Groups	705.6	1	705.6	13.226	5.317
Within Groups	426.8	8	53.35		
Total	1132.4	9			

Earning an independent income through credit access has shown to lead to an increase in women's ability to exercise 'voice' in the household decision-making process. The Malkanagiri experience categorically support the above view as the level of difference in the independent decision making process in the household shows a significant change between the periods of study (Table–11). This is important as it is a reflection of enhanced power at the household level resulting in greater choice in household resource allocation, especially for those who were previously disenfranchised (Kabeer, 1998:47).

Table 11
ANOVA
Independence in Decision Making in Household

Source of Variation	*df*	*SS*	*MS*	*F*	*F crit*
Between Groups	1	1406.25	1406.25	4.783	4.600
Within Groups	14	4115.75	293.982		
Total	15	5522			

Of course, when the division of labour and distribution of authority over resources remains uncontested, it is not easy to conclude that there has been a positive change in the degree of women's empowerment. In the tribal society of Malkangiri district, the control over the assets and its ownership is generally bestowed with the male member as per the Hindu Law and the situation could not be changed much though the economic empowerment. Table 12 shows a non-significant difference in the response over the attribute, control and ownership of the assets and resources.

Table 12
ANOVA
Control and Ownership Over Assets and Resources

Source of Variation	*df*	*SS*	*MS*	*F*	*F crit*
Between Groups	1	12.5	12.5	0.0583	5.987
Within Groups	6	1287	214.5		
Total	7	1299.5			

Within this divergence of opinions and research findings it needs to be reiterated that an ethnocentric approach cannot be adopted to analyze the issue of women's empowerment. These findings need to be located in the socio-political context of Malkangiri, a typical tribal backdrop and culture, where the household is seen as a joint venture with women responsible for household-based activities and men taking on the responsibility for all other activities outside the house. In other words, women place greater emphasis on the advantage of working inside home, leading to a complementary division of labour. This makes it virtually inevitable that a woman's loan will be used jointly by herself and by the productive men in the household.

Conclusion

MFPs and ME Programs provide women with the opportunity to contribute towards the household economy, leading to economic empowerment of women. This has ramifications at the personal and relational level. Further, participation in MFPs has resulted in most women experiencing increased mobility and a concomitant reduction in their traditional seclusion. More importantly, it addresses gender relations by increasing women's intra-household bargaining power and 'voice' in household decision-making processes. These in some cases, have resulted in women participating in collective socio-political processes challenging existing gender inequality.

With empowerment being closely inter-linked with women's lives, it is essential for all of us the to know various issues involved to explore the 'women's own vantage point,' taking into account their voices and strategies. However, at the dawn of the 21st century despite the global recognition of the importance of women's empowerment, MFPs and ME Programs should at least adopt the minimalist approach slowly and steadly to penetrating in to the male dominating society like India and achieve the goal of woman empowerment if not today but tomorrow with much confident. All attempt in this regard will certainly contribute to the betterment of not only the down trodden women of the society but at large to the socio economic development of the nation as a whole.

References

Ackerly B.A. (1995), *Testing the Tools of Development: Credit Programmes, Loan Involvement and Women's Empowerment. IDS Bulletin*, Vol. 26 No 3, pp. 56-68.

Amin R., S. Becker and A. Bayes (1998), *NGO-Promoted MicroCredit Programmes and Women's Empowerment in Rural Bangladesh: Quantitative and Qualitative Evidence. The Journal of Developing Areas,* Vol. 32, No. 2, Winter 1998, pp. 221-236.

Ardener S. & S. Burman (1995), *Money-Go-Rounds: The Importance of Rotating Savings and Credit Associations for Women.* Berg, Oxford.

Bastelaer T.V. (1999), *Does Social Capital Facilitate The Poor's Access to Credit? A Review of the Microeconomic Literature.* The World Bank, Washington DC.

Beijing Platform for Action, Fourth United Nations World Conference on Women (Beijing, 1995), paragraph 41.

Bennett L. & C.E. Cuevas (1996), *Sustainable Banking With the Poor. Journal of International Development,* Vol. 8, No. 2, pp. 145-151.

Bennett L. & M. Goldberg (1993), *Providing Enterprise Development and Financial Services to Women: A Decade of Bank Experience in Asia. World Bank Technical Paper* No. 236, The World Bank, Washington D.C.

Canadian International Development Agency (CIDA), "CIDA's Policy on Gender Equality" (Hull, Canada: CIDA, 1999), 5.

Christesen G. (1993), *The Limits of Informal Financial Intermediation. World Development,* Vol. 21, No. 5, pp. 721-731.

Coleman J.S. (1990), *Foundations of Social Theory.* Harvard University Press, London.

Convention on the Elimination of All Forms of Discrimination Against Women, Beijing Declaration and Platform for Action, and other documents on UNIFEM's Web site: www.undp.org/unifem

Craig G. & M. Mayo (1995), *Community Empowerment: A Reader in Participation and Development*. Zed Books, London.

Deshpanda, Rani (2001), Increasing Access and Benefits for Women: Practices and Innovations among Microfinance Institutions – Survey Results. New York: UNCDF.

Deshpanda, Rani (2001), Increasing Access and Benefits for Women: Practices and Innovations among Microfinance Institutions – Survey Results. New York: UNCDF.

Dichter T. (1999), *Non-governmental Organisations (NGOs) in Microfinance: Past, Present and Future*. Available from: www.esd.worldbank.org/html/esd/agr/sbp/end/ngo.htm (Accessed on: 20.08.99)

Eade D. & S. Williams (1995), *The Oxfam Handbook of Development and Relief*. (Vol. I), Oxfam, Oxford.

Ebdon R. (1995), *NGO Expansion and the Fight to Reach the Poor: Gender Implications of NGO Scaling-Up in Bangladesh. IDS Bulletin*, Vol. 26, No 3, pp. 49-57.

Edgcomb E. & L. Barton 1998, *Social Intermediation and Microfinance Programs: A Literature Review*. USAID, USA.

Friedmann J. (1992), *Empowerment: The Politics of Alternative Development*. Blackwell Publishers, Oxford, UK.

Goetz A. M. & R. Sengupta (1996), *Who Takes the Credit? Gender, Power, and Control over Loan Use in Rural Credit Programs in Bangladesh. World Development*, Vol. 24, No 1, pp. 45-63.

Hashemi S.M., S.R. Schuler & A.P. Riley (1996), *Rural Credit Programs and Women's Empowerment in Bangladesh. World Development*, Vol. 24, No 4, pp. 635-653.

Hindess B. (1996), *Discourses of Power: From Hobbes to Foucault*. Blackwell Publishers, Oxford.

Hulme D. & P. Mosley (1996), *Finance against Poverty*. Volume I & II, Routledge, London.

Hulme D. (1998), *Impact Assessment Methodologies for Micro-Finance: A Review. IDS*, Brighton.

Jain, P.S. (1996), *Managing Credit for the Rural Poor: Lessons from the Grameen Bank. World Development,* Vol. 24, No 1, pp. 79-89.

Johnson H. and L. Mayoux (1998), *Investigating Empowerment: Issues in Participatory Methods.* In Thomas A., J. Chataway and M. Wuyts 1998, *Finding Out Fast: Investigative Skills for Development Policy and Public Action.* Sage, London.

Johnson S. & B. Roglay (1997), *Microfinace and Poverty Reduction.* Oxfam, UK.

Johnson S. (1998), *Microfinace North and South: Contrasting Current Debates. Journal of International Development,* Vol. 10, No 6, pp. 799-810.

Johnson S. (1998), *Programme Impact Assessment in Micro- Finance: The Need for Analysis of Real Markets. IDS Bulletin,* Vol. 29, No 4, pp. 21-30.

Kabeer N. (1994), *Reversed Realities: Gender Hierarchies in Development Thought.* Kali for Women, New Delhi.

Kabeer N. (1998), *'Money Can't Buy Me Love'? Re-evaluating Gender, Credit and Empowerment in Rural Bangladesh. IDS Discussion Paper,* No 363.

Kabeer N. (1999), *Resources, Agency, Achievements: Reflections on the Measurement of Women's Empowerment. Development and Change,* Vol. 30, No. 3, pp. 435-464.

Kabeer N. The Conditions and Consequences of Choice: Reflections on the Measurement of Women's Empowerment, *UNRISD Discussion Paper* No. 108 (1999), 49; www.unrisd.org.

Karl M. (1995), *Women and Empowerment: Participation and Decision Making.* Zed Books, London.

Khandker S.R. (1998), *Micro-Credit Programme Evaluation: A Critical Review. IDS Bulletin,* Vol. 29, No 4, pp.11-20.

Marchand M.H. and J.L. Parpart (eds.) (1995), *Feminism: Postmodernism Development.* Routledge, London.

Mayoux and Naila (1998), Empowerment in Rural Bangladesh, *IDS Discussion Paper 363* (Brighton, England: Institute of Development Studies, University of Sussex).

Mayoux L. (1998b), *Women's Empowerment and Micro-Finance Programmes: Approaches, Evidence and Ways Forward. DPP Working Paper No 41.*

Mayoux L. (1998a), *Participatory Learning for Women's Empowerment in Micro-Finance Programmes: Negotiating Complexity, Conflict and Change. IDS Bulletin*, Vol. 29, No 4, pp.39-50.

Mayoux L. (1999a), *Collective Strategies Reconsidered: Social Capital, Women's Empowerment and Sustainability in West African Micro-Finance Programmes.* In The *'Third International NGO Conference on 'NGO in a Global Future,'* University of Birmingham 10th - 13th January, 1998.

Mayoux L. (1999b), *From Access to Empowerment: Gender Issues in Micro-Finance.* In *CDS Virtual Conference.*

Mayoux, Linda (1995), From Vicious to Virtuous Circles? Gender and Micro-Enterprise Development. *Occasional Paper No. 3.* UNIFEM. United Nations Fourth World Conference on Women .

McKee K. (1989), *Microlevel Strategies for Supporting Livelihoods, Employment and Income Generation of Poor Women in the Third World: The Challenge of Significance. World Development, Vol. 17,* No 7 pp. 993-1006.

Micro-Credit Summit (1997), *Declaration and Plan of Action.* Available from: http//www.microcreditsummit.org/declaration.htm (Accessed on:18.08.99).

Montgomery R., D. Bhattacharya and D. Hulme (1996), *Credit for the Poor in Bangladesh: The BRAC Rural Development Programme and the Government Thana Resource Development and Employment Programme.* In Hulme D. & P. Mosley 1996, *Finance against Poverty. Volume II,* Routledge, London.

Moser C.O.N. 1989, *Gender Planning in the Third World: Meeting Practical and Strategic Gender Needs. World Development,* Vol. 17, No. 11, pp. 1799-1825.

Moser C.O.N. (1993), *Gender Planning and Development: Theory, Practice and Training.* Routledge, London.

Narayan D. (2000), *Bonds and Bridges: Social Capital and Poverty. World Bank,* Washington DC.

Nelson N. and S. Wright (1995), *Power and Participatory Development: Theory and Practice. Intermediate Technology,* London.

Oakley P., B. Pratt and A. Clayton 1997 *Outcomes and Impact: Evaluating Change in Social Development. INTRAC,* Oxford.

Paul S. and A. Subramanian (1983), *Development Programmes for the Poor: Do Strategies Make a Difference? Economic and Political Weekly,* pp. 349-358.

Pitt & Khandker (1995), *Household and Intrahousehold Impacts of the Grameen Bank and Similar Targeted Credit Programmes in Bangladesh.* In a *Workshop on 'Credit Programmes for the Poor Household and Intrahousehold Impacts and Programme Sustainability'*, Dhaka, Bangladesh.

Price J. (1992), *Women's Development: Welfare Projects or Political Empowerment?. Amesterdam Conference,* Mimeo.

Rahman A. (1999), *Micro-Credit Initiatives for Equitable and Sustainable Development:Who Pays? World Development,* Vol. 27, No. 1, pp. 67-82.

Reinke J. (1998), *Does Solidarity Pay? The Case of the Small Enterprise Foundation. Development and Change,* Vol. 29, pp. 553-576.

Robinson M.S. (1996), *Addessing Some Key Questions On Finance and Poverty. Journal of International Development,* Vol. 8, No. 2, pp. 153-161.

Roglay B. (1996), *Micro-Finance Evangelism, 'Destitute Women', and the Hard Selling of a New Anti-Poverty Formula. Development in Practice,* Vol. 6, No 2, pp. 100-112.

Roglay B. (1998), *Combating Financial Exclusion Through Co-operatives: Is there a Role for External Assistance? Journal of International Development,* Vol. 10, No 6, pp.823-836.

Rose K. (1992), *Where Women are Leaders: The SEWA Movement in India.* Zed Books, London.

Rowlands J. (1997), *Questioning Empowerment: Working with Women in Honduras.* Oxfam. UK.

Rutherford S. (2000), *The Poor and Their Money.* Oxford University Press, New Delhi.

Sally Baden and K. Milward (1995), "Gender and Poverty," *BRIDGE Report,* No. 30 (Sussex: IDS).

Schmidt R.H. and C.P. Zeitinger (1996), *Prospects, Problems and Potential of Credit-Granting NGOs. Journal of International Development,* Vol. 8, No. 2, pp. 241-258.

Schuler S.R., S.M. Hashemi and A.P. Riley (1997), *The Influence of Women's Changing Roles and Status in Bangladesh's Fertility Transition: Evidence from a Study of Credit Programme and Contraceptive Use. World Development,* Vol. 25, No. 4, pp. 563-575.

Sen A. (1990), *Development as Freedom.* Oxford University Press, Oxford.

Sinha S. and I. Matin (1998), *Informal Credit Transactions of Micro-Credit Borrowers in Rural Bangladesh. IDS Bulletin,* Vol. 29, No 4, pp. 66-81.

Sinha S. (1998), *Introduction and Overview. IDS Bulletin,* Vol. 29, No4, pp. 1-10.

UNDP (1995), *Human Development Report* (New York, UNDP, 1996), 4.

UNIFEM (2000), *Progress of the World's Women* (New York: UNIFEM).

USAID. Microenterprise Development in a Changing World: U.S. Agency for International Development Microenterprise Results *Reporting for 2000* (Arlington, Va.: Weidemann Associates, 2001), 31.

USAID (2000), Reaching Down and Scaling Up: Focus on USAID's *Development Partners:* USAID Microenterprise Results Reporting for 1999 (Arlington, Va.: Weidemann Associates), 22.

Wieringa S. (1994), *Women's Interests and Empowerment: Gender Planning Reconsidered. Development and Change,* Vol. 25, p. 829-848.

Wood G.D. & I. A. Sharif (1997), *Who Needs Credit? Poverty and Finance in Bangladesh.* Zed Books, London.

World Bank, Engendering Development: Through Gender Equality in Rights, Resources, and Voice Summary (Washington, D.C.: World Bank, 2001); www.worldbank.org/gender/prr/ engender summary.pdf.

World Development Report (1996), World Bank, Washington DC.

World Summit for Social Development (1995), Policy Paper. Available from: http://www.un.org/esa/socdev/wssdoc-4.htm (Accessed on: 20.08.99)

Wright G.A.N. (1999), *Examining the Impact of Microfinance Services–Increasing Income or Reducing Poverty. Small Enterprise Development,* Vol. 10, No. 1, pp. 39-47.

Young K. (1993), *Planning Development with Women: Making a World of Difference.* Macmillan, London.

Chapter-25

Rural Women Entrepreneurs: A Study

K.A. Rasure

Women Entrepreneurs: - The prime propellers of development are not born, but are created. Entrepreneurship development among women may be looked at from two angles. One is to create the environment needed for healthy and sound entrepreneurship and the other is to organize more and more rational motivational campaigns for the women entrepreneur. When she takes on this challenging role and wants to adjust her personality needs, family, social life and economic independence to this new role.

A rural women entrepreneur plays a catalytic role in activating the factors of production leading to an overall economic development in any country. There is no bar or distinction on the basis of caste, creed, religion or sex to anyone becoming an entrepreneur. Women Entrepreneur was a person endowed with the qualities of judgement, perseverance and knowledge of the world as well as of business. (J.B.Say).The prime motive of the entrepreneur is to accumulated and without motive there should be no accumulation to facilitate capital formation and economic development (Devid Ricardo). Women Entrepreneur is an important change agent in every society. Although it is her purposive activity that bridges the gap between plan and reality (G.Wayne).

Women Entrepreneur is an enterpriser, risk taker, co-ordinator and initiator. She plays a major role in the creation of new business and hence is a major contributor to economic growth. She is a combination of thinker and doer. Women entrepreneur always searches for change, responds to it and exploits it as an opportunity. Thus they innovate. (Peter Drucker). Thus women entrepreneur has a business gambler's and is goal-oriented rather than means-oriented. Further, by acting as role performer corresponding to the role expected by the society, they form the important change agents in every society and help in catalyzing economic growth of a country which is recognized world over.

Keeping the above facts in views, the following study was attempted by framing the following objectives.

- To analyse the various factors influencing the rural women entrepreneurs.
- To identify the problems encountered by the women entrepreneurs.
- To suggest measures to promote large scale rural women entrepreneurship

Results and Discussion

The factors which influence the entrepreneurship among rural women were classified as technological, personal, economic, physical and market factors. The respondents were asked to indicate which factor under each influenced their entrepreneurship and the percentage analysis was worked out.

The above factors influence the entrepreneurship directly or indirectly. So relevant data on the factors influencing entrepreneurship were collected and the data are presented below.

It could be inferred that about three fourths of the respondents had expressed that availability of SHG's for consultancy as the technology factor influencing their entrepreneurship, followed by NGO which is expressed by 65 per cent of the respondents.

Among the personal factors, self-confidence was expressed by 95 per cent of the respondents. About 90 per cent of the respondents had expressed the personal factor–own interest as a factor influencing their entrepreneurship. Entrepreneurs are people with high self-confidence and personally driven and enthusiastic people to achieve something which they call us their own accomplishment. The above findings proved the same. Experience was another factor influencing entrepreneurship as expressed by 60 per cent of the respondents. For any profession experience is very important to become a maestro in that area. Of course experience is the best teacher that would have made them well-versed in their enterprise influencing their entrepreneurship. Among the economic factors, demand for the product was expressed by 80 per cent of the respondents. Higher demand results in higher economic gain from the enterprise. In anticipation of higher demand leading to higher economic gain and high potential of the enterprise, they take up the enterprise.

The next important economic factor as expressed by 55 per cent of the respondents was initial investment. Initial investment must be strong to set up or maintain or to expand the enterprise. High investment makes the enterprise viable and therefore the returns are high. Lastly, physical factors which influenced the entrepreneurship were good transport facilities and availability of inputs. Regarding market factors, responsive prices 83 per cent and good market potential 80 per cent were major factors influencing entrepreneurship. Potential market and responsive prices will influence one to set up the enterprise and expand.

Problems of Rural Women Entrepreneurs

The major problems faced by women entrepreneurs are discussed here under.

Financial constraint was expressed by nearly 85 per cent of the respondents. This was due to the poor family background. Marketing of products was one of the major problems 75 per 7cent of the respondents expressed their opinion. Lack of technical know-how and do-how was yet another problem expressed by 70 per cent respondents. Non-availability of space to keep the manufactured produce was expressed by 55 per cent respondents. Lack of government support in establishing EDP for rural women and delay in license were expressed by 30 and 25 per cent of the respondents. Lack of knowledge (various facilities offered by state & central govt.) and seasonal demand of the produce were expressed by 50 and 33 per cent of the respondents.

Table 1
Factors Influencing Entrepreneurship

Factors	*Percentage*
Technological Factors	
Guidance from private agencies	40
Guidance from extension personnel	08
Guidance from SHG	75
Guidance from NGO	65
Personal Factors	
Own Interest	90
Self-confidence	95
Eagerness to evaluate enterprise	43
Risk-taking ability	20
Achievement motivation	18
Anticipation of future possibilities	18
Experience	60
Educational qualification	20
Economic Factors	
Initial Investment	55
Possession of ancestral property	05
Demand for the products	80
Resource recycling	05
Physical Factors	
Availability of inputs	63
Good transport facilities	93
Own vehicle	03
Good roads	05
Market Factors	
Good market potential	80
Response prices	83
Nearness to the market	03

Table 2
Problems Encountered by Women Entrepreneurs

Category	*Percentage*
Delay in license	25
Lack of Knowledge (various facilities offered by state & central Govt.)	50
Lack of technology know-how & do-how	70
Lack of infrastructure facilities	55
Lack of marketing facilities	75
Seasonal demand of the produce	33
Financial constraint	85
Lack of Government support in established EDP for rural women	30

Suggestions to Promote Rural Women Entrepreneurs

1. Re-orientation of educational system for women with due emphasis on career guidance, entrepreneurship awareness should start with school curriculum itself.
2. Group entrepreneurship should be promoted to bring out the hidden talents of the individual entrepreneur.
3. Publicizing the various incentive schemes of government and other agencies to rural women entrepreneurs is a must, to promote entrepreneurship in far-flung (remote) rural areas.
4. Fellow-up support in marketing the products of women entrepreneurs should be properly executed.
5. The skill of the existing women entrepreneurs should be upgraded.

To conclude, the various factors influencing the entrepreneurship should be the dimensions for the Entrepreneurship Development Programmes. (EDP). This has to be considered by the Government and the NGOs to promote the entrepreneurship among rural women. Similarly the policy table should consider the perceived constraints to be averted for the development of entrepreneurship among rural women.

References

Canon, Mark (1982), *The Entrepreneurship, An Economic Theory,* Barnes and Noble Books, Totowa. p.23.

Drucker, Peter (1985), *Innovation and Entrepreneurship. Practice and Principles,* Heiaemann, London. p.15

David Ricardo (1962), *The Principles of Political Economy and Taxation,* J.M.Dent & Sons Ltd., London. p.73.

Say, J.B. (1927), *Catechism of Political Economy,* New York. p. 295.

Wayne, B.G. (1978), *The Village Entrepreneur,* Harvard University Press, London.

Chapter-26

Self-Help Groups: A Keystone of Microfinance in India–Women Empowerment and Social Security

M. Savithri

Introduction

The post-nationalization period in the banking sector, circa 1969, witnessed a substantial amount of resources being earmarked towards meeting the credit needs of the poor. There were several objectives for the bank nationalization strategy including expanding the outreach of financial services to neglected sectors (Singh, 2005). As a result of this strategy, the banking network underwent an expansion phase without comparables in the world. Credit came to be recognized as a remedy for many of the ills of the poverty. There spawned several pro-poor financial services, support by both the State and Central governments, which included credit packages and programs customized to the perceived needs of the poor. While the objectives were laudable and substantial progress was achieved, credit flow to the poor, and especially to poor women, remained low. This led to initiatives that were institution driven that attempted to converge the existing strengths of rural banking infrastructure and leverage this to better serve the poor. The pioneering efforts at this were made by National Bank for Agriculture and Rural Development (NABARD), which was given the tasks of framing appropriate policy for rural credit, provision of technical assistance backed liquidity support to banks, supervision of rural credit institutions and other development initiatives.

In the early 1980s, the GoI launched the Integrated Rural Development Program (IRDP), large poverty alleviation credit program, which provided government subsidized credit through banks to the poor. It was aimed that the poor would be able to use the inexpensive credit to finance themselves over the poverty line. Also during this time, NABARD conducted a series of research studies independently and in association with MYRADA, a leading non-governmental organization (NGO) from Southern India, which showed that despite having a wide network of rural bank branches servicing the rural poor, a very large number of the poorest of the poor continued to remain outside the fold of the formal banking system. These studies also showed that the existing banking policies, systems and procedures, and deposit and loan products were perhaps not well suited to meet the most immediate needs of the poor. It also appeared that what the poor really needed was better access to these services and products, rather than cheap subsidized credit. Against this background, a need was felt for alternative policies, systems and procedures, savings and loan products, other complementary services, and new delivery mechanisms, which would fulfill the requirements of the poorest, especially of the women members of such households. The emphasis therefore was on improving the access of the poor to microfinance rather than just micro-credit. To answer the need for microfinance from the poor, the past 25 years has seen a variety of microfinance programs promoted by the government and NGOs.

Some of these programs have failed and the learning experience from them has been used to develop more effective ways of providing financial services. These programs vary from regional rural banks with a social mandate to MFIs. In 1999, the GoI merged various credit programs together, refined them and launched a new programme called Swaranjayanti

Gram Swarazagar Yojana(SGSY). The mandate of SGSY is to continue to provide subsidized credit to the poor through the banking sector to generate self-employment through a self-help group approach and the program has grown to an enormous size.

MFIs have also become popular throughout India as one form of financial intermediary to the poor. MFIs exist in many forms including co-operatives, Grameen-like initiatives and private sector MFIs. Thrift co-operatives have formed organically and have also been promoted by regional state organizations like the Cooperative Development Foundation (CDF) in Andhra Pradesh. The Grameen-like initiatives following a business model like the Grameen Bank. Private sector MFIs include NGOs that act as financial services providers for the poor and include other support services but are not technically a bank as they do not take deposits. Recently, microfinance has garnered significant worldwide attention as being a successful tool in poverty reduction. In 2005, the GoI introduced significant measures in the annual budget affecting MFIs. Specifically, it mentioned that MFIs would be eligible for external commercial borrowings which would allow MFIs and private banks to do business thereby increasing the capacity of MFIs. Also, the budget talked about plans to introduce a microfinance act that would provide some regulations on the sector.

It is clear that objectives of the bank sector nationalization strategy have resulted into several offshoots, some of which have succeeded and some have failed. Today, Self-Help Groups and MFIs are the two dominant form of microfinance in India. This report focuses on the aspects of the SHG as an effective means to provide financial services to the poor.

Emergence of the SHG Movement

While no definitive date has been determined for the actual conception and propagation of SHGs, the practice of small groups of rural and urban people banding together to form a savings and credit organization is well established in India. In the early stages, NGOs played a pivotal role in innovating the

SHG model and in implementing the model to develop the process fully. In the 1980s, policy makers took notice and worked with development organizations and bankers to discuss the possibility of promoting these savings and credit groups. Their efforts and the simplicity of SHGs helped to spread the movement across the country. State governments established revolving loan funds which were used to fund SHGs. By the 1990s, SHGs were viewed by state governments and NGOs to be more than just a financial intermediation but as a common interest group, working on other concerns as well. The agenda of SHGs included social and political issues as well. The spread of SHGs led also to the formation of SHG Federations which are a more sophisticated form of organization that involve several SHGs forming into Village Organizations (VO) / Cluster Federations and then ultimately into higher level federations called as Mandal Samakhya (MS) in AP or SHG Federation generally. SHG Federations are formal institutions while the SHGs are informal. Many of these SHG federations are registered as societies, mutual benefit trusts and mutually aided cooperative societies. SHG Federations resulted in several key benefits including:

- Stronger political and advocacy capabilities
- Sharing of knowledge and experiences
- Economies of scale
- Access to greater capital

Some states have developed SHGs further than others. This report is based on the experience that APMAS has had in working with SHGs in Andhra Pradesh and limited experiences in other states.

The SHG Model

Structure of SHG

A SHG is a group of about 10 to 20 people, usually women, from a similar class and region, who come together to form savings and credit organization. They pooled financial resources to make small interest bearing loans to their members. This process creates an ethic that focuses on savings first. The setting of terms and conditions and accounting of the loan are done in the group by designated members.

SHG Federation

SHGs have also federated into larger organizations. In Figure 1, a graphic illustration is shown of a SHG Federation. Typically, about 15 to 50 SHGs make up a Cluster / VO with either one or two representatives from each SHG. Depending on geography, several clusters or VOs come together to form an apex body or an SHG Federation. In Andhra Pradesh, the Village Organizations, SHG Clusters and SHG Federations are registered under the Mutually Aided Co-operative Society (MACS) Act 995.

At the cluster and federation level, there are inter-group borrowings, exchange of ideas, sharing of costs and discussion of common interests. There are typically various sub-committees that deal with a variety of issues including loan collections, accounting and social issues.

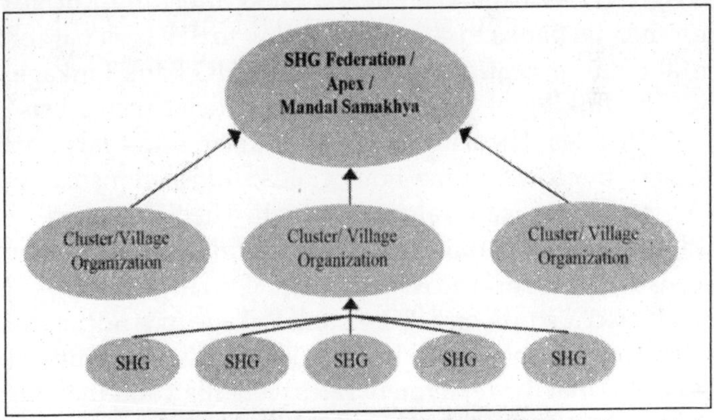

Figure 1: Illustrative SHG Federation

SHG Federations have presented some key benefits to SHGs as a result of their greater scale. Increasingly, SHG Federations are being seen as a key interface with the SHG movement because of their formal registration under the MACS and recognition from bankers. But, in addition to the benefits of SHG Federations, there are some drawbacks, or constraints, that should be noted.

An SHG Federation is a formal group of informal common-interest groups. As a result of its rather informal members, there are internal constraints that it faces. Namely, it has a poor capacity for self-governance, average to low quality managers and systems and process are poorly defined. Further, there is significant financial cost to organizing and registering a SHG Federation which has been estimated to be about Rs 7,000 per SHG member. To bridge these internal constraints requires savvy external assistance and there are few good quality NGOs to provide this assistance to a burgeoning number of SHG Federations.

SHG Bank Linkage

A most notable milestone in the SHG movement was when NABARD launched the pilot phase of the SHG Bank Linkage programme in February 1992. This was the first instance of mature SHGs that were directly financed by a commercial bank. The informal thrift and credit groups of poor were recognised as bankable clients. Soon after, the RBI advised commercial banks to consider lending to SHGs as part of their rural credit operations thus creating SHG Bank Linkage.

The linking of SHGs with the financial sector was good for both sides. The banks were able to tap into a large market, namely the low-income households, transactions costs were low and repayment rates were high. The SHGs were able to scale up their operations with more financing and they had access to more credit products. During 2003, APMAS conducted a study on SHG – bank linkage in Andhra Pradesh covering a sample of 400 bank linked SHGs. The study clearly indicated that the repayment rates were high and that the bank linkage made difference in the lives of the SHG members. However, the study also pointed out certain issues that require attention. These include adequacy of loan size, timeliness of credit and also the need for branch manager or the promoter undertaking a rating before the SHG is bank linked. The following were the major findings of the study:

- Average Savings per SHG – Rs. 23,000, average loan size Rs. 31,000.
- 50% of SHGs practice equal distribution of bank loan.
- Only 50% SHGs felt that the loan size was adequate and 54% studied SHGs were first time linked.
- 69% of SHGs got RLF, some got from multiple sources.
- It takes more than four months for an SHG to get a bank loan.
- No post linkage follow up by banker and others.
- 66% of bank linked SHGs are A grade as per CRI
- Only 22% of bank linked groups are appraised by banker, etc.
- Idle fund of bank linked SHGs average – Rs. 5,300
- Leaders dominate and have 30% loan on them.
- 12% SHG default to banks – repayment problem.
- 10% SHGs reported that they were forced to take loan.
- High percentage of SHGs participate in Government Programs.
- Bankers attitude is still an issues.

The State of SHGs in India

Before evaluating their impact and determine support solutions, it is important to examine the current state of SHGs in India today. And, it is certainly a mixed picture.

Overall Financial Snapshot

The table below indicates the number of SHGs and amount of financing they received through SHG Bank Linkage during the 12 month period ended March 31, 2005 (NABARD.

While figures do not indicate the total number of SHGs and the loans outstanding as at March 31, 2005, the table does reveal some interesting statistics. Specifically, SHGs are showing explosive growth as the number of new SHGs provided with financing under SHG Bank Linkage in the year 2004-05 represent about a third of total cumulative SHGs since

(in millions of Rs.)

	No. of New SHGs provided with Bank Loan during 2004-05	No. of Existing SHGs provided with repeat Bank Loan during 2004-05	Cumulative No. of SHGs provided with Bank Loan Upto Mar. 31, 2005	New Customer Bank Loans During 2004-2005	Repeat Customer Bank Loan During 2004-05	Cumulative Bank Loan Upto Mar. 31, 2005
Northern Region	33.622	3.381	86.018	927	145	2.395
North-Eastern Region	21.960	125	34.238	815	3	1.020
Eastern Region	107.391	24.557	265.628	2.101	477	5.183
Central Region	70.356	5.431	197.365	1.883	368	5.015
Western Region	41.451	5.837	96.266	1.319	223	2.951
Southern Region	264.585	218.761	938.941	10.221	11.461	52.421
Grand Total	539.365	258.092	1.618.456	17.266	12.676	68.985

the mid- 1990s. This also demonstrates the ease of duplication of the SHG model. In addition to the growth of the SHG movement, the table provides some scope of the financial size of the loans. Interestingly, the size of repeat loans is more than two-thirds of the new customer loans while the number of repeat SHGs is less than half the number of new SHGs. This indicates the accessibility of greater financing to SHGs who have shown strong repayment capability.

Financial Management

The financial management of SHGs has been found to be ranging from weak to average. Specifically, internal controls at SHGs and SHG Federations are lacking. Internal controls represents the systems and processes that manage the day to day transaction flow and ensure that roles and responsibilities are defined and executed to safeguard assets. Field studies have indicated that these systems and processes have been ill-defined and poorly executed by members. In addition to internal controls, how SHGs are managing their cash flows is especially important. Since SHGs are accessing external borrowings through SHG Bank Linkage and then lends these funds to its members, there has been a case of poor cash flow management to repay debts not just externally but also internally. The risk of overleveraging SHGs is high.

Governance

Since SHGs are an informal organization and a SHG Federation is a composition of informal groups, there is poor governance and the capacity of the members to enact good governance is weak. The members of SHGs do not have much experience with establishing formalized monitoring and review functions or complying with legal regulations. With the growing size of the loans being made to SHGs, a strong governance system is needed to ensure that there is accountability.

Human Resources

While the achievements of the women members to form common interest groups to help themselves is remarkable, there is a long way to go to build the capacities of the staff of SHGs. The role of NGOs to provide support is essential to many SHGs success stories. The support needed ranges from bookkeeping and accounting, organizational structure, governance and other areas.

Impact of SHGs

With the structure and model of SHGs and SHG Bank Linkage firmly established, the nature of the impacts of SHGs can be more closely examined and evaluated. The latest published estimates from NABARD state that, to date of March 31, 2005, 1.6 million SHGs have benefited from approximately Rs 69 billion in financing (NABARD, 2005). There is no doubt that there has been greater outreach of financial services to the poor through SHGs. Of course the outreach has been good in South India. However, there outreach has been limited in the rest of the country. In addition to the financial analysis of SHGs, the non-financial areas such as social security and gender dynamics are also effected by the SHG Movement. Indeed, poverty reduction is much less an issue of numbers but rather ideas and concepts. The following is an analysis of the non-financial impact of SHGs.

Political

Political engagement includes active involvement by SHGs in government including local assemblies, Lok Sabha or Panchayati Rai Institutions (PRIs) (APMAS, 2005). One of the key benefits of SHGs is women's empowerment and this can be seen with the number of women involved in public affairs. While the number of women actually involved in politics is still very low, research has indicated that of those women that stand for election, over 70% had won their seat (APMAS, 2005). And, the female contribution to civil issues ranges from issue of ration cards, laying of pucca roads, building of school, ensuring appointments in vacant positions in schools and health centres, recovery of river bank lands from encroachers and laying of drinking water pipes (APMAS, 2005).

As mentioned, the number of women involved in politics is low. But, the trend is definitely moving up. A mere 5 years ago, the likelihood of women contesting panchayat election was extremely low. Their presence today is affecting the perception of women and their role in the political arena. They are being recognized as an important group with serious concerns. The role of SHGs is both as an inspiration and as a financer. Impoverished women develop greater language and financial skills through the SHG which provides the building blocks for higher levels of confidence to engage the world. Also, the SHG sometimes finances the campaign of its members that stand for election. SHGs not only empower its members but also wield a powerful political role as a group as well. At local village meetings, the leaders of SHGs are often invited to attend and speak (APMAS, 2005).

Social Harmony

Broadly defined, social harmony encompasses the equality and integrity of relationships between different social groups. To frame the following analysis, SHGs typically consists of the following social groups:

- Schedule Caste (SC)
- Scheduled Tribe (ST)
- Minorities (MN)
- Backward Caste (BC)
- Other Caste (OC)

The composition of SHGs are sometimes exclusively one particular social group or a mix. The impact of SHGs on social harmony has also been mixed. While it has been observed that in groups with mixed membership had group leaders that came from a variety of the social groups. In the vast majority of instances, groups leaders were almost exclusively from the dominant social groups' category. This demonstrates a lack of equality and unity across caste divisions. Given the relatively young history of SHGs, it is to be expected that their impact on bridging centuries old divisions would be slow.

Social Justice

Social justice is the presence of moral and ethical conduct in areas that are historically typified with backward and abusive customs. There have been several occurrences of SHGs resolving disputes between members and the community at large. These instances include initiating legal action, arbitration, divorce and others. While there have long been dispute resolution mechanisms in villages, in the past it was controlled by men. Now, there are instances of women, SHG members, being involved in resolving disputes. Whether or not the women are working for their own interests or in the case for justice varies, regardless SHGs' impact on the political arena is certainly being seen also in social justice, albeit in a slow and evolutionary process.

Community

Being a group based organization of members of similar caste and geography, the community resources that are shared by are affected by the SHG. Recent analysis has shown that the impact that SHGs have on the community at large have been minor. There have been few instances of significant contributions from SHGs to education, family planning, eradication of child labour and hygiene. To interpret these findings further it should be noted that such community problems are often large financial commitments which SHGs simply do not have the capacity to afford. Also, of the few instances where there have been significant contributions from the SHGs to the community, the SHG demonstrated a clear leadership role and rallied the support of the entire village. This demonstrates that given the opportunity, SHGs, assuming they have the capacity, can act as a director of community development. The perception of taking of a women's based organization taking a leading role for the betterment of the greater good has monumental impacts on the local community. Gender dynamics begin to balance in instances such as these.

Livelihoods

Livelihoods, meaning a persons' economic activity, is an area that is vitally important to SHGs. The loans that SHG members receive are intended to improve their livelihoods so that they can receive greater and more steadier cash flows. In rural areas, livelihoods range from agriculture farming, animal husbandry, dairy and various other goods and services activities. Experience has shown that SHGs have had improved livelihoods to the extent of providing the leveraging needed to start an enterprise. However, the interventions to introduce new livelihoods or refine existing ones that could yield better economic results were done by external agencies.

Supporting the SHG Movement

The impact of the SHG movement on various aspects of civil society have been varied. The development of SHGs has varied from state to state but, regardless of the phase of evolution, SHGs require external help to continue to grow and have greater outreach and impact to civil society. It is clear from research that some of the obstacles to evolution are beyond the control of the SHGs. The following is a pointed analysis of where government, NGOs, Banks and others, including the private sector, can work together to help answer the needs to SHGs in a measured and effective manner in hopes of not overloading them leading to failure.

Political: Training on Governance

The impact of SHGs on women in the politics is clear; they have helped women enter the political area as they are being elected to various public offices and SHGs themselves are engaged in discussion with governing bodies. SHPIs need to be at least a few steps ahead of the SHGs, in order to be useful to them in their role in politics (APMAS, 2005). Specifically, there is a need to train women on good governance because the history of poor governance has been long established. If there is to be lasting change, women need to occupy the offices of where strategic planning is done.

Social Harmony: Creating a Mixed Caste Model SHG

SHGs do not appear to be managing social tensions well. The reason for this lack of unity is difficult to identify but it could very well be the deep rooted beliefs of the caste system which tends to exclude social disadvantaged groups. These are problems are ingrained in the ethos of the villages and it will take a very long time to change. For SHGs to better manage social tensions, there needs to be a perception among members of equity, or ownership, in a enterprise that exists for mutual benefit. Fostering this cohesiveness is very difficult in a given environment. SHPIs can encourage the formation of mixed groups of SHGs and make these "model" organizations for others to follow.

Social Justice: Awareness of Legal Rights and Entitlements

SHGs have played an important role in the lives of distressed members. Given the years of suppression of women in India, it is to be expected that SHGs take up the cause of their members. However, they are also responding from a desire to see justice done. Therefore, if helped to process the pros and cons of various situations and arriving at just and sustainable situations, women could be chosen by local communities as arbitrators. Arbitration in most villages is currently a male domain, but the experiences of women in negotiating for women's rights could be taken to the next logical step of involvement of women in local justice issues, whether or not a member is involved, and whether or not a member is "right" (APMAS, 2005). Similar to the political arena, SHPIs need to provide the technical support to help SHGs equip themselves as arbitrators.

Communities: Provide Strategic Support

SHGs have helped their members and their communities. By taking a leadership role in community development, SHGs are perceived to be a guiding force for the village. Though the instances of SHGs engaging in community development is low, given the capacity, there has been proven results. SHPIs could help facilitate processes whereby women made long-term plans for their villages as a whole, and worked steadily towards the transformation of their villages into modern and equitable hubs of creative and sustainable actions (APMAS, 2005). They might focus on some core issues in each set of plans that they make, and work towards the fulfillment of these. Having persons trained to work on a larger canvas can contribute to a new cadre of political activists. Women may choose to engage directly in party politics, or to play a watchdog role from the environs of civil society – either way, they will usher in a new era of more responsible politics and public life.

Livelihoods: Technical Livelihood Support

The support of livelihoods is increasingly being seen as an important area related to microfinance. Indeed, the term of livelihood finance has been coined and is in vogue at leading NGOs. The need for livelihood support is critical to SHGs development as livelihoods are typically financed by the loans that members receive from the SHG. The needs of SHGs varies from the introduction of new livelihoods to providing support such as market linkages or procurement techniques to refine existing livelihoods. State government programs such as Indira Kranthi Patham (IKP) in Andhra Pradesh have successful executed livelihood interventions on various non-timber forest products that have brought about increased cash flows to SHG members as they have been able to bypass middlemen and sell their goods at market and cut costs. Experience has indicated that these benefits would not be possible without external intervention. Thus, SHPIs can provide the technical livelihood support as needed to help develop SHGs.

Policy Considerations

In addition to actual technical support, government policy can help support the SHG movement in the previously mentioned areas. Poverty is invariably characterized by lack of public investment in infrastructure or dysfunctional public systems including education and health care and underdeveloped markets. Large scale investment is required to build infrastructure like roads and bridges so that there can be access to markets. These sorts of investment will have to be completed by the state government. The payoff such costs though is infinite. An improved infrastructure will help to increase investment and mobility of staff. Further, livelihoods can be enriched through greater access to markets. In some areas, there is reasonable amount of infrastructure that state-owned rural banks operate. As some SHGs have grown and matured to a sizeable scale, they need access to more financial services. Government can address this need through their state-owned banks by introducing flexible and easily accessible products. Specifically, products such as innovative savings products, micro-insurance, larger loans and enterprise financing can be introduced. Banks lending to SHG federations could also facilitate access to livelihood finance by the women SHG members. Not only will programs such as these address the service gap but it will also change perceptions among bankers. If the state-owned banks take the lead, other bankers will likely follow and make an investment to work with the poor and expand their services to them.

The Other Side of the Coin

This paper has outlined several areas of working with SHGs to further their impact on civil society. It should be noted though that the sustainability of SHGs to effect such change is directly linked to their financial sustainability. While this latter issue was not the intended focus on the report, any external intervention to SHGs should bear this issue in mind. Research has shown that SHGs financial management is average or weak (APMAS, 2005). Thus, it is vitally important that both government and NGOs work to bear all the costs in mind of interventions to make them sustainable otherwise the SHGs will be overburdened and destined to failure. Government regulations could help manage this risk and increase the emphasis on sustainability of SHGs. There are key areas of SHG financial management that need to be improved such as internal controls, accounting, management stewardship, organizational efficiency and others. If the government were to enact policy that would regulate the quality of SHGs and tied this to their eligibility for SHG Bank Linkage, then this would help bring about a more measured and responsible growth to the movement. Both for SHGs and SHG federations there is a need to aspire to attain standards following the best practices. As the SHG federations are emerging as community owned microfinance institutions, there is a need for significant investment in providing institution building support. These SHG federations being bodies like corporations as they are registered under an appropriate legal form, must comply with the prudential and legal norms. There is a need for a well developed third party rating system for SHG federations before they are linked with financial institutions to act as an intermediary as they handle large volume of funds from the bank linkage and also undertake savings from their members.

There is a need for establishing a computerized MIS for SHGs and SHG federations to monitor their performance on a regular basis. SHG Federations must be able to publish their annual reports and share those with all their members. Governance of SHG federations is a major challenge. For the SHG members to manage their own institutions with professional staff and large volumes of transactions will be difficult. SHPIs must provide the needed support for the SHG federations to develop into sustainable institutions of the poor. Considerable investments would be needed to facilitate and sustain SHG federations across the nation.

References

APMAS (2005), Optimizing SHGs, October.

IFAD (2003), IFAD Microfinance Project–India Chapter, September.

Kropp, Dr. Erhard W. & Suran, Dr. B.S. (2002), Linking Banks and (Financial) Self Help Groups in India–An Assessment, November.

NABARD (2005), SHG Bank Linkage Model-wise Cumulative Position upto 31 March.

Reserve Bank of India (2005), Report of the Internal Group to Examine Issues Relating to Rural Credit and Microfinance, July.

Singh, Kavaljit (2005), Banking Sector Liberalization in India: Some Distributing Trends, ASED, August 29.

Chapter-27

Gender and Displacement: A Study on Project Affected Families Under Various Irrigation Projects in Andhra Pradesh

K. R. Rama Mohan, V. Subramanyam

Introduction

State Sponsored Development Projects have created lot of human displacement by uprooting their traditional way of life. Most of the projects are designed and developed by the policy makers do not take into consideration the natives in the planning stage. The idea of construction of large and medium range irrigation projects to develop the agricultural output is considered as public good, but large numbers of families are displaced from their original habitats and their livelihoods are lost. Though the planners are careful in dealing with compensation and rehabilitating the victims to some extent, the policy guidelines are not clear with the gender issues involved in evacuating the natives from their homelands. The study deals with how tribal women suffer and experience the negative effects of their displacement and struggle to come to grips with an alien situation. Thus drawing the attention of the State, Media, Scholars to bring new ways in gender balancing in displacement due to the construction of irrigation projects especially in tribal areas.

Recently, the Government of Andhra Pradesh State has initiated several, medium and minor irrigation projects to enhance the access to Irrigation facility especially to a large number of small and marginal farmers in different parts of the state. A total of 83 medium irrigation projects have been completed in several districts in the state during 2004-2006. Currently another 31 medium irrigation projects are being planned in different districts, while seven projects are being constructed in the tribal areas of Vizianagaram, East Godavari, Adilabad and Kadapa districts. These ongoing reservoir projects are Peddagadda, Bhupatipalem, Musurumilli, Srikomarambheem, Gollavagu, Peddavagu, and Velligallu. A total of 1100 tribal families were affected in many ways. All these familes belong to different tribes such as Konda Dora, Mooka Dora, Manne Dora, Koya, Konda Reddy, Konda Kammara, Gond, Pardhan, Naikpod, Kolam, Sugali and Thoti. Due to Construction of Irrigation projects in these tribal areas, all the inhabitants of the Project Affected area are displaced from their original habitats to an alien surroundings. Apart from displacement of their original homes, they were displaced from their land and other means of livelihoods. The displacements have adversely affected their socio-cultural life, as all the tribal families depend on forest wealth in eking out their livelihood.

An alarming aspect of displacement of tribes from their habitats is the Gender Stratification where it has serious implications for the victims of Project Affect Families due to the construction of the irrigation projects in the tribal areas.

To define PAP, it is a generic term, which include all those who are adversely affected by a project. In case of an Irrigation project, the clearly recognized category is of people who are physically displaced by the construction of the reservoir project (dam). With the scarcely available official reports, it is considered that persons or families displaced by the construction of reservoir, as the only category of people affected by the dam.

Displacement of tribal families from their original habitats is really a traumatic experience for everyone undergoing it. If displacement is affecting everybody undergoing it, then why there is a need to focus on women separately?

So, how does displacement affects the tribal women per se?

Given the existence of gross gender inequality in India, whether the process of displacement is even adding more to the problem of gender inequality, especially with the tribal families.

Whether there are any biases in State's response to address the cause of women displacees?

How does the media respond to the cause of women displacees?

Nature of the Problem

Dearth of studies on the Project Affected families displacement especially with tribes. Population displacement caused by the construction of irrigation projects(dams) is an unique case of a mixture between development-induced and environment-induced displacement. Few attempts to place the debate of gender, displacement and resettlement within socio-cultural and historical processes. To ascertain the magnitude of the problem of displacement in tribal areas of Andhra Pradesh.

Lack of studies on the gender dimension of the problem of population displacement due to various irrigation projects constructed in tribal areas. Contextualising the questions with reference to some of the related studies on Gender Inequality

Lyla Mehta (2002) interestingly argues that there is a "double bind" which entraps displaced women.

Women suffer more during displacement because of lack of access to medical and health facilities, reduced nutritional and health status, lack of sanitation facilities, increased sexual and domestic violence, increased incidence of male migration, trafficking and prostitution, already existing gendered division of labour (Ganguly & Thukral, 1996).

It is not gender, but gender inequality which puts girls and women at risk when floodwaters rise in Bangladesh (Akhter, 1992).

Enarson and Morrow(1998) argue that because of race, class, ethnicity, age, sexuality, culture, the relationship between gender and disaster-induced displacement experiences is not a simple one.

Role of the State and the Media

The States in South Asia have failed to recognize that the displaced population is largely a feminine population and hence the rehabilitation programmes need to be gender-sensitive (Banerjee, 2005)

Because of the absence of any serious attempts at national or state level to look into the displacement issue from gender perspective, there is no data disaggregated along gender lines (Scudder, 1990; Fernandes and Raj, 1993)

The recent National Policy for Resettlement and Rehabilitation (2003) is only for the development displacement and the other displacees are out of its ambit.(Kumar, 2005).

The women who suffer the misery of displacement more by virtue of being mothers, wives and sisters and also because of the cultural erosion that hits them directly, have not been covered adequately by the media. Hardly any study shows the insensitivity of the mainstream towards people's rights and gender issues in sourcing and presenting news of those affected by the disasters.

The displaced Tribal under seven different irrigation projects are 1,100 families.

The number of affected families of the tribes in each Reservoir Project is shown below :

Pedda gadda Project	
Name of the Tribe	*No of Families Affected*
Konda Dora	43
Nooka Dora	4
Manne Dora	41
Bhupatipalem Project	
Name of the Tribe	*No of Families Affected*
Koya Dora	101
Konda Reddy	47
Konda Kammara	1
Musurumilli Project	
Name of the Tribe	*No of Families Affected*
Koya Dora	281

Konda Reddy	60
Konda Kammara	2

Sri Komarambheem	
Name of the Tribe	*No of Families Affected*
Gond	105
Pardhan	71
Naikpod	28
Kolam	56
Thoti	19

Velligallu Project	
Name of the Tribe	*No of Families Affected*
Sugali	139

Gollavagu Project	
Name of the Tribe	*No of Families Affected*
Naikpod	11

Peddavagu Project	
Name of the Tribe	*No of Families Affected*
Manne Dora	70
Koya Dora	17
Pardhan	4

Analytical Framework

The concepts used are 'development', 'ecological imbalance', 'displacement' and 'gender'.

Developing linkages among these in a specific case of women suffering from displacement due to construction of irrigation projects in the tribal areas.This is prompted by two powerful theoretical insights:

Development very often takes place at the cost of people.

Feminist theory which directs us to examine women's victim hood and vulnerability because of historical, social and natural processes.

The analytical categories that are used for this study are "socially significant personal (both ascribed and achieved) attributes" like age, religion, education and "household attributes" like asset owning(mainly land), presence of male members, number of times of displacement of the household etc. Whether Gender Inequality has increased? The dimensions at which women are most affected: Food Security, health, sanitation, education, migration alcoholism, domestic Violence, to some extent trafficking and the mundane household ativities

State Response and the Media Response

Faulty and gender-insensitive rehabilitation. Lack of sensitivity of the various schemes of the government. State's apathy towards the Tribes because of game of 'political ecology' and vote bank politics. Less and that too during a particular time of the year and not prolonged and sustained reportage in media (both audio-visual and print) about displacement caused by construction of irrigation projects in these tribal areas.

Women in general bear a negative feeling about media and their such feeling is due to a variety of reasons. Quite contrary to this, the civil society activists feel that the media have been quite active in reporting various issues on the Project Affected Families.

The local media, within their limited capacity, as for example *TV9,(State TV channel)* made a documentary on the plight of the Project Affected Families in some of the villages have tried their level best to focus on the problem of population displacement due to the construction of these projects in these areas.

Women become easy victims of displacement because of their role of home maker, looking after the children, caring for the old, sick and pregnant women.

Women are not a homogenous category and the degree of vulnerability of women in times of displacement depends on a number of factors like age, religion, and household characteristics.

News items in mainstream media are conditioned and dominated by target audience, consumerism, market considerations to the utter neglect of the human dimensions of life.

There should be proper consideration of ecological and human cost of every development project.

The people displaced by these construction of resevior projects come under ambit of National Policy for Resettlement and Rehabilitation for the they are also project-affected. If displacement is unavoidable, there should be proper planning on the part of the State as to how best the displaced persons can be rehabilitated in all senses.

Gender Sensitivity should be there in case of Rehabilitation Programmes

In prior planning to deal with unavoidable displacement and in post-displacement period, community processes must be taken into account so that the greater degree of adversity can be minimized.

More spending on rehabilitation than on construction of embankments or spurs, ie, focus on the human dimension of the problem.

Recognition of the tribal villages submerged under these constructions by the State can help a lot to remove plight of the victims.

Restoration of livelihoods for the tribal families and their income is equally important to women and men. Tribal women are considered as backbone of their economy, women are largely engaged in the gathering forest produce, working in the agricultural fields,taking care of household chores. Dislocation can result in loss of livelihood, adding to women's economic and household hardships. Therefore, it is important to enumerate women's economic and household activities in planning and executing resettlement programs

The Psychological and Social impact of dislocation tends to affect women more than men. Breakdown of community and other social networks as a direct result of dislocation can affect women more than men because women rely and depend on community and other social networks for emotional and practical support, such as taking care of children. Displacement can be extremely traumatic if these networks break down. As Tribes generally isolated from the mainstream society, they have restricted mobility and limited exposure affect women's ability to adjust. Being less mobile than men, women's universe is more restricted. Hence, they have limited ability to cope with and adjust to new situations and environments

Conclusions

Low negotiation skills and with no formal education among women limit the choice of alternatives. Rehabilitation packages may include compensation opportunities for alternative occupations. Choices for exploring alternatives and livelihood options for women are limited because of their low levels of skills, education, and exposure. Planning for occupational and livelihood options for women is important when the situation like this arise. Hence the need to strengthen the participation of women in all the rehabilitation process. The planners and policy makers should take into consideration all the possible women's involvement in preparation and review of resettlement plans. Further, importance should be given to women's involvement and participation in implementation and monitoring in the pre and post planning process.

References

Akhter, K.R. (1998), *Gender and Society in Bangladesh's Flood Action Plan,* Govt of Bangladesh.

Banerjee (2005), *Internal Displacement in South Asia,* Sage Publications, New Delhi.

Enarson and Morrow eds. (1998), *The Gendered Terrain of Disaster: Through Women's Eyes* Westport, CT: Greenwood Publications/ Praeger.

Fernandes (1993), *Development-induced Displacement and Tribal Women in Tribal development in India:* The contemporary debate

Ganguly Thukral, Enakshi (1996), 'Development, Displacement and Rehabilitation: Locating Gender ', *Economic and Political Weekly,* 41(24).

Kumar, Manis Verma (2004) *Development, Displacement and Resettlement,* Rawat Publications, New Delhi

Lyla Mehta ed. (2009), *Displaced by Development Confronting Marginalisation and Gender Injustice, SAGE Publications Pvt. Ltd.*

Resettlement and Gender - Asian Development Bank (1991) The Akha Heritage Foundation.

Scudder,T. (1990), "Development Induced Relocation and Refugee Studies: Thirty-Seven Years of Change and Continuity Among Zambia's Gwembe Tonga", *Journal of Refugee Studies,* Vol. 62 pp.123 -152.

CHAPTER-28

Empowering Women through Micro Finance

Vineeth Sahadevan, A.P. Prajina

Introduction

The post-nationalization period in the banking sector, circa 1969, witnessed a substantial amount of resources being earmarked towards meeting the credit needs of the poor. There were several objectives for the bank nationalization strategy including expanding the outreach of financial services to the neglected sectors (Singh, 2005). As a result of this strategy, the banking network underwent an expansion phase without comparables in the world. Credit came to be recognized as a remedy for many ills of the poverty. There generated several pro-poor financial services, support by both State and Central governments, which included credit packages and programmes customized to the perceived needs of the poor. The very fact that almost 50% of the world (49.66%) and Indian (48.45%) population comprises of women, it becomes imperative to financially empower women so as to enable them to make meaningful contributions towards the development of the economy. The problem of financial empowerment becomes even graver when it comes to poor women which again are a sizeable population in India as well as in the other developing nations.[1]

A significant development in recent years has been the mushrooming of community-based organizations and initiatives at the local level for women. Self-help groups intermediated by micro credit have been shown to have positive effects on women. A SHG is a small economically homogeneous affinity group of the rural poor voluntarily coming together to save small amount regularly, which are deposited in a common fund to meet members emergency needs and to provide collateral free loans decided by the group (Abhaskumar, Jha 2000). They have been recognized as useful tool to help the poor and as an alternative mechanism to meet the urgent credit needs of poor through thrift (V. M. Rao 2002). SHGs enhance the equality of status of women as participants, decision-makers and beneficiaries in the democratic, economic, social and cultural spheres of life (Ritu Jain 2003). In India, micro finance scene is dominated by Self Help Groups (SHGs) – Bank Linkage Programme, aimed at providing a cost effective mechanism for providing financial services to the "unreached poor". Recently, microfinance has acquired significant worldwide attention as being a successful tool in poverty reduction. Microfinance has evolved over the past quarter century across India into various operating forms and to a varying degree of success. One such form of microfinance has been the development of the self-help movement. Based on the concept of "self-help," small groups of women have formed into groups of ten to twenty and operate a savings-first business model whereby the member's savings are used to fund loans.

From the early 1970s women's movements in a number of countries became increasingly interested in the degree to which women were able to access poverty-focused credit programmes and credit cooperatives. In India organizations like Self-Employed Women's Association (SEWA) among others with origins and affiliations in the Indian labour and women's movements identified credit as a major constraint in their work with informal sector women workers. The concept of women empowerment and its practical implications has been matured and developed considerably over the years. From 1980, onwards issues raised by Women-in-Development (WID) and lately, Gender and Development (GAD) approaches have acquired greater importance both for government and Non Governmental Organizations (NGOS) (Devika and Binitha, 2007). Empowerment is a continuous process and it is going on at the grass root level. It implies strengthening of life chances, collective participation in different spheres of life cultural, social, political economic development process, decision making etc. The empowerment of women is an integral and inseparable part of wider process of social transformation. The concept of power recognized that it is multi–locational and exists in multiple domains changes in power relations pertaining to gender therefore call for empowerment of women (Malthotra and Mather 1997 cited in Subrahmaniam, Mangala.2007). Micro-finance is promoted as an entry point for women's economic and social empowerment, it is an important institutional device for providing small credit to the rural poor in order to alleviate poverty. Alleviation of poverty, the core of all developmental efforts has remained a very complex and critical concern among developing countries. The innovation in participatory development in early and mid 1990's ,the government of Kerala inspired and initiated Kudumbasree (prosperity of the family) in 1998 to alleviate poverty in the state by 2008 by empowering women through collective action.

According to Blumberg, (cited in Subrahmaniam, Mangala.2007) economic empowerment is generally defined as the ability to earn income. Empowerment in the economic sphere therefore involves both earnings and controlling. Earnings in terms of personal autonomy can involve both economic and non–economic transactions. Understanding the social context and social basis of inequality is central to examining power relations and therefore approaches to empowerment. In this context, to study women empowerment at micro level in a development perspective is quite relevant. (1988).

This paper aims at examining the socio-economic impact of "Kudumbasree" among the Kurichiya, one of the Scheduled

Tribes in Kerala. Kurichiyans are divided into four divisions according to the place of distribution. *Kurichiyan of Wayanad, Kurichiyan of Kannavam, Anchilla Kurichiyan of Thirunelli, and Pathiri Kurichiyan* is the four divisions. Kurichiyans are a matrilineal tribe of Kerala distributed mainly in Wayanad and Kannur districts. They are also known as 'Hill Brahmins'.The word Kurichiyan is derived from two words*'kuri'* and *'chiyan'*. The word *'kuri'* means target and *'chiyan'* means people. So Kurichiyans are the people who can shoot at the target. This is an indication that they are experts in archery (Ramachandran, Bindu 2003). The Kurichiyan society is divided into exogamous clans called *'kulam'* and inheritance of the *'kulam'* as well as the property is matrilineal. They consider themselves to be superior to all the tribes in Kerala. Community endogamy and *kulam* exogamy are practiced as customary in the society. The traditional economy of the *Kurichiyan* is based on agriculture and they were also shifting cultivators and hunters. They were loyal fighters under the Pazhassi Raja who led a historical revolt against the British early in the 19thcentury. Both women and men of the Kurichiya community have maintained the habitat for several species of medicinal plants through the preservation of sacred groves and associated areas. Kurichiyas use different plant species to make winnowing pans, baskets, grain storage units, umbrellas, mats, bows and arrows. These activities are carried out by men, since they are considered too strenuous for women[2].

Kudumbasree Project–An Overview

The success of SEWA (Self Employed Women's Association) of Ahmadabad, Myrada of Mysore, and several other experiments in different parts of the country has attracted many states for replicating this strategy. It has been widely accepted that the programmes it taken up and implemented in the right sense would effective in poverty eradication and women empowerment. Community Development Society (CDS) strategy–a modified version of SHGS (Self Help Groups) was introduced in 1993 as part of implementation of centrally sponsored Urban Basic Services for Poor (UBSP) UNICEF–

assisted Community Based Nutrition Programme (CBNP). Kudumbasree in local language meaning 'prosperity of the family' launched by the state government of Kerala with the active support of the central government of India and the National Bank for Agriculture and Rural Development(NABARD), aiming at removing absolute poverty within ten years with the full co-operation of local self governments. The mission of the Kudumbasree, therefore, states: "to eradicate absolute poverty in ten years through concerned community action under the leadership of local governments, by facilitating organization of the poor by combining self – help with demand led convergence of available services and resources to tackle the multiple dimensions and manifestations of poverty, holistically (Devika and Binitha.2007).

Women identified from the poor families were organized Neighborhood Group (NHGS) of 15-40 families. The NHGS organized at the grass root level are co-coordinated at ward level through Area Development Society (ADS) by 8 to 10 NHGS. To co-ordinate the activities at the Panchayat level there is an apex body called Community Development Society (CDS) which would be a registered body at the municipality / district level. The entire 3 tier structure is envisaged as an extension of the Panchayat Raj System providing a support system as well as delivery mechanism for the unified implementation of all poverty eradication programmes. The success of the CDS model in urban Alapuzha and in rural Malappuram led the government of Kerala to start up to the whole of the state in 1998 under the name *'Kudumbasree'*. The programme began with the organization of the poor women folks to form the neighbourhood groups.

In Kerala Kudumbashree have organized 2340 Neighbourhood Groups (NHGs) among 5 primitive tribal groups, namely Koragas of Kasargod, Paniyas and Kattunaikans of Waynad and Malappuram, Kadar of Thrichur and Kurumbar of Attappadi – Palakkad Districts.[3] Government of Kerala established Kannavan Colony in the year 1961 keeping the vision of improving the living condition of Kurichiya, and at the same time maintaining their customs and practices.

There are 8 colonies of Kurichiyan in Kannavam forest, which is in Patyam Grama Panchayat of Kannur district of Kerala State. The early inhabitants of this colony were the families from the nearest tribal areas like hill of *Parambu Kavu, Chenna Poyil, Narikod, Punneri, Kadave, Elamangel, Vellonni, Kolakkat, and Kaniyoor*. Among the 48 tribal extension offices in Kerala, one is situated in the Kannavam colony, which is now working in the Block Panchayath office.

Methodology

Two Kudumbasree Units of Kurichiya Community were selected for the study. For the purpose 12 members from each unit were interviewed. Observation technique was used to understand their involvement in the day to day activities and weekly meetings. Statistical evidences are drawn from the Grama Panchayath offices. Interviewed S.T. promoters within the colony, who played a major role in the development of the Kurichiya community.

Microfinance Operations in Kannavam Colony

Microfinance is an intervention uniquely beneficial to the needs of women. There are two broad motivations for adding the delivery of social services to the provision of microfinance services. First, the provision of certain services such as business training or livelihood counseling can directly benefit the households as this would allow them to take up an activity with improved practices. These "plus" activities can provide customers with enhanced skills relating to important aspects of production, marketing, and financial management, which directly benefits the MFI as increased productivity of households, improves repayment rates and reduces risk for the MFI. A second and complementary motivation is that microfinance can be an effective and sustainable delivery channel for services which have high social impact and benefits. This is consistent with the overall objective of most microfinance institutions, which is to contribute to poverty reduction and development of their clients[4].

Table 1
Basic Data about Kannavam Colony

Name of Colony	*No of Houses*	*Family*	*Male*	*Female*	*Population*	*SSLC*	*PDC*	*DC*
Kannavam	127	146	201	235	436	69	28	8
Arayakkal	26	34	44	63	107	11	7	1
Chandroth	14	18	22	32	54	12	8	0
Elamangal	5	5	11	11	22	6	1	1
Vengalam	85	98	158	176	334	47	9	14
Kadavil	14	17	27	27	55	6	3	0
Athyara	5	5	7	11	18	2	0	0
Mundayod	53	60	115	105	220	5	8	0
Total	329	383	585	660	1246	178	64	24

Source: Patyam Grama Panchayath.

Microfinance is banking through groups. The essential feature of the approach is to provide financial services through the groups of individuals, formed either in joint liability or co-obligation mode. The other dimensions of the microfinance approach are:

- Savings/Thrift precedes credit
- Credit is linked with savings/thrift
- Absence of subsidies
- Group plays an important role in credit appraisal, monitoring and recovery.

The Thrift and credit societies are formed with the objectives of encouraging the poor women to save. Women bring their little bit for saving when they come to attend the group meeting. In every week the members pay 20 rupees as Thrift. The money is entrusted to the community volunteer, who in turn deposits it in the Patyam Service Co-operative Bank. The members can avail loans to meet their urgent needs like medical treatment, purchase of school book and uniform for children, to pay off their old debt etc. The interest of their credit collected and uses it for their own group purposes, like banana cultivation; they escaped from the private money lenders for their high interest rate, it is a great relief as far as Kurichiya women are concerned. We can say it as the loans without interest.

The present paper is based on the study in one colony, i.e., Kannavam. This colony has 127 houses with 436 inhabitants of whom 235 are females and 201 males. Females are more in number. There is only a single tribal upper primary school in the colony. There are 8 colonies in Kannavam based on the name of place. These colonies are *Vengalam colony, Kannavam colony, Araykal, Chandroth colony, Elamangal colony, Kadavil colony, Mundayod colony.*

Population is also high compared to neighbouring Kurichiya colonies. The government takes initiative to satisfy the basic facilities and infrastructures. The houses are registered in the name of the female member. This is infact a strategy of empowering the women. Women played a major role in housekeeping, education of the children etc. Earlier the Kurichiya women had no interaction with outsiders, untouchability was also practiced. Because of the government's intervention with special access of Kudumbasree programme in colonies, a change in the minds of Kurichiya women was noticed. The major aim of the SHGs is to promote savings and to credit for the productive and consumption purposes. This is true because people in the study area join the SHGs for getting loan and promote their personal savings. The group formation has totally changed and the women become more active and started involving in social issues. The thrift and credit societies are formed with the objectives of encouraging the poor women to save. Women bring their little bit income for saying when they come to attend the group meeting. Every week the members pay 20 rupees as thrift. The money is entrusted to the community volunteer, who in turn deposits it in the Patyam Service Co-Operative Bank. The members can avail loans to meet their urgent needs like medical treatment, purchase of school books and uniform for children, to pay off their old debt etc. The interest of their credit is collected and used for their own group purposes. In fact this is a safe way to escape from the private money lenders for their high interest rate, and a great relief for women especially from economically weaker sections of the population.

The Kudumbasree units were started in the *Kannavam* area in 2002, and there are three Kudumbasree units in the colony, named *oruma, poornima, sruthilaya vayottukavu*. All these are in the 11th ward of Patyam Grama Panchayat. The *sruthilaya vayottumkavu*, one Kudumbasree unit has 24 members registered at the beginning and more number of members. The main task of this unit is to start a goat farm. For this purpose they took 2.5 lakhs as loan from Patyam Service Co-operative Bank and they brought 16 cents of land for the working of farm. The 50 goats are sponsored by the government. Then they started sharing the goats, because they were lacking leadership. The shortage of members in weekly meetings is identified as a major problem. Most of the members are daily waged labourers. The main problem is that they have no possibility to market the goat meat. Gradually, due to lack of leadership, time, co-operation, and market accessibilities the working of goat farm is continued at their home. They take profit for their own purpose. It is the case, they become empowering at the same time, they were lacking support from their home, most of the men are addicted to alcoholism, women protested through their collective action, which is very necessary to create awareness in the community.

Conclusion

Kudumbashree has enabled the women to share their personal experiences and this in turn has given perspective to the individual situation of many women and transformed their personal feeling of hopelessness into a feeling of being part of a collective spirit. They have been able to develop a social network in the neighbourhood area, which to some extent has evoked a feeling of social security. Through their involvement in micro enterprise activities, the women are now more confident and independent. Even today the Kudumbasree units are working in the colony but they are not getting the required potential and profit from the activities. Now the Kurichiya women are also members in ADS (Area Development Society) and CDS (Community Development Society) in the midst of their domestic and economic responsibilities. Every week discussions will be conducted, record it and present it in front of the officers. The Kurichiya women are now active not only within the community but outside also. Earlier they were not aware of their rights but now they are well aware. As a Kudumbasree member the main advantage they get is responsive attitude. They started reacting to the problems around them, and develop a habit of acquiring income and earnings. It is very essential to empower Kurichiya women for the better future of the community. It is understood that Kudumbasree became the lifeline to Kurichiya women and it has proved without any doubt that women empowerment is the best strategy for the community development. The process of empowerment becomes a beacon light to their children, their families and to the society at large.

References

Abhaskumar, Jha (2004), *Lending to the Poor. Designs for Credit. EPW.* Vol XXXV (8).

Devika and Binitha (2007), *Between Empowerment and Liberation: the Kudumbasree Initiative in Kerala. Indian Journal of Gender Studies* 14 (1).

Ramachandran, Bindu (2003), *Fertility Concept in a Ritual an Anthropological Explanation of "Pandal Pattu". Studies of Tribes and Tribals* 2(1).

Rao, V.M. (2003), *Women Self Help Groups, Profile Andhra Pradesh and Karnataka, Kurukshetra,* 50 (6).

Ritu Jain (2003), *Socio-Economics Impact Through Self Help Groups. Yojana.* 47(7).

Singh, K.S. (2002), *People of India, Vol. XXll,* New Delhi: East West Press Private Limited.

Subrahmaniam, Mangala (2007), *The Power of Women's Organising.* New Delhi: Rawat Publications.

Singh, Kavaljit (2005), Banking Sector Liberalization in India: Some Distributing Trends, ASED, August 29.

Footnotes

1. Dr. S. Kaptan, Mrs. Lata Swaminathan. Microfinance Through Women Co-Op Banks To Achieve Milennium Development Goals In Developing Nations.

http://www.nabard.org/databank/IARD%20Web/csidfiles/Microfinance%20through%20women%20co-op%20banks.pdf

2. *Gender and biodiversity management :India*
http://tcdc.undp.org/SIE/experiences/vol5/Gender.pdf
3. Kudumbashree at a glance
http://www.kudumbashree.org/Publication/Article/KS_ short_article.pdf.
4. Does the Addition of Social Objectives to Microfinance Enhance Program Impact?
http://ifmr.ac.in/cmf/research/so/mf-and-social-objectives.pdf.

Chapter-29

Sustainable Development of Women–Issues and Problems

R.V.L.N. Ratnakar Rao, V. Krishna Murthy

Introduction

"Inclusive Growth" in the Eleventh Five Year Plan envisages respecting the differential needs of all women and children and providing them with equal access to opportunities. This can happen only when women are recognized as agents of socio-economic growth with autonomy of decision-making and also when the rights of women and children are recognized, respected and upheld. The Eleventh Plan proposes a Five-fold agenda for gender equity: Economic Empowerment, Social Empowerment; Political Empowerment; Strengthening Mechanisms for Effective Implementation of Women-Related Legislations; and Augmenting Delivery Mechanisms for Mainstreaming Gender. Recognizing that women are not homogeneous categories, the Eleventh Plan aims to have not just general programmes, but also special targeted interventions, catering to the diffential needs of different groups. Thus during the plan period (2007-12), specific pilots for girl children, and Muslim women will be taken up (GOI, XI Five Year Plan, 2007-12)

National Mission for Empowerment of Women

The Government has prepared a proposal for setting up the National Mission for Empowerment of Women to ensure convergence of various schemes for their development. A detailed note on the Mission has been circulated among other Ministries for comments said Krishna Tirath, Minister for Women and Child Development. The Mission, aimed at a holistic empowerment of women will be a decentralized scheme at the National, State, District and Village Levels. It will be governed by the National Mission Authority, headed by the Prime Minister and will function as an umbrella body to achieve coordination, synergy and convergence in the activities of select Ministries which have either women centric or pro-women programmes. It will review and strengthen capacities of exiting schemes, identify gaps and recommend new schemes, ensure convergence among States and other institutional bodies, and lay down set of gender related monitor-able out come indicators. The Minister said the government was contemplating an insurance scheme for women, under which parents would pay premium instead of giving dowry to enable daughters meet exigencies like widowhood and domestic violence.

Integrated Child Development Services (ICDS): For Children Up to 6 Years of Age & Pregnant and Nursing Mothers

Integrated Child Development Services (ICDS) launched in 1975 is a Centrally Sponsored Scheme implemented by the Ministry of Human Resource Development (MHRD). The Central Govt. is responsible for programme planning and operating costs while State Governments are responsible for programme implementation and providng supplementary nutrition out of their own resources. ICDS integrates supplementary nutrition with primary health care and in formal education. It is one of the largest child intervention programmes in the world with a holistic package of six basic service for children upto 6 years of age, and for pregnant and nursing mothers.

The package of services under the ICDS scheme include: supplementary nutrition, immunization, health check-up, treatment of minor ailments, referral services, pre-school education, nutrition and health education and convergence of other supportive services such as safe drinking water, sanitation etc. The ICDS network covered (1995) 176.04 lakh children below six years of age and 38.78 lakh pregnant and nursing mothers.

Aims: The complimentary package of services are delivered to the beneficiaries with the basic aim of achieving improvement in the nutritional and health status of children up to six years of age; reduction in the incidence of mortality, morbidity, malnutrition and school dropouts; laying the foundation of proper psychological, physical and social development of the child and enhancing of capacibility of mother to look after the normal health and nutritional needs of the child through health and nutrition.

Adolescent Girls: The scope of the ICDS scheme has also been enlarged to include adolescent girls under its cover. The scheme for adolescent girls focuses on school drop -out of girls in the 11-18 years. It envisages to make them better future mothers and tap their potential as social animators. The scheme has been sanctioned in 507 selected blocks of the country (1995).

National Programme for Education of Girls at Elementary Level (NPEGEL)

This programme is aimed at enhancing girls education by providing additional support for development of a "model girl child friendly school" in every cluster with more intense community mobilization and supervision of girls enrolment in schools. Under NPEGEL, 35,252 model schools have been opened in addition to supporting 25,537 Early Childhood Care and Education (ECCE) centers.

National Programme of Mid-Day Meals (MDM) In Schools

1. National programme of Mid-Day Meals (MDM) covers approximately 9.70 crore children studying at the Primary stage of education in 9.50 lakh schools: Government including local bodies, Government aided schools and the

centers run under Education Guarantee Scheme (EGS) and Alternative and Innovative Education (AIE) Scheme.

2. The programme provides a mid-day meal of 450 calories and 12 grams of protein to children at the Primary stage. For children at the Upper Primary stage , the nutritional value is fixed at 700 calories and 20 grams of protein. Adequate quantities of micro - nutrients like iron, folic acid, and vitamin-A are also recommended under the programme. To meet the nutritional norms, the Central Government Provides food grains @100 grams per Primary school child/school day and 150 grams per Upper Primary school child/school day.
3. In 2007-08, the Central Government also approved the inclusion of Inflation Adjusted Index (Consumer Price Index) for calculation of Central Assistance toward cooking once in every two years. This will be applicable from 2008-09 for Primary and Upper Primary stages.
4. The programme has helped in promoting school participation, preventing classroom hunger, instilling educational values, and fostering social and gender quality (Government of India, Economic survey 2007-08, New Delhi).

Gender Focus in the District Primary Education Programme–DPEP

The District Primary Education Programme (DPEP) has been taken up in 42 districts of seven States, all of which are educationally less developed, with low levels of female literacy. The decentralized implementation plans include specific interventions for girl.

DPEP is a major initiative aimed at achieving the goals of Universal Elementary Education (UEE) in a replicable, cost-effective and sustainable manner. The programme builds on the experience of earlier efforts for UEE which brought home the need to redesign Primary education as a whole, instead of a piece meal implementation of schemes. The major strengths of this programme are its sensitivity to local conditions rather than a rigid frame work. The approach is contextual, tailored to meet local situation and needs. Planning and management are decentralized and the emphasis is on involving local communities.

A gender perpective has been incorporated in all aspects of planning and implementation and is an integral part of the programme. Programme goals include a specific focus on reduction of gender disparities in education, as reflected in lower enrolment, lower retention and lower achievement of girls particularly those from socially and economically disadvantaged groups.

Interventions for Girls Education Initiated Under the Programme Include:

- Alternative schooling.
- Flexible school timings to accommodate girls needs.
- residential schools.
- Gender sensitive curricula and text books.
- recruitment of women teachers.
- Improved school building with toilets for girls.
- Educational incentives
- Gender sensitization of teachers and project managers.

Apart from these specific strategies designed to enhance girls' access, enrolment and retention in the school system, the programme recognizes the crucial importance of enabling local communities, particularly women to play an active role in every aspect of the programme. They include the following:

- Formation of village-level women's collectives and training of local women activists to catalyze collective action around educational issues.
- Empowerment of local bodies such as Village Education Committees (VEC's), Mother–Teacher Associations (MTA's) and women's groups, to enable them to take the responsibility for promoting education in their areas.
- Intensive capacity building for community and women's groups to focus on issues of education for girls.

- Involvement of community and women's organizations in mobilization and school management, and in monitoring enrolment, retention, levels of achievement and classroom transactions, with emphasis on girls.
- Mobilizing informed and active participation at the local level to build and sustain an environment supportive to girls education (Dept. of Education Government Of India).

Kasturiba Gandhi Balika Vidyalaya (KGBV)

Kasturba Gandhi Balika Vidyalaya (KGBV) Scheme was launched in July 2004 for setting up residential schools at Upper Primary level for girls belonging predominantly to the SC, ST, OBC and minority communities. The Kasturba Gandhi Balika Vidyalaya scheme ran as separate scheme for two years, but was merged with Sarva Shiksha Abhiyan (SSA) w.e.f. April 1, 2007. About 2180 KG BVs were sanctioned by Government of India up to March 2007.

Training Rural Youth for Self Employment: TRYSEM Scheme (A minimum of one-third rural youth to be women)

TRYSEM was initiated in 1979 with the objective of tackling unemployment problem among the rural youth. It aimed at training about 2 lakh rural youths every year to enable them to become self-employed. Under this scheme, 40 youths were to be selected from each block and for being eligible for selection, the person should belong to a rural family having an income less than Rs. 3500 per year. In making selection, members of Scheduled Castes and Scheduled Tribes were given preference. Under the scheme, a minimum of one-third of the rural youths trained were to be women. The TRYSEM was merged into Swarna Jayanthi Gram Swarozgar Yojana in April 1999.

National Rural Employment Guarantee Scheme: NREGS (At least One–third of the beneficiaries are to be women)

The National Rural Employment Guarantee Act (NREGA) was enacted in September 2005, and brought into force with effect from February 2, 2006 in 200 most backward districts of the country. The Act seeks to provide 100 days of guaranteed unskilled wage employment to each rural household opting for it. National Rural Employment Guarantee Scheme (NREGS) is different from other wage employment programmes as it bestows a legal right and guarantee to the rural population through an Act of Parliament and is not just a scheme like other wage employment programmes. The ongoing programmes of Sampoorna Grameen Rozgar Yojana (SGRY) and National Food For Work Programme (NFFWP) have been subsumed in NREGS.

The Focus of NREGS is on works relating to:

- Water Conservation.
- Drought proofing including a forestation tree plantation.
- Land development.
- Flood control/protection including drainage in waterlogged areas and
- Rural connectivity in terms of all-weather roads.

Panchayats have a key role in planning, implementation and monitoring of NREGA through preparation of perspective plan, approval of shelf of projects, execution of works at least to the extent of 50 percent in terms of costs. At least one-third of the beneficiaries are to be women. The Director of Centre for Environmental Concerns, K.S. Gopal points out quite correctly that work becomes an asset only if it is of any productive use and the majority of the NREGA Projects end up being unproductive. Ponds leak, bushes are eaten away with no one responsible, and the projects are closed (Hindustan Times, May 8, 2008, P.14).

Gender Budgeting

Gender Budgeting is a process that entails incorporating a gender perspective at various stages of planning:

- Policy/Programme formulation.

- Assessment of needs of target groups i.e. girls (school-going age) and women (adults).
- Allocation of resources.
- Implementation
- Impact assessment
- Reprioritization of resources etc.

Gender budgeting is not an end itself. It is a tool or means of achieving gender equality and women's empowerment. The Planning Commission of India has always focused on women's issues as per the perceptions of their members from the First Five Year plan (1951-56); Welfare, Development, Education, Health and Nutrition of Women and Children has been given attention. In the following Plan periods "Women Empowerment" has been given top priority. During the Eleventh plan period utmost care was taken to specify for the development of Dalit, Tribal and marginalized women through financial inclusion, to attain gender equality and to receive women rightful share from all the women related general developmental sectors. Establishment of a Gender Budget Monitoring Cell at the national level is also proposed (The Hindu, September 12, 2009).

Union Budget

Union Budget takes Gender Budgeting forward to ensure gender responsive health care system, maternal health services will be improved, an urgency and compulsory obstetrics care will be made available within a travel time of two hours. Targets for halving prevalence of anemia and malnutrition among women and children have been set and the ICDS scheme is being restructured and reoriented towards this end. A new component of conditional maternity benefits is proposed to target fetal malnutrition, ensure better care for pregnant women and encourage breast feeding. Universalisation of Anganwadis will be carried out, and Panchayat and Mothers Groups will be given resources to ensure effective implementation of the scheme. Need-based, community-run crèches will also be introduced to tackle malnutrition.

The Union Budget has brought out statement on Gender Budgeting which indicates Budget Provision for:

- 100% Women Specific Programmes: 14 ministries / Departments indicate Rs. 87,953 million as 100% allocation and the 100% allocation Ministries are traditional sectors with women related programes (2007-08).
- 30% Women Specific Programmes: 13 ministries indicate 223825 millions as 30% allocation.

Concluding Remarks

Women targeted special interventions and schemes represent a major endeavour on the part of the Government of India in improving the nutritional and health status of vulnerable sections- girls and women and form a key element of the human resource development strategy which combines health, education and counseling. The expanding coverage of such schemes bring into the forefront the country's development effort is ameliorating the condition of poor children and woman and encourage the girl child to complete at least primary education by reducing the dropout rate of girl students.

References

Kurukshetra Special Issue, August 1995.

Economic Survey 2007-08, Government of India, Oxford University Press, New Delhi, 2008.

Misra and Puri (2008), *Indian Economy, 26th Revised Edition,* Himalaya Publishing house, Mumbai.

Chapter-30

Women Entrepreneurship in India–Problems and Prospects

P. Jayanand Kumar, M. Sridevi, P. Raj Kumar

Introduction

Entrepreneur's fast reinforcing the capitalist tendencies in the context of globalization. The economic history reveals that it is the entrepreneurs who holds key of economic development. But unfortunately innovative entrepreneurs as conceptualized by Schumpeter are a rare tribe to be found equally in all parts of the globe. The large the number of entrepreneurs the greater the economic growth rate is the experience of the advanced countries like U.K., U.S.A., Germany, France and Japan.

The supply of insufficient number of entrepreneurs is holding back economic development in developing countries like India. For entrepreneurial activity is an adventure backed by resource endowment to fully exploit the markets at local, National and Global levels. Entrepreneurial traits are rather not widely visible in the Indian context and not to speak of women entrepreneurs in particular.

Although women's population is almost equal to that of men, their active participation in economic development seems to be insignificant till 1990. The women in India did not enjoy social freedom so as to freely mingle with the mainstream of life sharing the nation building activity through realizing their full potentials.

Keeping the above background, it is very clear that the entrepreneurship for women group is essential and it is to be developed. In deed, there have been several women in the history of our country who have successfully ruled their kingdoms. Even in the modern times also there have been several women leaders such as Mrs. Sorojini Naidu, Mrs. Durgabai Deshmukh, Miss. Padmaja Naidu, Mrs. Sucheta Kriplani and Madam Indira Gandhi who could equal their men counterparts in intellectual capabilities and statesmanship. Now-days there are several women political leaders in our country who could show their talents and abilities in the administration on par with men. All these would only prove that women are in no way inferior to men in any walk of life and they can be as good entrepreneurs as men.

Having realized the importance of the role of women in the Nations development, in the Sixth Five year plan, a special chapter on women's development has been included and the chapter explains the plan of action for "Integration of women in development". Further, the New Industrial Policy of Government of India has especially highlighted the need for conducting special entrepreneurship programmes exclusively for women group. These programmes would be in the nature of product/process oriented courses meant for women entrepreneurs to enable them to start small-scale industries. It shows that the objective of this course is to give representation to women group in the field of small industry development with view to uplift the economic and social status of women.

Indian society, though tradition bound in the past, now it is undergoing through a change and women are seeking gainful employment in all fields in increasing numbers. Even then it cannot said that women entrepreneurship movement has taken off the ground and it is felt that the movement is still in a transition period. It is during the last 10-15 years women have started becoming entrepreneurs and started industries and business and they are yet to go a long way to be on par with men. The situation is quite understandable, as women have to play a dual role as a housewife and also as an income earner. Despite the modernization and other factors mentioned above, the weight of tradition and the responsibilities of the women have to discharge to their children as mother slow down this movement. Further, occupational backgrounds of the families and the educational attainment of the husbands have a direct bearing in the development of women entrepreneurship. Limiting the size of the family help the women entrepreneurs to some extent to enable them to enter business in such a manner that husband's prestige is not affected in any manner.

It is believed that entrepreneurs are born not made. However, some recent researches on promoting entrepreneurs seem to show that this view is not really correct. Entrepreneurship can be planned and developed and the need for providing appropriate importance in the case of prospective women entrepreneurs. The spirit of entrepreneurship can be nurtured to some extent by an appropriate pattern of education and training programme. The curriculum design for women's education needs re-orientation and the philosophy of "Good enough for women" should be given a go-by.

For instance, the present emphasis in any women's polytechnic is on stitching, embroidery, house decoration, etc., which are the women's traditional role rather than aiming at imparting new skills which would help them to become entrepreneurs by starting small-scall industries or setting up business. Some recent researches conducted indicate that several women are now willing to become entrepreneurs due to various factors. These factors can be broadly classified under heads, namely, "pull factors" and "push factors". Under the first category, the women entrepreneurs choose a profession as challenge and adventure with an urge to do something new and to have an independent occupation. The other category of women take-up business enterprises to get over financial difficulties and responsibility is thrust on them due to family circumstances.

However, in sum, the problem of entrepreneurship among women is a question of the family outlook on the role to be played by the women, and the estimation of capabilities by women themselves. Much depends upon the courage and determination of women to become entrepreneurs and with the facilities offered by Government, Banks and Financial Institutions to women, they should now start setting up business ventures in large number in many parts of the country.

Definition of Women Entrepreneurship

The term women entrepreneurship refers to socio-economic and political upliftment of women-folk making them equal to their men counterparts in all respects. These include social status, self-sustenance and participation in decision-making mechanism starting from gross-root level to the national level. In this context International Labour Organization (ILO) describes that "entrepreneurs are people who have the ability to see and evaluate business opportunities, to gather the necessary resources to take advantage of them and to initiate appropriate action to ensure success".

World Bank defines empowerment as "the process of increasing the capacity of individuals or groups to make choices and to transform those choices into desired actions and outcomes. Central to this process or set of actions which both build individual and collective assets and improve the efficiency and fairness of the organizational and institutional context which govern the use of those assets".

This definition explains freedom of choice and action in all spheres to shape one's life and the life of fellow citizens. Women must have to secure control over resources and decisions. Due to gender inequality, such control is often severely curtailed. Hence, at the individual level, women empowerment require a set of assets and capabilities like health, education and employment and at the collective level they secure the ability to organize and mobilize to take action to solve their problems.

A women entrepreneur is one who owns and controls an enterprise having a share capital of not less than 51 per cent as partial/shareholder/directors of private limited company/ members of co-operative society. The functions performed by a women entrepreneur are categorized as risk-bearing organization and innovation. In India, where its population maintains almost equal ratio of male and female, the emergence of women entrepreneurs have great relevance and importance. Otherwise it will be amounting to neglecting 50 per cent of the entrepreneurial talent of the country.

Confidently speaking the creative entrepreneur is the back-bone of a nation's industrialization and economic development. There is no gender for the entrepreneur. Women entrepreneurs are managing the fast developing USA's 40 per cent business and it is likely to be further more in the Third Millennium.

Need for Women Entrepreneurship

Primarily, the Indian women are generally under valued and considered inferior to males. Creating and developing more women entrepreneurs in India is nothing but giving them their due share of recognition and social respect. Under the suppressed socio-economic conditions women entrepreneurs did not prosper in the 50 years of independence. There has been a little movement in the growth of women entrepreneurship. With the advent of liberalization policy, there is lot of scope for the growth of entrepreneurship under the private sector and at the same time the circumstances to develop women entrepreneurship have become congenial.

With growing awareness and spread of education over the years, women have started engrossing to modern activities like engineering, electronics and energy. In certain business, women entrepreneurs are doing exceedingly well. Most of the women entrepreneurs carry on small or medium sized business and many of them operate in the informal sector. The management styles adopted by women differ from men's due to differences in skills and experience. The prosperity of women entrepreneurs largely depends on association, net working and mutual support.

Functions of Women Entrepreneurs

The women entrepreneur is a key to economic development.

Frederick Harbison has enumerated the following five functions of a women entrepreneur:

- Exploration of the prospects of starting a new business enterprise.
- Undertaking of risks and the handling of economic uncertainties involved in business.
- Introduction of innovations or imitation of innovations.
- Coordination, administration and control.
- Supervision and leadership.

The emergence of women entrepreneurs in a society depends to a great extent on the economic, religious, cultural, psychological and other factors. For developing countries like India, the presence of entrepreneurs, that too women entrepreneurs are of vital necessity, to achieve a rapid, all round and regionally and socially balanced economic growth through industrialization. It also helps in tapping the inherent talents prevailing among them and act as a panacea for many problems faced by them, such as dowry death, low recognition in society, poverty, unemployment and excessive dependence on male members.

Characteristics of Entrepreneur

To be a successful entrepreneur, a person has to acquire and develop certain qualities, which can be included by training and motivation. The essential entrepreneurial traits/qualities are:

1. High achievement motivation
2. Insatiable drive and persistent enthusiasm
3. Readiness to face challenge
4. Persistent problem solving
5. Goal setting
6. Dealing with failure
7. Technical background

8. Experience in the line
9. Willingness to introduce something new (Sprit of innovation)
10. Taking initiative and seeking personal responsibility
11. Competing against self imposed standards
12. Tolerance to ambiguity and uncertainty
13. Hard working
14. Regularity and dedication to work
15. Self control
16. Self confidence
17. Confidence in self capability
18. Use of feed back
19. Willingness to take advice
20. Time management
21. Money as a measure
22. Drive and energy
23. Long term involvement
24. Total commitment and immersion

Types of Women Entrepreneurs

Women entrepreneurs may be broadly categorized under the following four groups.

1. *Natural Entrepreneurs:* Those who take business as profession on their own either by self planning or motivated through many factors and also for keeping themselves busy.
2. *Generated Entrepreneurs:* Those who have been encouraged and trained through specialized training programmes such as the Entrepreneurial Development Programme (EDP), to set up independent business.
3. *Forced Entrepreneurs:* Those who are compelled by circumstances such as the death of father or husband with responsibilities failing on them to take over the existing business, and

4. *Benami Entrepreneurs:* Those who are acting as a façade for business of their husband or brother.

Entrepreneurship development among women can be considered a possible approach to economic empowerment of women. A women as entrepreneur is economically more powerful than as a mere worker because ownership not only confers control over assets (and liabilities) but also gives her the freedom to take decisions. This will also uplift her social status significantly.

Status of Women Entrepreneurs In India

It is evident that women constitutes around 50 per cent of the world's population, do the two-third of world's work hours, receive 10 per cent of world's income and own less than one per cent of world's property (ILO Report 1980). Women owned business are becoming increasingly important in the economies of almost all countries. To the U.S. economy, they contribute more than $250 billion annually and create new business opportunities at two to three times the rate of their male counterparts.

Similarly, in India, women constitute nearly 50 per cent of national population and a very important human resource for the nation's development. According to Survey Report on Indian women, women entrepreneurs constitute 47 per cent of the total urban population. The participation of women in the economy's GDP is as low as 8 per cent, though their work participation was 19.7 per cent in 1981. In India, according to the census 2001, the female labour force participation, rated in their total population, is 25.7 per cent but it is 31 per cent in rural and 11.6 per cent in urban areas. They are engaging in different sectors.

It is estimated that the invisible work of housewives contributes nearly one-third of Indian's GNP. Over the last few decades, women have come forward to establish their own enterprises. Earlier studies revealed that economic role played by women couldn't be isolated from the framework of development. The contribution of women in the socio-economic development particularly in the rural areas has been vital. Around 77 per cent of the total female population of the country lives in rural areas. Out of the main workers as many as 80 per cent are in rural areas and the percentage of women engaged in cultivation was 33.2. As major part of the agricultural operations like breaking clods of earth, manage wading, transplanting, harvesting, threshing and winnowing. Women do most of the work of caring the dairy animals and marketing of their products. In household industries, it is 46 per cent against the male percentage of 43.7 working in the same sector. They also extend their helping hand in other small industries like rope and basket making. Pottery, handloom, weaving and food processing indicating that women playing multi-dimensional role in the society. However except some cases, it is an indisputable fact that out of more than 370 million women in the country almost 150 million are below the poverty line.

The national policy for empowerment of women was adopted in 2001 with the objective of ensuring women their rightful place in society by empowering them as agents of socio-economic change and development. Empowerment of women is therefore, an important approach adopted in the Tenth Five-year plan for development of women. The new industrial policy has stressed the need for conducting a special Entrepreneurship Development Programme (EDP) and some other programme supporting and promoting entrepreneurial skill. Government financial institutions and national banks also have special cells to assist women entrepreneurs.

Problems of Women Entrepreneurs

Apart from the facit assumption that women are frail and indecisive, women entrepreneurs encounter many problems in their efforts to develop the enterprises they have established. The main problems faced by the women entrepreneurs may be analysed as follows:

Shortage of Finance

Women and small entrepreneurs always suffer from inadequate financial resources and working capital. They are lacking access to external funds due to absence of tangible security and credit in the market. Women do not generally have property to their names.

Inefficient Arrangements for Marketing and Sale

For marketing their products, women entrepreneurs are oftern at the mercy of the middlemen who pocket large a chunk of profit. Although the middlemen exploit the women entrepreneurs, the elimination of middlemen is difficult because it involves a lot of running about.

Shortage of Raw Materials

Women entrepreneurs find it difficult to procure raw materials and other necessary inputs.

Stiff Competition

Many of the women enterprises have imperfect organizational setup. They have to face stiff competition from organized industries and male entrepreneurs.

High Cost of Production

Another problem, which undermines the efficiency and restrict the development of women enterprises, is the high cost of production. Government assistance in the form of grants and subsidies to some extent enables them to tide over this difficulty.

Low Mobility

One of the biggest handicaps for women entrepreneurs is mobility or traveling from place to place. Women on their own find it difficult to get accommodation in smaller towns. A single woman asking for a room is still looked upon with suspicion.

Family Responsibilities

In India it is mainly a women's duty to look after the children and older members of the family. Her involvement in family leaves little energy and time for business. Married women entrepreneurs have to make a fine balance between business and home. Their success in this regard also depends up on supporting husband and family.

Social Attitudes

The biggest problem of a women entrepreneur is the social attitude and the constraints in which she has to live and work. Despite constitutional equality, there is discrimination against women in a tradition-bound society, women suffer from male reservations about a women's role and capacity.

Low Ability to Bear Risk

Women have comparatively a low ability to bear economic and other risks because they have led a protected life. Sometimes they face discrimination in the selection for entrepreneurial development training, and some of them lack entrepreneurial initiative or specialized training.

Lack of Education

In India literacy among women is very low. Due to lack of education, majority of women are unaware of technological developments, marketing knowledge etc., lack of information and experience creates further problems in the setting up and running of business enterprises.

In addition to the above problems inadequate infrastructure, shortage of power and technical know-how and other economic and social constraints have retarded the growth of women entrepreneurship in India.

Suggestions for Improving the Status of Women Entrepreneurs

The problems of women workers in India are multifarious and multidimensional. These problems can be solved through changes in the attitude of family, society and nation towards the women. Some suggestions are given below:

Financial Cells

Special cells may be opened for providing easy finance to women entrepreneurs in various public financial institutions and banks. These cells should be manned by women officers and clerks. Efforts should be made to provide finance at the local level.

Marketing Cooperatives

Encouragement and assistance should be provided to women entrepreneurs for setting up cooperatives. These cooperatives will pool the inputs of women enterprises and sell them on remunerative prices. Such cooperatives will help to eliminate the middlemen.

Supply of Raw Materials

Scarce and imported raw materials may be made available to women entrepreneurs on priority basis. A subsidy may also be given to make the products manufactured by women entrepreneurs as cost effective measure.

Training Facilities

Training and skills are essential for the development of entrepreneurship. Training schemes should be so designed that women can take full advantage. Family members do not like women to go away to far off places for training. Women have the potential and the will to establish and manage enterprises of their own. What they need is encouragement and support.

Education and Awareness

Many efforts were taken to improve the position of women by increasing the literacy rates. Now, both government and non-government organizations are taking steps to promote entrepreneurship among women. But the results are not in commensurate with the efforts. A recent study of the Town and country planning reveals that self-employment is a powerful motivating factor. It should motivate her to set up an enterprise.

It is necessary to change negative social attitudes towards women. Elders particularly, mothers and mother-in-law need to be made aware of the potential of girls and their due role in society. There shall be compulsory education for women. When she is educated, she can manage her dual responsibility of home and work.

Seminars

More seminars, conferences and workshops on women should be organized. They should be encouraged to participate in them and express their views.

Part Time Jobs

Another suggestion is to increase part time jobs for women in various organizations, which will give a sense of dignity and identity to the women.

Wage Gap and Medical Facilities

Wage gapes between men and women should be reduced. Better medical facilities and congenial atmosphere should be provided to them. Maternity benefit schemes should be enhanced in private sectors.

Change the Attitude

The attitude of the husband and family members should be changed towards the working women. Husband should come forward to share her burden. Women should change their attitude about themselves. They should be self confident in their approach.

Baby Care Centres

Baby care centres should be opened at the work place where she can leave her child.

Constitutional and Legal Rights

Women should be made aware of their constitutional and legal rights both in their work and in the social sphere.

Conclusions

Now working women have become a major part of labour market of India and hence their problem cannot be ignored. When they are engaged in gainful employment and contributing to the household and national economy, they should be given the due respect and status they deserve in the family and the society. In the changing socio-cultural environment of India, women are entering in a new era. But they are still over burdened with the household cores. So some measures should be introduced to reduce their household burden. This requires a drastical change in the mind set of the men folk towards women in general and working women in particular.

Hence, it becomes necessary for the society and Government to find remedies for the problems of women entrepreneurship. Already the Central and State Governments and non-governments organizations have taken so many steps to solve the problems of women entrepreneurs, yet they have to provide special incentives and subsidy. As entrepreneurship opportunities will be more in small and medium scale industries, the sector should be given prominence and proper marketing strategy of such products should be planned and implemented, which will give scope for women entrepreneurs. If Indian women's talent will be utilized properly, one day India will become an ideal country to others.

References

Bhatia, B.S. and Batra, G.S. (2003), *Entrepreneurship and small Business Management,* Deep and Deep Publications Pvt. Ltd., New Delhi.

Birley, S. (1989), "Female Entrepreneurs: Are they Really any Different", *Journal of Small Business Management,* 27 (1), pp.32-37.

Dhameja, S.K. (2004), *Women Entrepreneurs,* Deep and Deep Publications Pvt. Ltd., New Delhi.

Garg, R.B.L. (2004), "Women Entrepreneurs: Problems and Prospects", *Social Welfare,* 50 (12), March, pp.16-18.

Khurana, I.R. (1988), "Strategy for Rural Development", *Khadi Gram Udyog,* 34 (8), pp.335-344.

Mohiuddin, A. (1987), "Entrepreneurship in Rural Women", *Kurukshetra,* 35 (12), pp.22-25.

Nelson, R.E.(1985), *Entrepreneurship and Self Employment Training, Asian Development Bank,* Manila.

Rao, S.K. (1976), Entrepreneur Development in India- Is Achievement Training the Aanswer, *Laghu Udyog,* 4. pp.9-12.

Sinha, Poonam (2003), "Women Entrepreneurship in the North East India: Motivation, Social Support and Constraints", *Indian Journal of Industrial Relations,* 28 (4), April, pp.425-41.

Sundaram, I. Satya (2004), "Encouraging Women's Entrepreneurship", *Social Welfare,* 50 (12), March, pp.15-19.

Vidyu Lata (1990), *Developing Rural Women,* Discovery Publishing House, New Delhi.

Vitz, M.D. (1987), *Women Entrepreneurs in India,* Mittal Publications, New Delhi.

Chapter-31

Empowerment of Muslim Women Entrepreneurship in Visakhapatnam City

B. Ratna Kumari, G. Zilani Begum

Introduction

The Socio-Economic status of a country is reflected in the Socio-Economic development of its people. Now everywhere entrepreneurship is acknowledged as mechanism for socio-economic development. However, entrepreneurship was prevalent even before this formal recognition. In fact, entrepreneurship was born with the first human being on the earth. Especially in Muslim women they have imbibed skills such as suing, stitching, embroidery and fashion designing etc. However, the status of Muslim women in our country is relatively low compared with other women. Hence there is a need to study the Muslim women entrepreneurship much essential in the context of women empowerment.

Entrepreneurship is regarded as one of the most crucial factors in the economic development of every region of the country. It widens the horizons of economic development even in the socially and industrially backward regions. Dynamic entrepreneurs are considered to be the agent of change in a society. Entrepreneurs play a very important role in generating new employment and setting up of new business. The problem of poverty, inequality and regional imbalances can be tackled with the development of entrepreneurship. Entrepreneurship among women is more suitable because it is possible to do work when she has free time. A self-employed woman is gaining better status. It enables her to pool the small capital resources and skill available with women. It paves the way for fuller utilization of capital and also mobilizes the female human potential. Entrepreneurship development among women offers, mental satisfaction and provides diversion to women and enhanced identity in the psychological satisfaction to women and enhances identity in the society. Further, emergence of women entrepreneurs in the economy is an indicator of women's economic independence.

Women entrepreneurs may be defined as the women or a group of women who initiate, organize and operate a business enterprise. However such innovators are rarely sound in the underdeveloped countries, the enterprises for these people may be small and unimpressive when judged by standards of the developed countries. But the high propensity to imitate can set in motion the chain reaction which leads to cumulative progress. Thus in the Indian context, entrepreneur are an adopter and imitator than a true innovator.

According to the government of India, a women entrepreneur is defined as "an enterprise owned and controlled by women and having a minimum financial interest of 51% of the capital and giving at least 51% of the employment generated in the enterprises to women". Enterprises set up by women should be provided with incentives and support on the basis of their ownership and management characteristic and not linked with employment of women. *'Entrepreneurship'* broadly stands for self-employment. It mainly involves identification of opportunities with in the economic system. It involves assumptions of risks and responsibility in designing and executing a business strategy of starting a new business venture. Entrepreneurs are skilled organizers of various activities such as identifying the needs for various products or services, originating or generating ideas on how to provide the desired products are services, evolution of well thought out ideas and present a business enterprise opportunity, and finally, a plan of action to translate idea into a commercially viable proposition. Entrepreneurship has been attracting more and more attention of policy makers, academicians and business practitioners since early nineties. The main reason behind this is that the creation of new enterprises has a great potential to contribute to a balanced and accelerated economic growth and creation of employment opportunities.

Need of the Study

So many women were migrated from rural areas of Visakhapatnam district and a number of women have been engaged with in self employment, hence there is an activities need to find out the status of women entrepreneurs especially Muslim women entrepreneurs in the City.

Objectives

The present study examines the growth of Muslim women entrepreneurship to the empowerment level. It studies *inter alia, the educational background, motivation to initiate to entrepreneurial career, and their problems.* It also further observes the trend of income and employment generating capacity and the constraints of women entrepreneurship.

The Specific Objectives of the Study are as follows:

- To study the socio-demographic profile of the Muslim Women Entrepreneurs;
- To observe the factors which contribute income and employment generation of the women entrepreneurs;
- To analyze the role conflict and constraints of the Muslim Women Entrepreneur;
- To suggest for policy implications to strengthen their growth with economic empowerment;

Research Methodology

Sample

The study is based on primary data. The Muslim women entrepreneurs of chaitanya sravanthi an NGO were selected on *purposive basis*. There are nearly 700 Muslim women entrepreneurs in chaitanya sravanthi which is located in I town area of Visakhapatnam city. For the present study 150 women were selected on randomly basis.

Tools

The selected samples were administered with structured schedule and necessary information has been collected from them. The Andhra Pradesh state minority finance corporation (APSMFC) of Visakhapatnam.

The study has used the simple percentage method to find out the above objectives.

Findings of the Study

Table.1. Percentage distribution of the Muslim women entrepreneurs by age:-

The Table-1 explains that the distribution of the age of the respondent Muslim women. Out of the total respondent 46.7 percent of respondent are in 21-30 years age group 26 percent of the respondents are in 31-40 years age group. 14 percent of the respondents are in 41-50 years of age group. A small percentage (13.3) respondent is in 10-20 years and age group.

Table 1
Age of the Respondents

Age Group	*Frequency*	*Percent*
10-20	20	13.3
21-30	70	46.7
31-40	39	26.0
41-50	21	14.0
Total	150	100.0

Table.2. Percentage distribution of the Muslim women entrepreneurs by education qualifications:-

The Table-2 explains that the distribution of the education qualification of the respondent Muslim women. Out of the total respondent 50.7 percent of respondent are secondary education, 24.7 percent of the respondents are primary education, 18.7 percent of the respondents are illiterate, 4 percent of the respondents are degree, 1.3 percent of the respondent are intermediate and a small percentage (0.7) respondent are PG and above education .

Table 2
Education Qualification of the Respondents

Education Qualification	*Frequency*	*Percent*
illiterate	28	18.7
primary education	37	24.7
secondary education	76	50.7
intermediate	2	1.3
degree	6	4.0
PG and above	1	.7
Total	150	100.0

Table.3. Percentage distribution of the Muslim women entrepreneurs by martial Status:-

The Table-3 explains about respondent Muslim women Martial Status. 92.7 percent respondents were married, 3.3 percent respondents are unmarried and 2 percent of respondents were widows and separated.

Table 3
Martial Status of the Respondents

Martial Status	*Frequency*	*Percent*
Un married	5	3.3
married	139	92.7
widow	3	2.0
separated	3	2.0
Total	150	100.0

Table.4. Percentage distribution of the Muslim women entrepreneurs by family size:-

Table 4
Family Size of the Respondents

Family Size	*Frequency*	*Percent*
1-5	118	78.7
6-10	32	21.3
Total	150	100.0

Table 4 indicates about the respondent's family size. 78.7 percent of them had 1-5 members' family. 21.3 percent of them had 6-10 members in a family.

Table.5. Percentage distribution of the Muslim women entrepreneurs by Type of house:-

Table 5 indicates the respondent's house type. 42.7 percent of them were staying in semi-pucca. 29.3 percent of them were residing in Pucca house. 28 percent of them were staying in kuccha house.

Table 5
Respondents House Type

Type of House	*Frequency*	*Percent*
kuchha	42	28.0
pucca	44	29.3
semi pucca	64	42.7
Total	150	100.0

Table.6. Percentage distribution of the Muslim women entrepreneurs by Source of drinking water:-

Table 6 gives the information about the source of water for respondent's domestic use. 71.3 percent of them fetch the water from public tap. 22.7 percent of them had tap at their houses. 6 percent of them hand pump at their house premises.

Table 6
Source of Drinking Water by Respondents

Source of Drinking Water	*Frequency*	*Percent*
hand pump	9	6.0
piped water(public tap)	107	71.3
piped water (own tap)	34	22.7
Total	150	100.0

Table.7. Percentage distribution of the Muslim women entrepreneur's toilet facilities of house:

Table 7 reveals the information about the toilet facility at the respondent's house. 47.3 percent of them have pit type toilet at their house. 24 percent of them have own flush toilet, 20.7

percent of them have shared flush toilet at their house. 5.3 percent of them have shared pit toilet at their house and 2.7 percent of them have public toilet.

Table 7
Toilet Facilities at the Respondent's House

Toilet Facilities	*Frequency*	*Percent*
own pit toilet	71	47.3
own flush toilet	36	24.0
shared flush toilet	31	20.7
shared pit toilet	8	5.3
public toilet	4	2.7
Total	150	100.0

Table.8. Percentage distribution of the Muslim women entrepreneurs' professional/vocational qualification and link with present entrepreneurial activity:-

Out of the total respondent women (150), 93.3 percent do not have any professional/vocational qualification and link with present entrepreneurial activity and only 6.7 percent professional/vocational qualification and link with present entrepreneurial activity.

Table 8
Professional/Vocational Qualification and Link with Present Entrepreneurial Activity

Professional Qualification	*Frequency*	*Percent*
Yes	10	6.7
No	140	93.3
Total	150	100.0

Table.9. Percentage distribution of the Muslim women entrepreneurs' Professional/vocational qualification:-

Out of the total respondent women (150), 5.3 percent have government recognized technical vocational qualification, 1.3 percent of respondent have unrecognized diploma or certificate and 99.2 percent of the respondents do not have any professional vocational qualification

Table 9
Professional/Vocational Qualification of the Respondents

Professional/Vocational Qualifications	*Frequency*	*Percent*
govt.recongnised technical	8	5.3
unrecognized diploma or certificate	2	1.3
none of the above	140	93.3
Total	150	100.0

Table.10. Percentage distribution of the Muslim women entrepreneurs' previous business experience:-

Table explains the distribution of the sample Muslim women in the three districts with their previous business experience. Out of the total Muslim women entrepreneurs from 58 percent of the respondents do not have any business experience, 42 percent of the respondent have business experiment.

Table 10
Business Experience of the Respondents

Business Experience	*Frequency*	*Percent*
Yes	63	42.0
No	87	58.0
Total	150	100.0

Table.11. Percentage distribution of Muslim women entrepreneurs husbands Occupation:-

Table 11
Occupation of the Respondent Husbands

Occupation of the Respondent Husband	*Frequency*	*Percent*
self employed	40	26.6
Business	10	6.6
organized sector	10	6.6
unorganized sector	40	26.6
Urban labour	50	33.3
Total	150	100

It is evident from this table 31.3 percent of respondents were self-employed, 50 percent of the respondents involved in business, 8.3 percent of the respondents were involved in unorganized sector and 8.3 percent of respondents were involved in other occupational filed. 2.1 percent of respondent women not involved in any previous occupation and remained as housewives.

Table.12. Percentage distribution of the Muslim women entrepreneurs information about the minority commission:-

The Table 12 indicates about the 28.7 percent of the respondent women got the information family members, 27.7 percent got the information women groups, 25.3 percent got the information self help groups 15.3 percent got though Kazi/ ulamas. 3.3 percent of the respondents got the information through friends.

Table 12
Information About the Minority Commission

Information about the Minority Commission	*Frequency*	*Percent*
kazi ulamas	23	15.3
family members	43	28.7
women groups	41	27.3
self help groups	38	25.3
friends	5	3.3
Total	150	100.0

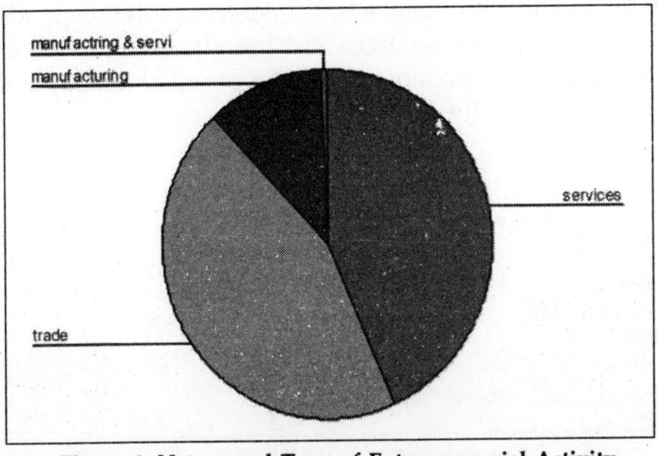

Figure 1: Nature and Type of Entrepreneurial Activity

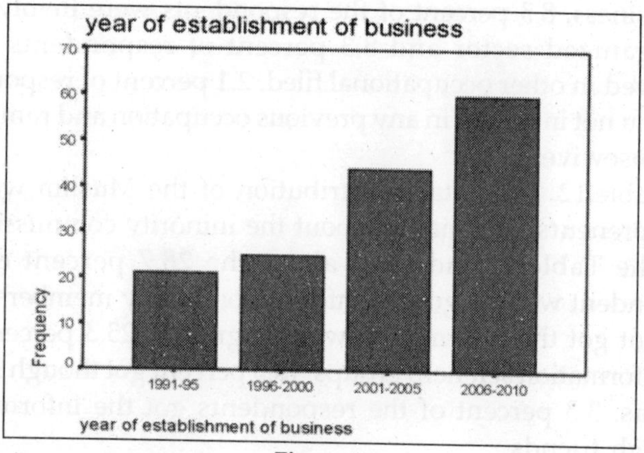

Figure 2

Table 13 explains the various source of credit facility offered to the respondent women to start their entrepreneurial activity. Broadly these sources are from financiers; Relatives and friends; APSMFC (Andhra Pradesh State Minority Federation Corporation); and respondent own money. Out of 150 respondents from study area 46.7 percent of the respondents took the credit from bankers for their entrepreneurial activity. 37.3 percent of the respondent took the credit from APSMFC for their entrepreneurial activity. 6.7 percent of the respondents took the credit from financials, 5.3 percent of the respondents took the credit from relatives and friends, 3.3 percent of the started with their own money and 0.7 percent of the respondent took credit from others help.

Table 13
Sources of Credit Facilities

Credit Facilities	*Frequency*	*Percent*
Financial	10	6.7
relatives friends	8	5.3
Bankers	70	46.7
APSMFC	56	37.3
Own	5	3.3
Others	1	.7
Total	150	100.0

Table.14. Percentage distribution of the Muslim women entrepreneurs' initial investment:

The table indicates that 50.7 percent of the respondents invested less than Rs.4000-10,000 initially, 41.3 percent of them invested Rs.11000-15,000, 6.0 percent of the respondents invested 16,000-20,000. 1.3 percent of them invested 21,000-25,000 and 0.7 percent of them invested only Rs.31, 000-35,000 initially to start their entrepreneur activity.

Table 14
Initial Investment of Respondents

Initial Investment	*Frequency*	*Percent*
4000-10,000	76	50.7
11,000-15,000	62	41.3
16,000-20,000	9	6.0
21,000-25,000	2	1.3
31,000-35,000	1	.7
Total	150	100.0

Table.15. Percentage distributions of the Muslim women entrepreneurs get raw materials:

The table indicates the 61.3 percent of the respondent women get raw materials from wholesale market for their entrepreneurial activity and 38.7 percent of the respondent women get raw materials form retail market for their entrepreneurial activity.

Table 15
Get the Raw Materials of Respondents

Get Raw Materials	*Frequency*	*Percent*
wholesale market	92	61.3
retail market	58	38.7
Total	150	100.0

Table.16. Percentage distribution of the Muslim women entrepreneurs, details of source of materials:

The table indicates out of the total respondent women 80 percent source of raw materials from with the district for their entrepreneurial activity and 20 percent of the respondent women source of raw materials other parts of the state for their entrepreneurial activity.

Table 16
Details of Source of Materials of Respondents

Source of Raw Materials	*Frequency*	*Percent*
from within the district	120	80.0
from other parts of the state	30	20.0
Total	150	100.0

Table.17 Percentage distribution of the Muslim women entrepreneurs faced by marketing problem:

Table 17 shows various marketing problems faced by the respondent women entrepreneurs. In out of total respondent (150) 38 percent of the respondents have not faced any problem, but 62 percent of the respondents from this district faced some problems in marketing the goods.

Table 17
Marketing Problem Faced by the Respondents

Marketing Problem	*Frequency*	*Percent*
Yes	57	38.0
No	93	62.0
Total	150	100.0

Table.18. Percentage distribution of the Muslim women entrepreneurs faced by financial problem:

Table 18
Financial Problems Faced by the Respondent

Financial Problem	*Frequency*	*Percent*
Yes	69	46.0
No	81	54.0
Total	150	100.0

Table 18 shows various financial problems faced by the respondent women entrepreneurs. Out of 150 entrepreneurs

46 percent of them have faced various financial crises (problem). 54 percent of them have not reported any financial problem during their entrepreneurial activity.

Suggestions and Policy Implications

- Entrepreneurship is found to be at very low ebb in Muslims. Existing policies for the growth of Muslim women entrepreneurship in need to be further strengthened.
- Muslim Women prefer to establish home-based enterprises. Efforts should be made to provide information on various business opportunities available to potential Muslim women entrepreneurs, which can be started at their home place.
- The present study recommends that banking policy needs to be implemental in favor of women with greater amount of flexibility. It would assist women further if banks educate Muslim women through awareness programmes of the various loans/credit facilities available.
- The study recommends that if the loans are though agencies with which women groups, anganwadi worker, State advisory boards and women's development corporations.
- The government has to allot space for the sales Muslim women entrepreneurs in order to face competition from the rivals or encourage them in this sector.
- The present study observed the existence of variation in the earnings of the Muslim women in different occupations in the Informal sector in order to rectify this problem, we have to prepare evaluation studies on various developmental progrmmes for Muslim women. Thus, these studies will find out the inter linkage within the different activities as well as with the rest of the economy.
- Motivational courses for housewives to earn additional income. Change of attitude in society towards Muslim women entrepreneurs.

References

Anil Kumar (2007), *Women Entrepreneurship in India,* Regal publications, New Delhi.

Asghar Ali Engineer (2001), *Islam Women and Gender Justice* – (Religion, Gender, women), published by Indian Gyan Publishing House.

Dr. P.V.L Ramana (2002), *Women in Slums-A Study of Women in Muslim Slums of Visakhapatnam* Published by Serials Publications, Delhi.

Sami Uddin (1989), *Entrepreneurship Development in India* Published by K.M.Mittal publications, Delhi.

S.K. Modi (2008), *Socio-Economic Development of Delits in India,* Navyug publishers & distributors, New Delhi.

www.google.com

CHAPTER-32

Women Empowerment and Gandhi's Contribution

V. Krishna Murthy, R.V.L.N. Ratnakar Rao

Introduction

Gender equality became a global agenda in the 21st century. The concept of women's empowerment was introduced at the International Women's Conference in Nairobi in 1985 where empowerment was stated to be a "distribution of social power and the center for resources in favour of women". The status of woman in Gandhi's eyes was that of equal standing as man. This was clearly indicated through his words and actions. It was through his leadership that more women came into Indian Politics, which ultimately produced two women ministers in the first cabinet of Independent India.

Gandhi's organization based on respect through truth and non-violence, placed women on an equal if not higher platform with men. He communicated with them throughout the nation, and even the world. His rapport with women, including, his written correspondence to the ashram women, displays a sincere sense of dignity for women. In fact in some ways he regarded women as superior to men. For him bravery lay in dying and not killing (M.K.Gandhi, 1958, P.3) and since in courage of self sacrifice women are superior to men in non-violent struggle women could make a greater contribution than men (S.C Biswas, 1967, P.116). He believed that when women do a thing in the right spirit, they can move mountains. He said that if non-violence is the law of our being, the future is with women for they can make the most effective appeal to the heart (J.B.Kripalini, 2005, P.403)

Gandhi's Sources of Inspiration: His Mother and Wife

For Gandhi to fight endlessly for women's equality. He had to be inspired, like many great men, by his mother and wife. His inspiration to lead India's women to a better life came from the first women in his life and later his beloved wife, namely, his loving mother and Kasturba respectively. These two figures inspired him and his understanding of women was through his interaction with them. His mother impressed him most: "The outstanding impression my mother left on my memory is that of saintliness" (M.K. Gandhi, *An Auto biography,* 1998). His mother and wife were his intimate influences of his life and the relationship he had with these two figures in his life was "a most ennobling influence" on him (Kamladevi Chattopadhyay 2003, 'Woman the Comrade', P.9)

These two women did everything for him: his mother gave him here consent to go to England despite that he could be considered as an outcast for going overseas, and his wife sold most of her jewelry to raise the funds to so. According to Kapadia, Gandhi credited his wife for his moral strength and personal growth that his wife demonstrated by example. Gandhi's own words confirmed this, "My wife made the orbit of all women. In her I studied all women." This illustrates how Gandhi respected his wife and his long partnership with her even after 62 years of their marriage. Through these two women, who had the most profound impact on his life, he paid his tribute to them, and woman- kind: 'I have worshipped woman as the living embodiment of the spirit of service and sacrifice".

Ba and Bapu (Kasturba and Gandhi)

Among other sources, Gandhi learned about woman's potential from his wife, also known as Ba. Gandhi was married in childhood, and he states that he grew up with his wife. He wrote to a woman on women. When Gandhi wrote to Raj Kumari Amrit Kaur from Wardha on 21st October 1931, it was an invitation for women like her rise up and save themselves from the unfair treatment they received. In his letter, he wanted her and the rest of her woman kind to realize that they are just as dignified as the man, and their worth to mankind:

"write to the papers and invite other women to do likewise. If you women would only realize your dignity and privilege, and make full use of it for mankind, you will make it much better than it is. But man has delighted in enslaving you and you have proved willing slaves till the slaves and the slave - holders have became one in the crime of degrading humanity. My special function from child hood, you might say, has been to make woman realize her dignity. I was once slave-holder myself but Ba proved an unwilling slave and thus opened my eyes to my mission" (1961, Pp. 100-101).

An old photograph of Gandhi taken upon his return from South Africa in 1915 shows him and his wife, Kasturba, standing side by side (website on Mahatma Gandhi Album, *http://wwww.kamat.com/mmgandhi/wedding.htm*). Although her face was solemn, and most probably she was camera shy, standing next to her husband was an indication of her status in her husband's eyes. As a husband, Gandhi had elevated her to his equal status and the proof is the photograph with her standing next to him. Both were still young but the future that awaited them would put Gandhi on the map to change India's future, with her by his side, and to shape the future of Indian women in particular.

Ba and Bapu are the two sides of the same coin. They stand for a culture of truth and non-violence, i.e. a culture of pursuit of ethical perfection as the ultimate goal of life and pursuit of selfless ethical life of universal love as it means! The essence of Gandhian Philosophy is that Truth is the ultimate goal of life and non-violence is its means.

Bapu's Letters to Ashram Sisters

The letters written as far back as 1926 through 1929 demonstrate that even as early as the 20s Gandhi valued the abilities of women. He clearly saw the women in the role of a leader. Kalelkar, Gandhi's co-worker, later compiled Gandhi's letter to the ashram women published as Gandhi's Letter's to Ashram Sisters". In the preface of this book, Kalelkar writes regarding Gandhi's letters to the women that:

"There runs all through his letters, like the accompaniment of a Tambura, the theme of freedom for women. That women is in fact not weak; that there is no eternal rule that leadership in society should always remain in the hands of men; that women can shape and develop her life in the manner she choses for herself, and thus only can she help in achieving human progress" (1952, p, xii).

In his own ashram he practiced in every way that which he had preached in public. Women there had equal rights in every respect with men. They voted on all important matters along with the men (C.F Andrew, 1996, p.321)

Gandhi's View on Equality

Gandhi's view on equality was not limited to women taking on work previously seen as 'men's work'. His beliefs on equality applied to men doing work that was socially seen as 'women's work' as well. 1927, in a letter written to the women in charge of the common kitchen of the ashram where many families stayed, Gandhi explained, "you may free yourselves from kitchen work when the men have acquired as much skill as you have at present, but certainly not before" (1952, p.22).

Gandhi Said: "I am uncompromising in the matter of women's rights. In my opinion she should labour under no legal disability not suffered by men. I should treat the daughters and sons on a footing of perfect equality" (Young India, 17 October, 1929).

Regeneration of Women

Gandhi realized that many movements stop half way because of the bad condition of Indian women and the lot of women needs regeneration (M.K.Gandhi, 1958, p. 3). He clearly stated that all that is printed in the name of scriptures need not be taken as the word of God or the inspired word (M.K.Gandhi,

1942, pp.14-15). He did not accept the ancient law giver Manu's word that for women there can be no freedom. He accepted that women have been suppressed under custom and law made by men and asked his countrymen to help women play their part as equals (M.K.Gandhi, 1959, pp.5-7). He believed that women should labour under no legal disability not suffered by men (M.K. Gandhi, 1959, P.7). His reconstituted family was a place where both father and mother assume shared duties. He extended the obligations of fathers into new realms and insisted that women must move beyond domesticity (Naresh Dadhiuch, 2003, p.51)

To the Women of India

Gandhi in an article titled "To the Women of India", stated:"...call woman the weaker sex is a libel; it is man's injustice to woman. If by strength is meant brute strength, then indeed woman is less brute than man. If by strength is meant moral power, then women is immeasurably man's superior. Has she not greater intuition, is she not more self-sacrificing, has she not greater powers of endurance, has she not greater courage? With out her man could not be. If non violence is the law of our being, the future is with woman" (1971, CW.Vol. XLIII, pp.219-220).

Women Leaders

Gandhi believed in women and therefore guided them into leadership roles. He often shared with the women his leadership wisdom on a personal level. He wrote to the women on leader and power: "A leader should have few powers and many responsibilities; she should always be thinking of the good of the institutions and try to increase its capacity for service" (1952, p.23).

In order to take on leadership responsibilities, it is essential to be courageous and have faith in oneself. In another letter to the ashram women, Gandhi wrote of equality and courage. He stated, "always keep cheerful; be calm; and make it a point to carry on your share of all the activities of the Ashram equally with men, and as well as men. This is not at all beyond your capacity. You need only desire it, and strive for it" (1952, P.62)

Gandhi's leadership created a great number of women leaders. In fact, Gandhi believed that without support from women, the vision of Swaraj was impossible to attain.

As a result of his conviction and dedicated work in freeing the women of India, thousands of Indian women partook in several of Gandhi's movements. His entourage, including his walk out to the sea known as the Dandi March of 1930, against the Salt Tax imposed by the British Government, included women from all walks of life, Hindus and Muslims included. Although Gandhi had not wanted women to be included in the walk, the women protested as they wanted to be part of the historic event. Such was the strong support from women; all in their appreciation to him for speaking out for them.

Numerous women groups were formed in India as a result of his act of empowering the women in India. Indian women today have inherited the freedom and dignity. Gandhi, a modern thinker and feminist, spoke for the women of India, and his words can still be heard and remembered in the 21st century. Savita Singh testifies that the socio-political philosophy of Gandhi is feminist. The non-violent way that he advocated was to encourage women's participation.: "...the beauty of non-violent war is that women can play the same part in it as men. In a violent war women have no such privilege".

Gandhi trusted the future, the household, the work place and society to women. Gandhi believed that women by nature are much more sensible regarding many issues including family and child welfare, and that the family and children gain much from women. But he also hoped for a future in which women would be men's "Co-workers and collegues, (who) enjoy the same rights and privileges as the women" (1971, CW, Vol. XL VIII, P.65).

In the preface of the collection of Gandhi's letters written to princess Amrit Kaur, the princess writes of Gandhi's belief in family relationships. She writes about Bapu (Gandhi) and Sabarmati ashram:

"I wanted to join him in Sabarmati but I was not at all well and when he asked me what my parents would feel about it I had of course to say that they would resent it. He then said,

'You must not hurt them and you can work for me in your own environment without necessarily joining my Ashram'. In 1924 when my mother passed away he said it was incumbent on me to stay with my father. Not until my father passed away in 1930, and I had settled all our family affairs according to the wishes of my brothers and Bapu was again out of jail, did I have the chance to take up active work with him" (Gandhi, 1961, p.vi)

Gandhi admired the qualities, be they socialized or biological, in both women as well as men and believed that these qualities should exist in both genders. He clarified: "A man should remain a man and yet should learn to become a woman; similarly a woman should remain women and yet learn to become man. This is to say that men should cultivate the gentleness and the courtesy of women and women should cast off their timidity and become brave" (1952, p.94)

Four Indicators of the Status of Women

Four indicators are used to judge the status of women in the Global gender gap index: a) Economic Participation, b) Educational attainment, c) Political empowerment and d) health and survival. In 2007, India's over all ranking was a dismal 114 on of 128 counties surveyed i.e. Just 14 countries below India, as if this was not depressing enough, its ranking in the specific areas is even worse.

1. In economic participation and opportunities for women, it is 122 (Just 6 countries below it in economic participation)
2. In Educational attainment it is 116, and 41 Percent of Indian women in the 15-49 age group have never been to School (Just 12 countries below it in Educational attainment)
3. in health and survival it is 126 and India's maternal mortality rate is 301 per 100000 live births with only Azerbaijan and Armenia lower.
4. Only in Political empowerment does it a score higher at 21, probably thanks to the million and more women elected to Panchayat Raj institution.

Political Role of Women

Women participated in large numbers in every political movement launched by Gandhi including the non-cooperation movement of 1920; civil disobedience movement of 1930-32; and quit India movement of 1942. Women from every part of India i.e. north, south, east, west, and every section i.e., royal, common, rich, poor, urban, rural, educated, illiterate, Hindu, Christian, Sikh, Parsi, were drawn not just as followers, but also as leaders. Annie Besant and Sarojini Naidu became the Presidents of the Congress Party.

Women in the Freedom Movement

He called upon women to join the freedom struggle and the constructive programme. There was a breath taking abruptness about the entry of women into political life due to his influence. One moment they were not there, the next they were in the fore front of the scene (B.Kumarappa, 1957, P.20). They could do so because Gandhi choose a particular form of struggle which suited women. They did not feel limited or unequal to men. He mobilized women through his speeches, writings and personal example. Vijaya Laxmi Pandit, the first woman Minister in India, accepts that her life changed when she first heard Gandhi speak. Gandhi was soliciting funds and she donated her gold bangle. She says that Gandhi's oratory bordered on sheer magic (Raj Kanwar et al, 1998, Pp.13-14). Due to Gandhi women participated in the freedom movement and their presence in the public sphere gained acceptability. It was made possible because men know that the honour of their women is safe in a nonviolent struggle guided by Gandhi (J.B. Kriplani, 2005, P.403)

Women's Participation in Mass Movements, Gandhi's Efforts

On the whole, Gandhi's consistent efforts for the liberation of women and his immense faith in women's moral conduct made women's struggle for rights and equality as an integral part of the struggle for national independence. Women's participation in large numbers in mass movements led by him made a big break through in Indian women's lives.

In 1885 the Indian National Congress was founded and in its 1889 Bombay session, ten women participated. Gandhi's call to women and large scale participation of women in the freedom movement brought about changes in the perception of other nationalist leaders as well. Many women who fought for the country's freedom also became active on the issues of women's rights. This period saw the emergence of many women's organizations. The Women's India Association (WIA) was founded in 1917 by Margaret Cousin, an Irish and Indian Nationalist, the National Council of Indian Women (NCIW) in 1926 and All India Women's Conference (ALWC) in 1927. In the 1920's and 1930's women participated actively in the Civil Disobedience Movement. Thousands of women were jailed during their participation in "Salt March" when Gandhi urged people to break the salt law by making salt themselves. Hence, women's participation in the national movements helped in breaking several of the old barriers of tradition and custom. To begin with, Gandhi did not advocate an 'active role for women in the public sphere, However, when the 'issue of women's suffrage was first raised in 1921, Gandhi supported it and even felt that the success of the Satyagraha movement and the Dandi March was inextricably linked with the active participation of women. Burning of foreign cloth and picketing of liquor shops were activities which were predominantly undertaken by women. In 1939, Gandhi was thoroughly convinced that if the national movement had to be elevated to the level of a mass movement, then women lad to be included as active participants. Gandhi said, "I would love to find that my future army contained a vast preponderance of women over men. If the fight come, I should then face it with greater confidence, then if men predominated. I would dread the latter's violence. Women would be my guarantee against such an outbreak". Equality between men and women was accepted as one of the objectives in the Fundamental Rights Resolution of the Indian National Congress in 1931.

Jawaharlal Nehru, influenced by the western suffragettes and exposed to liberal views on women's question in the west felt that without economic freedom other aspects of women's equality would not be realized. He disagreed with the limited view that women's education alone can bring about the desired changes and wanted women to be trained in all human activities (Simmi Valecha, "Gandhi and women Empowerment", *Journal of Gandhi Studies,* Jai Narain Sharma, Ed., Vol VI, No's I and II, 2008, pp.216-224).

Women's Status in Post - Gandhian Era (Kalpana Sharma, The Hindu, September 6, 2009).

Most people cheered when the government announced that it would raise the percentage of reserved seats for women in Panchayats and Nagar - palikas from the current one - third to half. Ironically, the state that has led the way in this is Bihar, one that is hardly ever held up as an example. Three year ago, Bihar enhanced the percentage of reserved seats for women to 50 percent.

Now with the rule applying all over India the number of elected women representatives is Panchayati Raj institutions alone will jump from the current 1,038,989 (2006 data) to an estimated 1,400,000. To do this, the government plans to amend Article 243 D of the Constitution that relates to reservation of seats for women, in the winter session of Parliament. There is some talk of the Women's Reservation Bill for seats in Parliament also being tabled at the same time although no one is placing any bets on it. Numbers, however, never tell the full story. The participation of women in Panchayats has been a fascinating and flawed story. Fascinating because it has shown that even deprived, illiterate, marginalized women can become competent and concerned elected representatives. But flawed because the women have to function in a society that will not accept that they can think independently, understand matters of governance, and take responsibility outside the four walls of their homes.

Kerala has been a pioneer in training women in Panchayats and its Kudumbashree Initiative is rightly lauded as imaginative and effective (http./www.kudumbashree.org/). Studies and surveys have established that without such specific input, the majority of elected women would not have been able to function effectively. The Panchayati Raj ministry also initiated with the National Commission for women a Panchayat Mahila Shakti Abhiyan specifically to inject a level of confidence in the women. The Ministry's report on "The state of the Panchayats" (2006) states, "At Present, many women in Panchayats feel isolated and powerless, particularly because of the persistence of gender prejudices and gender discrimination in the social mores of village life". Apart from prejudice, these women function against the background of the reality of women's status in the country. An increase in the number of elected women does not necessarily alter this reality. Only in political empowerment does India score higher at 21, probably thanks to the million and more women elected to Panchayat Raj institutions.

Handicaps

The women who enter politics through the Panchayat route mainly because there are seats reserved for them do so in an environment where they have to struggle between their role as primary care takers of their homes and their responsibilities as elected officials, where they can only contest if there is spousal or family support and where once the reserved seat reverts to a general seat as a result of the system of rotation of reserved seats, they inevitably have to step down.

A survey initiated by the Panchayati Raj Ministry in 2008 revealed that 89 Percent of the women interviewed did not contest a second election and that 11 Percent who did so, lost. Nearly half the women said that they felt the work was 'unsuitable' and that they felt incompetent and a third said their spouses had discouraged them from contesting a second time. These studies and data bring about two crucial points: 1) that even if the number of women elected to office increases because more seats are reserved, these women do not necessarily continue their participation in politics, partly due to social attitudes. 2) They have to struggle because of lower qualifications, the majority of women are less educated then their elected male counter -parts, the lack of training and the system if self. The rotation of seats, for instance, appears to work against the interests of women who might have been encouraged to contest again. In fact, one of the recommendations in the survey quoted above 'Elected Raj Institutions' (available on the Ministry's website) is that this particular system needs to be rethought.

Changing Perceptions

On the positive side, more women doing things that they have not done before will contribute to society's perceptions of what women are and what they can do. Reservation certainly encourages women to enter polities. Imagine a whole generation of girls growing up seeing their mother as Pradhans, or Mayors, giving orders, conducting meetings, speaking in public, sorting out problems, being out of the home, or having people coming to the house seeking help. In a society where the women's voice is most often ignored, or over-ruled in the home, such imagery is quite revolutionary. It challenges entrenched ideas of what women can and cannot do.

Concluding Remarks

Much has been written about Gandhi's political work and the creation of passive resistance as an engine of reform. Gandhi helped change the status and path of Indian Women through his peaceful and firm ways. His views on Indian women were modern for his contemporaries so much so that his dedication to fight for the women's causes brought out the women of India who were empowered by his words and actions to take part in freeing India from the British. The essence of Gandhi's perception of women as individuals, wives and freedom leaders were not only positive and encouraging but also guiding and directing into the role of leadership and comradeship on equal footing.

References

Andhrew, C.F. (1996), *Mahatma Gandhi: His Life and Ideas,* Radha Publications New Delhi.

Biswas, S.C. (1967), *Gandhi Theory and Practice:* Social Impact and Contemporary Relevance, Indian Institute of Advance Study Shimla.

Farridah Noor Mohammed Noor (2006), 'Understanding the Status of Women through the Eyes of Gandhi' in Ravindrakumar , Ed. *Mahatma Gandhi, in the beginning of 21st Century*, Gyan Pub. House, New Delhi.

Gandhi, M.K. (1942), *Women and Social Injustice*, Navjivan Publishing House, Ahmedabad.

Gandhi, M.K. (1952), *Bapu's Letters to Ashram Sisters*, K.Katelkar, Ed., Navjivan Publishing House, Ahmedabad.

Gandhi, M.K. (1958), *Women*, Navjivan Publishing House, Ahmedabad.

Gandhi, M.K. (1959), *Women's Role in Society*, Navjivan Publishing House, Ahmedabad.

Gandhi, M.K. (1961), *Letters to Raj Kumari Amrit Kumar*, R.A. Kaur, Ed., Navjivan Publishing House, Ahmedabad.

Gandhi, M.K. (1950-1984), *Collected Works Mahatma Gandhi*. Volumes I through XC, the Publication Division, Ministry of Information and Broad Casting, Government of India, Patiala House, New Delhi.

Kamaladevi, Chattopadhyay (2003), *Woman The Comrade*, Janta Weekly, 16 Nov.

Kripalani, J.B. (2005), *Gandhi : His Life and Thought*, Publication Division, New Delhi.

Kumarappa, B. (1957), *Gandhi Towards Non-violent Socialism*, Navjivan, New Delhi.

Naresh Dadhiuch (2003), *Women Conflict Resolution and Culture Gandhian Perspective*, Aavishkar Publisher, Jaipur .

Raj Kanwar, Rameshwari Devi, Romila Purthi (1998), *Women and the Indian Freedom Struggle*, Vol. 6, Pointer Publisher, Jaipur.

Savita Singh, *Empowerment of Women: Miles to Go.*

Index

Z